Praise for *Unfree Labour?*

"The authors of *Unfree Labour?* have done us a great service, reporting and theorizing from the front lines of migrant and immigrant worker organizing in Canada. They've produced an internationally important book. The specific stories resonate with a global narrative, in which workers in poorer countries are freed to bring their labour to serve the rich, and are then rendered permanently vulnerable through the collusion of employers, police and government agencies. This bitter liberty is, however, being fought: look for inspiration in the reflections by organizers on resisting racialized capitalism, and the victories they've achieved, far from the media's gaze, in fields, factories, the fast food sector, and homes."
—Raj Patel, author of *The Value of Nothing* and *Stuffed and Starved*

"Analyzing the contemporary production of 'unfree' labour in Canada's immigration and neoliberal economic policies, this book makes an excellent contribution to the fields of labour and migration studies. Grounded in the struggles of migrant workers against racialized bondage, the studies presented by Choudry and Smith draw much needed attention to one of the most important movements of our times. A must read for all concerned with labour rights and economic justice in an increasingly polarized world."
—Sunera Thobani, author of *Exalted Subjects: Studies in the Making of Race and Nation in Canada*

"Choudry and Smith have put together an impressive collection of authors who reveal the ugly truth about Canadian so-called values: that Canada is a willing participant and leader in the exploitation, racialization, and commodification of human labour on stolen land. They reveal much about a human dignity that shines a light on the Canadian hubris and myth of being a champion of 'human rights' as families and people are torn asunder in the name of profit and privilege."
—David Bleakney, second national vice president, Canadian Union of Postal Workers

"*Unfree Labour?* systematically shows how rapacious capitalists and the state thrive and secure profits through the systematic subordination of women,

nonwhite, and migrant labourers. The chapters document that exploitation, so reminiscent of feudalism and early capitalism are ever-present in our modern capitalist system in the West. The chapters in this book provide chilling accounts of the constrained lives of domestics, agricultural labourers, and the growth of temporary foreign workers, so dependent on removing and denying rights that were achieved over the past two centuries. Choudry and Smith have assembled a comprehensive and outstanding book that is essential for all scholars of the labour movement."
—Immanuel Ness, editor of *New Forms of Worker Organization: The Syndicalist and Autonomist Restoration of Class-Struggle Unionism*

Unfree Labour?

Unfree Labour?
Struggles of Migrant and Immigrant
Workers in Canada

Edited by Aziz Choudry and Adrian A. Smith

Unfree Labour? Struggles of Migrant and Immigrant Workers in Canada
Edited by Aziz Choudry and Adrian A. Smith
© 2016 by Aziz Choudry and Adrian A. Smith
This edition © 2016 by PM Press

ISBN: 978-1-62963-1-493
Library of Congress Control Number: 2016930961

Cover by John Yates/Stealworks.com
Interior by Jonathan Rowland

10 9 8 7 6 5 4 3 2 1

PM Press
PO Box 23912
Oakland, CA 94623
www.pmpress.org

Printed in the USA on recycled paper, by the Employee Owners of Thomson-Shore
in Dexter, Michigan.
www.thomsonshore.com

Contents

LIST OF TABLES AND FIGURES

Acknowledgments

THIS BOOK WAS BORN OUT OF OUR SCHOLARLY AND ACTIVIST ENGAGEMENT with migrant and immigrant workers' struggles and is very much a collaborative endeavour. First we would like to thank all of the contributors to this collection. This builds on many years of conversations, debates, and discussions in both academic and organizing contexts. Many thanks to the Immigrant Workers Centre, Montreal, for hosting the May 2013 workshop that brought together most of the participants in this book. We are also deeply grateful to Sarah Mostafa-Kemal, Lily Han, and Désirée Rochat for their hard work in different aspects of the life of this project. We gratefully acknowledge the support of a Social Sciences and Humanities Research Council Connection Grant for this project. Thanks to those readers who offered constructive reviews of earlier drafts of this book and to the PM Press team. Perhaps most importantly, we are inspired by both the historical and present struggles of migrant and immigrant workers, organizers, and movements, who have carved a path in local and global struggles against unfree labour, and for labour and immigration justice in Canada and around the world.

All royalties from this book will be donated to the Immigrant Workers Centre, Montreal.

Introduction
Struggling against Unfree Labour

Aziz Choudry and Adrian A. Smith

AT THE START OF THE TWENTY-FIRST CENTURY, CANADA HAS EXPERIENCED considerable growth and change in labour migration. Temporary labour migration has replaced permanent immigration as the primary means by which people enter Canada. Using the rhetoric of maintaining competitiveness, Canadian employers and the state have ushered in an era of neoliberal migration (Arat-Koç 1999) alongside an agenda of "austerity" flowing from capitalist crisis. Labour market restructuring renders labour more flexible and precarious, and in Canada as in other high-income capitalist labour markets—where "guest" or temporary labour programs proliferate—employers are relying on migrant and immigrant workers as "unfree labour." We use the term *unfree labour* deliberately, provocatively, and analytically to contend that the formal lines of distinction between "free" and "unfree" labour, long since questioned within capitalist societies (Pentland 1981; Miles 1987; Satzewich 1991; Brass 1999), remain blurred in the period of neoliberal migration. The tendency of some to relegate the term to the past (referring, for instance, to historical forms of slavery and indentured labour) or to reject its ongoing explanatory utility sits in stark contrast to the contemporary claims and struggles of migrant and immigrant workers and organizers.

The current relevance of this book is indisputable. The years 2013, 2014, and 2015 saw renewed and sustained media attention on Canada's Temporary Foreign Worker Program (TFWP), changes to several foreign worker programs, and official announcements of reforms and promises of further changes. Yet while some of this debate reflected concerns about the

1

actual and potential exploitation of foreign workers, most demands hinged on the preservation of Canadian jobs. Very few acknowledged the broader historical and contemporary feature of Canada's capitalist economy—its systemic reliance upon exploitation through race, immigration status, and shifting forms of "unfree labour" (for exceptions, see Ramsaroop and Smith 2014). Public pressure led the federal government at the time (Stephen Harper's Conservatives) to ban the restaurant industry from using the TFWP (e.g., Harper 2014). Opposition parties and labour unions called for the moratorium to be extended to the entire program. But the moratorium placed on the use of migrant workers in this sector forms a knee-jerk reaction that fails to address the racist foundations of Canada's temporary labour migration regime, and the role of capitalist restructuring and broader transformations of work in contributing to the pronounced use of temporary foreign workers across many sectors. Although a change of government followed Justin Trudeau's Liberal Party victory in the October 2015 federal election, there is little sign of any substantive departure from this model.[1]

The uniqueness of this collection derives from its grounding in activist and organizing experiences, its cross-Canada scope, and the interdisciplinary scholarly perspectives that it assembles. Contributors are directly engaged with the issues emerging from the influx of temporary foreign workers and what Galabuzi (2006) describes as Canada's "creeping economic apartheid"—the ongoing racialization of economic inequality for many workers of colour, including permanent residents and citizens. With the erosion of trade union power, the rolling back of many employment standards and the re-regulation of the labour market to render all workers more readily exploitable (Camfield 2011), increasing numbers of workers—especially immigrant and temporary migrant workers—have suffered disproportionately from low-wage employment and welfare state retrenchment.

Equally in Canada as elsewhere, many unions have failed to mobilize mass rank-and-file militancy to resist the deterioration in workplace conditions and the systematic erosion of workers' power (Camfield 2011). Critical labour scholars such as Camfield argue that to build a working-class movement, unions need to radically reinvent themselves ideologically and structurally, and to learn lessons from other forms of labour organizing—not least migrant and immigrant worker organizing outside of union structures

---

1   As we go to press, the TFWP is under review by a parliamentary standing committee on human resources, skills, and social development.

and bureaucracies. While some unions have proactively supported migrant and immigrant worker organizing, others have been hostile or indifferent to migrant workers, including refraining from supporting their struggles for decent work, respect, and immigration justice. Alternative forms of organizing have proven essential to advancing migrant workers' rights, often outside of, and sometimes in tension with, established unions.

Besides the real difficulties and challenges that daily confront migrant and immigrant workers, there are pivotal stories of resilience, resistance, and partial victories. While examples of innovation and dynamism may exist at the outer edges of union tactics and strategies in relation to organizing migrant workers, this book largely focuses on community-entrenched organizations that support low-wage migrant and immigrant workers.

Drawing on critical scholarship as well as insights from knowledge produced in labour activism, this introduction sets up the book's central dialogue among scholars and organizers, identifies interconnecting themes that run throughout the collection, and introduces the chapters. In taking up "unfree labour" as a useful conceptual frame of analysis, we place migrant and immigrant workers' struggles for dignity and justice at the heart of this collection. Alongside an outline of the global context for labour migration, we highlight the role of migrant and racialized immigrants in the labour market, the expanded role of temporary foreign workers, and how changes or gaps in labour market legal regulation and social policy have intensified the socioeconomic risks that these workers face.

In many countries, including Canada, border controls are increasingly geared toward managing flows of largely temporary migrant workers— what some liken to a rotating-door labour market geared to just-in-time production or services. Kundnani's (2007, 145) reflections on recent British immigration history arguably hold true for the Canadian context when he writes that in contrast to the reserve army of manual workers in the post– Second World War period:

> the new post-industrial migrant workforce [is] characterized by several distinct streams—reserve regiments of labour—each adapted to the specific needs of different sectors of the economy. The intricacies of the system would be kept subject to constant review and adjustment, so that the numbers, character, and entitlements of workers entering the economy under different schemes could be changed as

necessary. Each of these various routes provide[s] employers with a different package of exploitation.

Immigration and Temporary Labour Migration to Canada

Canada's im/migration policies provide an exemplary model of how "reserve regiments of labour" are constructed and adapted to the specific needs of Canadian employers and subjected to "a different package of exploitation." Historically, racialized qualifications have defined the settlement rights of certain immigrant workers. Most notably, the arrival of workers from China beginning in the 1880s, primarily tasked with building the Canadian Pacific Railway, led to restrictive measures designed to halt immigration of people from China, then later Japan and India. The preferential treatment of "white" immigrants from Britain, the United States, France, and later western and northern Europe was well entrenched in the formation of Canada and extended well into the twentieth century. The celebrated points system, instituted in 1967 and held out as the basis of nondiscriminatory immigration, merely extended racialized immigration into the contemporary moment (Simmons 1998). In turn, Canadian immigration policy has also produced undocumented workers through draconian rules on temporary residence and sponsorship.

The categorization, regulation, and racialization of migrant work in Canada occurs through the Temporary Foreign Worker Program, which includes the Caregiver Program (which in November 2014 replaced the Live-in Caregiver Program, or LCP), bringing in care workers, once Caribbean women and now mainly Filipinas; the Seasonal Agricultural Worker Program (SAWP), dominated by Mexican and Caribbean workers; the Stream for Lower-Skilled Occupations (formerly the Pilot Project for Occupations Requiring Lower Levels of Formal Training); and the Agricultural Stream, with both streams recruiting from various countries including Guatemala, the Philippines, and Thailand. In 2012, according to Citizenship and Immigration Canada (CIC) 213,573 foreign workers entered Canada, a 12 percent increase over the previous year (CIC 2013). Of these, 6,242 workers entered through the LCP, 25,414 through the SAWP, and 20,636 through the Pilot Project, although there is a discrepancy in numbers given CIC's failure to report on the occupational classifications of 153,668 workers.[2]

---

2   An overhaul in the TFWP in June 2014 led to a change in reporting of holders of work permits. Whereas earlier data identifies a category of permit holders under the TFWP, more recent

Through Canada's TFWP, migrant workers labour in fields, restaurants, factories, nursing homes, and households, among myriad other sectors and places. These workers grow, process, and serve food; attend to the young and elderly; build, fix, and provide—all at a time when permanent residence is being offered to fewer people. They are commodities, labour units to be recruited, utilized, and sent away again as employers require. Tied to a specific employer through a combination of their immigration status and labour permits, migrant workers may be stuck with little recourse to improve their often deplorable conditions. Critical commentators remark that Canada's temporary migrant worker schemes amount to a condition of "indentured labour" (e.g., Stasiulis and Bakan 2003, 52). The Alberta Federation of Labour (2009) described these schemes as "entrenching exploitation" of migrant workers.

While in power, the Harper government promoted the expansion of temporary foreign worker programs to further institutionalize a "cheap," disposable migrant workforce, with its system of hierarchies and exclusions in a range of jobs. This recent expansion along a more employer-driven and employer-directed, privatized model expands a class of workers for whom it is more difficult to gain permanent status. Hiring temporary foreign workers is a way of meeting labour-market demand without incurring high administrative costs. Employers can easily fire such workers without incurring social costs when employment declines. Discrimination and exploitation based on race, immigration status, class, and gender work in concert. Women migrant workers are particularly impacted, as they make up the majority in sectors with the least protections, lowest wages, and most-demeaning conditions. As Stasiulis and Bakan (2003, 14) note, they are particularly affected by "the neoliberal realignment of the public/private divide" as care shifts more into households due to shrinking state commitments to funded childcare and health care. Typically, live-in caregivers and other migrant workers have not been permitted to join unions and thus lack collective bargaining power. While the TFWP requires payment of a minimum or prevailing wage, as a number of the cases in this book illustrate, workers are not always paid on time or maybe not paid at all. They may endure unsafe and unhealthy

---

data distinguishes between, on one side, TFWP permit holders who require a Labour Market Impact Assessment (LMIA—formerly Labour Market Opinion [LMO]) and permit holders in the International Mobility Program (IMP) who are exempted from the LMIA requirement. This policy change renders it quite difficult to make comparisons across time.

working conditions, receiving wages below the going rate for equivalent work while toiling long hours. There is also inadequate enforcement and monitoring of conditions for migrant workers. They may be subject to abuse from employers and perhaps be more willing to accept this situation because of the relatively short duration of their employment abroad.

Notwithstanding the difficult circumstances in which they work, many migrant and immigrant workers are fighting back. For example, in November 2013, Canada's Federal Court of Appeal ordered new hearings for 102 migrant farmworkers in Ontario who had their employment insurance parental benefits claims denied. In the same month in Quebec, a new Temporary Foreign Worker Association was launched with the support of Montreal's Immigrant Workers Centre. On October 10, 2010, migrant workers with the support of Justicia for Migrant Workers undertook the historic Pilgrimage to Freedom trek from Leamington, Canada's self-described Tomato Capital, to the Tower of Freedom "Underground Railroad" Monument in Windsor, Ontario. This protest march was followed up a year later with the Pilgrimage to Freedom Caravan, which, over two autumn weekends, made stops in Windsor, Leamington, Chatham, Dresden, Simcoe, Brantford, Hamilton, and Toronto.

Yet scholars in Canada have devoted relatively little sustained attention to migrant and immigrant worker organizing, activism, and resistance. Even as significant critical scholarship has emerged on the restructuring of paid work and on capitalist restructuring and austerity, the interconnections between neoliberal public policies of immigration, low-wage work, and the political actions of migrant and immigrant workers have yet to be adequately explored. Nor, with a few notable exceptions, such as the work of Galabuzi (2006), Sharma (2006), and Zaman (2005, 2012), has scholarly work sufficiently accounted for the impact of racialization on shifts in the nature of work in Canada. Alongside the racialized nature of temporary foreign worker programs, a recent study has shown that the work secured by racialized Canadians is more likely to be insecure, temporary, and low paying (Block and Galabuzi 2011). We believe there are important—even necessary—reasons to bring reflexive activist perspectives on labour migration and precarious work more squarely into view. In this collection, academics and activists look to deepen understanding of racialized neoliberal migration, and examine recent labour organizing efforts and the prospects for improving the economic and social conditions of migrant and immigrant workers in Canada.

This volume explores contemporary labour migration to Canada and how public policies of temporary worker programs function in the global context of work and capitalist restructuring. Chapter contributors examine the racialized effects of neoliberal migration to explore how these play out in labour markets and workers' lives. They examine how migrant and immigrant workers have organized for justice and dignity. As opposed to a large swath of current scholarship that downplays or ignores the struggles of racialized migrant and immigrant workers, and that tends to focus mainly on trade unions, we contend that migrant and immigrant workers, labour organizations, and migrant worker allies have engaged in a wide range of organizing initiatives with meaningful political and economic impacts. These have included political marches and demonstrations; public shaming of "bad bosses" and public officials; court challenges to secure legal rights to unionization; and grassroots alternatives to traditional forms of unionization through worker centres and community unionism models. Traditionally, work-related issues have been the concern of the labour movement, acting on the assumption that the best way for workers to have a strong voice and bargaining power is through unions. While there are unresolved tensions between the differing forms of labour organization, in particular due to the bureaucratic and top-down approach characteristic of trade unions and to the marginalization of racialized workers and organizers, increased collaboration and mutual support will be a crucial component in future workers' struggles in Canada, especially in confronting the "different package[s] of exploitation" experienced by workers. We turn to the concept of unfree labour as a tool for thinking through the political and legal conditions and struggles of migrant and immigrant workers.

Labour Unfreedom in Contemporary Canada

The term *unfree labour* frames the interventions of contributors. In *Capital V.1*, Marx (1967, 874) outlines key conditions necessary for capitalist wage labour. Specifically, wage labour relies upon the existence of "free" labourers; that is, workers who are free in a "double sense": specifically, "they neither form part of the means of production themselves ... nor do they own the means of production." Being "free" from legal constraints that would prevent them from selling their labour power (i.e., slavery) and "freed" from the means of production, the only way free wage labourers are able to ensure their subsistence is to sell their labour power. While this system of free wage labour appears as a fair exchange between two equal parties, Marx's aim was to make visible its deeply exploitative nature.

Conceptually, unfree labour captures the use of extraeconomic compulsion, alongside what Marx termed the "dull compulsion of economic relations," to exact labour power. By "extraeconomic," we mean the use of political and legal compulsion specifically rooted in heavily restrictive citizenship and migratory status. This understanding helps to shed light on the ways in which "ordinary" labour exploitation becomes intensified, even transformed, under neoliberal migration, into super- or hyperexploitation.

The term *unfree labour* also invites interpretation on how historical change unfolds. It is not used here to enforce a binary distinction with "free" labour. Sociolegal historians among others have developed more nuanced understandings reflective of an intricate continuum of compulsions (e.g., Hay and Craven 2004). Neither is it meant to suggest a linear historical trajectory toward inevitable freedom, nor does it counterpose "free" labour as an object of desire or aspirational objective. Indeed, within capitalist relations, as demonstrated so forcefully by Marx and others, free labour is highly problematic as those so categorized must sell their labour power for subsistence wages and are therefore subjected to expropriation of the wealth they produce.

Because we need tools or concepts to interpret our unfolding history, unfree labour signifies a conceptual interpretation of the historical record on labour controls in capitalist societies. It provides a conceptual linkage between contemporary and historical experience. Far from novel, the general thrust behind neoliberal migration, we contend, is ongoing or continuous. In other words, "unfree labour" serves to recognize the historically entrenched use of politico-legal compulsion to hyperexploit and pacify labour (Smith 2013) while in the context of these patterns or continuities, leaving conceptual space for examination of specific qualities of and differences between migrant and immigrant workers and corresponding regimes of regulation. Thus we regard unfree labour as signaling an intricate and nuanced continuum of modes of economic and politico-legal compulsion. As such, sociologist Vic Satzewich's (1991) schema of twentieth-century migrant labour incorporation in Canada, which identifies four such modes—free immigrant, free migrant, unfree migrant, and unfree immigrant—remains instructive for contemporary analysis (see Thomas, this volume).

Although the use of migrant workers through temporary foreign worker programs relies on economic compulsion generally, migratory status is the fundamental politico-legal mechanism of labour unfreedom. The pivotal instrument is the temporary work permit or authorization, which subjects noncitizens to the constant threat of repatriation. Unfree migrant labour is deployed in Canada on a time-limited basis, anywhere from several weeks to several years, depending on the relevant scheme. These migrant workers are tied exclusively to a specific employer within a defined geographic locale.

In acknowledging the contemporary persistence of unfree labour, we acknowledge the crucial role assumed by capitalist states in labour unfreedom. States play a necessary and constitutive role in producing unfree labour. As an imperialist force, the Canadian state deserves particular scrutiny (see Smith 2015b).

Racialized Capitalism and Migration to Canada

Capitalism is a racialized phenomenon evidenced in immigration, labour market, and wider social policies in Canada.[3] The management of migration under neoliberalism is characterized by exclusionary practices of racialized othering. The Canadian state actively produces and reproduces unfree migrant and immigrant labour in distinctly racialized terms. Filtering workers from source countries in the global South through labour unfreedom, neoliberal migration in Canada relies upon, reinforces, and even extends global economic apartheid (Galabuzi 2006; Sharma 2006; Walia 2010; Smith 2013). Further, this contemporary system of migration is contingent upon the racialized formation of the Canadian state and its project of nation-building, which are infused with what Abigail Bakan (2008, 5) calls "a racialized culture of hegemonic whiteness."

McNally (2002, 137) argues that "the fundamental truth about globalization—that it represents freedom for capital and unfreedom for labour—is especially clear where global migrants are concerned." In addition to the neoliberal underpinning of domestic policy, in international forums such as the Organization for Economic Cooperation and Development

---

3   We consider the colonization of Indigenous Peoples and territories to be the foundational element of racialized capitalism in Canada. The displacement of Indigenous Peoples and the concomitant dispossession of lands served as Canada's original "civilizing mission." To these ongoing processes we would add Canada's im/migration policies. For a discussion see Smith 2015b.

(OECD) and the World Trade Organization (WTO), Canada actively supports the expansion of free market capitalist policies—not least in agriculture—which have undermined traditional societies and livelihood opportunities, and driven many people to migrate, in the name of a model of development through export-driven, market-oriented growth.

Migration continues to be shaped by interconnected economic, political, and social factors. As Razack (2004), Thobani (2007), and others contend, Canada's role in creating or exacerbating the conditions that drive people to leave their communities and become migrants needs close scrutiny. Such factors include structural adjustment programs imposed in the global South by international financial institutions, and often supported through bilateral official aid; "development" projects; and restructuring of economies along neoliberal lines through trade and aid arrangements in which Canadian international trade, aid, development, and economic policy play active roles. Akers Chacón (2006, 90) describes "neoliberal immigration" as "displacement accompanied by disenfranchisement and often internal segregation in host countries." Neoliberal policies force people from their farms, jobs, families, and communities and into circuits of migration as migrant workers in other countries. Deindustrialization and the downsizing and privatization of essential services, increasing user fees, and conflicts over land, water, and natural resources add to the reasons behind the growing numbers seeking work abroad. The material conditions in workers' countries of origin, as well as the structures of labour markets in migrant-receiving countries, shape the place of migrant workers. Free trade and investment agreements such as the North American Free Trade Agreement (NAFTA) between Canada, Mexico, and the United States push farmers off their land as common lands are privatized—often to facilitate corporate export-driven agricultural production. This forces people into low-wage labour in maquiladora assembly plants or to migrate north across an increasingly dangerous, militarized US-Mexico border. Likewise, Canadian corporations operating in the Philippines, India, Guatemala, Colombia, and elsewhere shape and benefit from liberalized natural resource policy regimes, which have led to the displacement and impoverishment of communities who are then forced to migrate to seek livelihoods elsewhere.

Many economies have become increasingly dependent on remittances in the wake of loss of foreign exchange earning capacity, takeovers by privatization, and massive public sector cuts. Early in the last decade, Sutcliffe (2004, 273) observed that "individual decisions of individual migrant workers lead to considerably more money being transferred to poorer countries than all the development aid provided by the world's richest countries (including the multilateral agencies)." Migrant workers and financial remittances are a key area of interest to the World Bank, the European Commission, the International Organization for Migration (IOM), and other international agencies. These institutions increasingly promote the concept of migrant workers' family remittances to keep their countries of origin from collapsing. Growing dependence on remittances as part of what Kapur (2004) calls "the new development mantra" puts many countries at the mercy of the vagaries of anti-immigrant sentiment and immigration (and other) policies of other countries, not least in times of economic crisis and uncertainty. Growth of remittances has outpaced that of private capital flows and official development assistance (ODA) during the last fifteen years. Some estimates (Ratha et al, 2015) project worldwide remittances from migrant workers to reach over US$636 billion by 2017.

Locked into a neoliberal model, countries that have grown dependent on exporting workers often have shrinking policy space to pursue other options for economic development. One international site of policy discussion (and contestation) is the Global Forum on Migration and Development (GFMD), established after the 2006 UN high-level dialogue on migration and development as a venue for labour-sending and labour-receiving governments to discuss strategies on instituting temporary labour migration programs. Rodriguez (2010, 53) notes:

> Pegged as a win-win-win, for both sets of governments and migrants themselves, temporary labour migration programs are being celebrated as the best solution to labour-receiving governments' demand for cheap foreign workers to whom they are unwilling to extend full citizenship rights, to labour-sending governments' need to address domestic unemployment, and to bolster foreign exchange reserves, and migrants' and their families' need for livable wages.

Rodriguez (2010, 55) contends that the migration-as-development approach promoted by the World Bank, IOM, and the GFMD through temporary labour migration programs "allow employers to exploit foreign workers, absolve developing states from introducing truly redistributive developmental policies and relieve states from extending the full benefits of citizenship to immigrants." Remittances have been a way of downloading state responsibility to individual workers and their families, as well as serving as a social safety valve for masses of unemployed or underemployed workers in many countries. In both migrant-sending and migrant-receiving countries, a more general trend of state withdrawal of responsibility for provision of social services adversely impacts local and migrant workers alike.

Highlighting the historical and ongoing experiences of workers characterized as unfree labour forms a strategic dimension of this book's agenda. That said, we do not claim to write for immigrant and migrant workers, or even from the standpoint of these workers, in any sort of reductionist way. We write from our locations as engaged academics and organizers, contemplating what we see as the conditions and relations of labour unfreedom in which migrant and immigrant workers find themselves in Canada. As a defining feature of production relations in Canada, unfree labour is enforced at the level of everyday social life and on the human body.

Yet recognition of unfree labour is not meant to undermine the resistance struggles of workers. Asserting resistance as a crucial feature in explaining social change is not to claim that migrant and immigrant workers exist in a state of perpetual or existential rebelliousness. Resistance is integral to the human condition but the forms in which resistance occurs are complex and varied. The challenge therefore rests with judging its efficacy, mobilizing for its most concerted forms, and consolidating disjointed forms of it. We do not claim a monopoly on knowledge about the ways forward for migrant and immigrant worker justice. Nor do we aim to (over)determine resistance struggles of im/migrant workers or the wider working class. The way forward will only emerge from self-reflexive struggle with deep reflection on action in ways that assist in the undertaking of future action.

Care, Reproduction, and Neoliberal Migration

Another key feature of neoliberal migration in Canada and a theme raised in this book is its particular structuring of relations of production and reproduction. The work of social reproduction, generally characterized as the tasks associated with reproducing the labouring population on a daily and generational basis, has long been recognized as fundamentally gendered (Luxton and Bezanson 2006; Bakker and Silvey 2008). A more recent concern with care work extends the critique of gendered inequalities in paid and unpaid work on a global scale (Hochschild 2000; Yeates 2005). Disproportionately charged with carrying out the crucial tasks of social reproduction generally and care work specifically, privileged women in the global North shift the burdens of care work onto marginalized women of the global South, who in turn must find ways to meet their own care obligations.

The gendered impacts of neoliberalization play out in contemporary migration. Here we are cognizant of the impacts on racialized women, and migrant and immigrant workers specifically. A critical appreciation of unfree migrant and immigrant labour requires keen attentiveness to social reproductive labour; to the privileging of the productive sphere over the reproductive within capitalist societies; to the co-constitutive nature of productive and reproductive spheres within capitalism; and to the shifting of burdens and accordant devaluing of labour through the global care chain. Socially reproductive labour is both subordinated within capitalist relations of production and, following Burawoy's (1976) classic account, largely externalized to the states from which migrant and immigrant workers arrive to Canada. This means that the social reproduction and educational costs of producing migrant workers is borne by their countries of origin, and from there are further downloaded onto workers and their families and communities. This externalization produces stratified social reproduction with transnational and racialized effects felt upon motherhood and other caring labour (Arat-Koç 2006). An attentiveness to care work and social reproduction invites us to take labour, work, and economy not merely in narrowly individualistic terms, but rather in much wider and interconnected ways. It calls for recognition that the adverse impacts of labour unfreedom and employment precarity extend across families, households, and the communities in which they are embedded. Family or household units, as crucial sites for organizing, provisioning, and subsuming social reproduction, are integral to the analysis, especially in response to neoliberal capitalism's gendered shifting of certain social burdens away from capital and the state and onto labour. For these reasons, Sedef Arat-Koç concludes this book with a reflection on the chapters, revisiting concepts of social reproduction and unfree labour and their contributions to understanding and organizing for migrant and immigrant workers' struggles in Canada.

Margins and Centre

The significance of the work of activists in worker centres, and in other forms of organizing largely outside of traditional postwar trade unionism lies not simply in organizing a smaller vulnerable workforce, but also in the larger context of the fight-back against the on-the-ground impacts of, and the economic crises wrought by, global capitalism. We see real benefits in reflexive activist engagement as a means to deepen understanding of racialized neoliberal migration. Organizers are strategically situated to engage with the relatively rapid, complex, and intense nature of local neoliberal restructuring. They are involved in initiatives that, in contesting the growing assault on the labour movement, serve as testing grounds for alternative approaches to collective action. Meaningful consideration of activist perspectives is motivated by aims to construct an inclusive labour movement that perceives migrant and immigrant workers' struggles as more than marginal or secondary. Worker centres, national and transnational migrant worker alliances and networks such as MIGRANTE and the Coalition for Migrant Worker Rights, and activist collectives including Justicia for Migrant Workers are testing grounds for new and alternative approaches to or models of collective organization, and are grounded attempts to work through the issues, debates, and tensions around the shifting centres and margins of labour market regulation and workers' struggles in contemporary Canada. Hearn and Bergos (2010, 13) hold that:

> organized migrant workers pose two of the greatest threats to employers and the hierarchical and divisive way in which the segmented labour-market has been constructed and accepted. Their low wages and working conditions "offer the greatest potential for worker dissatisfaction and protest" (Strikwerda and Guerin-Gonzales 1998, 20). In addition, if they become integrated into the indigenous union structure, in the process radicalizing it by bringing their raw experiences of exploitation and marginalization, they realize the capitalists' worst nightmare, a united working class.

Migrant and racialized workers, and other precarious workers, can no longer be seen as existing at the margins. Their struggles are central to fight-backs against austerity and neoliberalism. A fundamental question is *not* whether traditional union structures and practices can carry this fight forward—the experiences of many of the contributors suggest otherwise—but rather *how the labour movement will rebuild to adapt to the new understandings of the ways capitalism reshapes work and migration, and what it might learn from community-based im/migrant labour struggles.* The need to deepen understanding demands that we reshape and reimagine class and struggle in this moment to effectively combat myriad forms of exploitation. A deep and broad-based solidarity of migrant and nonmigrant workers within Canada and across borders is urgently needed. This kind of solidarity cannot be built without meaningful engagement with the racialized and gendered nature of class articulations in Canada and elsewhere. It cannot be conducted within outmoded confines of business unionism and its devotion to nationally bounded labour policies. Nor can it be found within social democratic politics, which imprison Canadian left thinking and action in the neoliberal moment, demanding, at most, only piecemeal social welfare reforms within a national context—demands directed only at citizens and permanent residents.

Organization of the Book

While some chapters attend to the historical and political economic context for, and working conditions within, specific temporary foreign worker programs, as well as broader impacts of these programs on work and labour markets, critical discussion of migrant and immigrant worker organizing and the prospects for real change are central throughout the book.

In focusing on the SAWP, Mark Thomas examines conditions of employment and the terrain of labour organizing for migrant agricultural workers, focusing specifically on recent efforts to secure freedom of association rights through a court challenge supported by the United Food and Commercial Workers union. Thomas explores both the potential and limitations of this legalistic strategy, and concludes by situating this struggle within the broader context of the global expansion of temporary labour migration.

Jah-Hon Koo and Jill Hanley consider the problematic position of live-in caregivers in Canada. They explore the ways in which domestic workers take control over their situations through social networks, ethnic and community associations, and, increasingly, community-labour initiatives.

Abigail Bakan notes that systemic discrimination is a widely employed but little understood concept. The Canadian state has formally acknowledged systemic discrimination in one area of federal labour policy dedicated to its redress: that associated with employment equity, the federal Employment Equity Act (EEA). Bakan addresses the apparent contradiction regarding systemic discrimination evident in the EEA and LCP. She unpacks the meaning of systemic discrimination in liberal ideology, in the context of a political economy that enables but rhetorically denies the persistence of unfree labour characteristic of live-in domestic care as well as other sectors. Bakan highlights the role of organized resistance among foreign domestic workers as an example of an effective means to challenge systemic discrimination.

Geraldina Polanco examines the turn to migrant labour by employers such as Tim Hortons in western Canada. Polanco argues that the recent expansion of the TFWP has significant implications for dynamics within worksites and wider social relations, particularly given the degree to which employers of low-wage workers have embraced this strategy.

Adriana Paz Ramirez and Jennifer Chun revisit how South Asian farmworkers—permanent residents and citizens—in British Columbia (BC) struggled to challenge harsh and exploitative working conditions in the late 1970s and 1980s, founding the Canadian Farmworkers Union and winning unprecedented reforms in employment standards and occupational health and safety policy. Paz Ramirez and Chun assess the relationship between previous struggles and current organizing efforts among today's farmworkers recruited through the TFWP. They write that interrogating how past histories of resistance and struggle shape current organizing efforts, as well as the ways in which unions and community groups learn and relate to that history, is crucial for understanding the limits and possibilities of effecting structural transformation through popular struggle.

Chris Ramsaroop argues that the absence of discussion on expanding social entitlements for precarious populations such as migrant agricultural workers is connected to the absence of desire to expand who is included in organized labour's understanding of who belongs and who does not belong in Canada. Examining the role of organizing and transnational solidarity with migrant workers to expand access to entitlements, Ramsaroop addresses the resistance undertaken by migrant workers to demand rights and entitlements from nation-states.

Deena Ladd and Sonia Singh of the Toronto's Workers' Action Centre examine new organizing strategies emerging in campaigns to improve wages and working conditions and build a collective voice for precarious workers. They draw lessons from US and Canadian organizing models for connecting and building a broad movement for migrant and precarious worker organizing in Canada.

Joey Calugay, Loïc Malhaire, and Eric Shragge discuss how Montreal's Immigrant Workers Centre (IWC) supports temporary foreign workers in resisting the conditions they face, through organizing and building supportive allies. They explain how the IWC has helped workers make claims for various programs and benefits, and how workers have challenged their employers and made gains. Finally, the authors ask how to move forward in the organizing process, recognizing both the barriers and the opportunities.

The penultimate chapter is adapted from an insightful dialogue between organizers from prominent activist organizations and movements working with migrant and immigrant workers, where they discuss strategies, models, and dilemmas of labour organizing, including relationships with trade unions.

In conclusion, Sedef Arat-Koç articulates themes and strands that connect the chapters. Arat-Koç theorizes the contemporary context of temporary labour migration and activism through reconsideration of the concept of unfree labour, emphasizing racialization and social reproduction dimensions. This chapter ties the threads of the book together, suggesting ways forward for further scholarship and implications for organizing.

References

Alberta Federation of Labour. 2009. *Entrenching Exploitation*. < afl.org/upload/ TFWReport2009.pdf>.

Arat-Koç, Sedef. 2006. "Whose Social Reproduction? Transnational Motherhood and Challenges to Feminist Political Economy." In Meg Luxton and Kate Bezanson (eds.), *Social Reproduction: Feminist Political Economy Challenges Neo-Liberalism*. Montreal and Kingston: McGill–Queen's University Press.

_____. 1999. "Neoliberalism, State Restructuring and Immigration: Changes in Canadian Policies in the 1990s." *Journal of Canadian Studies* 34, no. 2.

Bakan, Abigail. 2008. "Reconsidering the Underground Railroad: Slavery and Racialization in the Making of the Canadian State." *Socialist Studies* 4, no. 1.

Bakker, Isabella, and Rachel Silvey (eds.). 2008. *Beyond States and Markets: The Challenges of Social Reproduction*. London: Routledge.

Block, Sheila, and Grace-Edward Galabuzi. 2011. *Canada's Colour Coded Labour Market: The Gap for Racialized Workers*. Toronto: Canadian Centre for Policy Alternatives and the Wellesley Institute.

Brass, Tom. 1999. *Towards a Comparative Political Economy of Unfree Labour: Case Studies and Debates*. London: Frank Cass.

Brass, Tom, and Marcel van der Linden (eds.). 1997. *Free and Unfree Labour: The Debate Continues*. Bern: Peter Lang.

Burawoy, Michael. 1976. "The Functions and Reproduction of Migrant Labor: Comparative Material from Southern Africa and the United States." *American Journal of Sociology* 81, no. 5.

Camfield, David. 2011. *Canadian Labour in Crisis*. Halifax: Fernwood.

Fudge, Judy, and Rosemary Owens. 2006. "Precarious Work, Women and the New Economy: The Challenge to Legal Norms." In Judy Fudge and Rosemary Owens (eds.), *Precarious Work, Women and the New Economy: The Challenge to Legal Norms*. Oxford: Hart.

Fuller, Sylvia, and Leah Vosko. 2008. "Temporary Employment and Social Inequality in Canada: Exploring Intersections of Gender, Race and Migration." *Social Indicators Research* 88, no. 1.

Galabuzi, Grace-Edward. 2006. *Canada's Economic Apartheid: The Social Exclusion of Racialized Groups in the New Century*. Toronto: Canadian Scholars' Press.

Harper, Tim. April 24, 2014. "Jason Kenney Suspends Food Services Sector from Foreign Worker Program." *The Toronto Star*. <thestar.com/news/canada/2014/04/24/a_flood_of_foreign_workers_drives_up_western_unemployment_tim_harper.html>.

Hay, Douglas, and Paul Craven. 2004. "Introduction." In Douglas Hay and Paul Craven (eds.), *Masters, Servants, and Magistrates in Britain and the Empire, 1562–1955*: 1–58. Chapel Hill: University of North Carolina.

Hearn, Julia, and Monica Bergos. 2010. "Learning from the Cleaners? Trade Union Activism among Low Paid Latin American Migrant Workers at the University of London." Identity, Citizenship and Migration Centre, University of Nottingham.

Hochschild, Arlie Russell. 2000. "Global Care Chains and Emotional Surplus Value." In Tony Giddens and Will Hutton (eds.), *On the Edge: Globalization and the New Millennium*. London: Sage Publishers.

Hughes, Christine, and Patti Lenard (eds.). 2013. *Legislating Inequality: Canada's Temporary Migrant Worker Program*. Montreal: McGill–Queen's University Press.

Kapur, Devesh. 2004. "Remittances: The New Development Mantra?" *G-24 Discussion Paper Series*. United Nations Conference on Trade and Development. <unctad.org/Templates/Download.asp?docid=4855&lang=1&intItemID=2103>.

Kundnani, Arun. 2007. *The End of Tolerance: Racism in 21st Century Britain*. London: Pluto Press.

Luxton, Meg, and Kate Bezanson. 2006. *Social Reproduction: Feminist Political Economy Challenges Neo-Liberalism*. Montreal: McGill–Queen's Press.

McNally, David. 2002. *Another World Is Possible: Globalization and Anti-Capitalism*. Winnipeg: Arbeiter Ring.

Miles, Robert. 1987. *Capitalism and Unfree Labour: Anomaly or Necessity?* New York: Tavistock.

Pentland, H. Clare. 1981. *Labour and Capital in Canada, 1650–1860*. Toronto: J. Lorimer.

Ramsaroop, Chris, and Adrian A. Smith. May 21, 2014. "The Inherent Racism of the Temporary Foreign Worker Program." *The Toronto Star*. <thestar.com/opinion/commentary/2014/05/21/the_inherent_racism_of_the_temporary_foreign_worker_program.html>.

Ratha, Dilip, Supriyo De, Ervin Dervisevic, Sonia Plaza, Kirsten Schuettler, William Shaw, Hanspeter Wyss, Soonhwa Yi and Seyed Reza Yousefi. 2015.

Migration and Development Brief, 24. Migration and Remittances Team, Development Prospects Group, World Bank (April 13). <https://siteresources.worldbank.org/INTPROSPECTS/Resources/334934-1288990760745/MigrationandDevelopmentBrief24.pdf>.

Razack, Sherene H. 2004. *Dark Threats and White Knights: The Somalia Affair, Peacekeeping and the New Imperialism*. Toronto: University of Toronto Press.

Rodriguez, Robyn Magalit. 2010. "On the Question of Expertise: A Critical Reflection on 'Civil Society' Processes." In Aziz Choudry and Dip Kapoor (eds.), *Learning from the Ground Up: Global Perspectives on Social Movements and Knowledge Production*. New York: Palgrave Macmillan.

Satzewich, Vic. 1991. *Racism and the Incorporation of Foreign Labour: Farm Labour Migration to Canada since 1945*. London: Routledge.

Sharma, Nandita. 2006. *Home Economics: Nationalism and the Making of 'Migrant Workers' in Canada*. Toronto: University of Toronto Press.

Simmons, Alan. 1998. "Racism and Immigration Policy." In Vic Satzewich (ed.), *Racism and Social Inequality in Canada*. Toronto: Thompson Educational Publishing.

Smith, Adrian A. 2013. "Pacifying the 'Armies of Offshore Labour' in Canada." *Socialist Studies* 9, no. 2.

_____. 2005. "Legal Consciousness and Resistance in Caribbean Seasonal Agricultural Workers." *Canadian Journal of Law and Society* 20, no. 2.

Stasiulis, Daiva K., and Abigail B. Bakan. 2003. *Negotiating Citizenship: Migrant Women in Canada and the Global System*. New York: Palgrave Macmillan.

Strikwerda, Carl, and Camille Guerin-Gonzales. 1998. "Labor, Migration and Politics." In Camille Guerin-Gonzales and Carl Strikwerda (eds.), *The Politics of Immigrant Workers: Labor Activism and Migration in the World Economy since 1830*. New York: Holmes & Meier.

Sutcliffe, Bob. 2004. "Crossing Borders in the New Imperialism." In Leo Panitch and Colin Leys (eds.), *Socialist Register 2004: The New Imperial Challenge*. London: Merlin Press.

Thobani, Sunera. 2007. *Exalted Subjects: Studies in the Making of Race and Nation in Canada*. Toronto: University of Toronto Press.

Thomas, Mark. 2010. "Labour Migration and Temporary Work: Canada's Foreign-Worker Programs in the 'New Economy.'" In Norene Pupo and Mark Thomas (eds.), *Interrogating the New Economy: Restructuring Work in the 21st Century*. Toronto: University of Toronto.

Vosko, Leah. 2007. "Gendered Labour Market Insecurities: Manifestations of Precarious Employment in Different Locations." In Vivian Shalla and Wallace Clement (eds.), *Work in Tumultuous Times: Critical Perspectives*. Montreal: McGill–Queen's University Press.

_____. 2006. "Precarious Employment: Towards an Improved Understanding of Labour Market Insecurity." In Leah Vosko (ed.), *Precarious Employment: Understanding Labour Market Insecurity in Canada*. Montreal: McGill–Queen's University Press.

Walia, Harsha. 2010. "Transient Servitude: Migrant Labour in Canada & the Apartheid of Citizenship." *Race & Class* 52, no. 1.

Yeates, Nicola. 2009. *Globalizing Care Economies and Migrant Workers: Explorations in Global Care Chains*. Basingstoke, UK: Palgrave Macmillan.

Zaman, Habiba. 2012. *Asian Immigrants in 'Two Canadas': Racialization, Marginalization, and Deregulated Work*. Halifax: Fernwood.

Producing and Contesting "Unfree Labour" through the Seasonal Agricultural Worker Program

Mark Thomas

RECENT NEWS MEDIA REPORTS HAVE DRAWN ATTENTION TO THE PRESENCE OF "temporary foreign workers" in the Canadian labour market. With much criticism directed at the decision of the Royal Bank of Canada (RBC) to displace employees who are Canadian citizens with noncitizen labour contracted through an outsourced employment agency, these reports have largely focused on the "scandal" of replacing Canadian workers with non-Canadians at a time of employment insecurity (CBC 2013). Through these reports, awareness of the significant recent expansion of Canada's Temporary Foreign Worker Program (TFWP) has brought scrutiny to bear on how the federal Conservative government had designed this program to enable employers to seek alternative sources of labour to Canadian workers. Less consideration was given to understanding the underlying sociological and political-economic conditions that drive the demand for workers who are not Canadian citizens. Specifically, these include the differential treatment experienced by migrants employed in Canada, the predominance of migrant workers in precarious and low-wage jobs, and the ways in which these two conditions are legitimated by both employers and the state.

These experiences are set in a much broader context of global labour migration. The social processes that shape the dynamics of labour migration and the wide range of ways in which migrant workers are integrated into "host" labour markets have received growing scholarly attention in recent years (Castles and Miller 2003; Freeman 2004; Hollifield 2004; Sharma 2006). With the differential social, economic, and political rights of migrants as they cross borders and enter "host" societies a central question (Schuster and Solomos 2002; Balibar 2004), the expansion of temporary foreign worker programs may be seen as one of the most significant contemporary developments in global migration.

This chapter examines Canada's Seasonal Agricultural Worker Program (SAWP), which regulates the entry of agricultural workers from Mexico and the Caribbean for seasonal employment on Canadian farms, and which was used as a model for the TFWP's expansion. With attention to both the political economy of labour market incorporation and the role of nationalist discourses in legitimating differential treatment of those categorized as "foreigners" within a nation-state, the chapter outlines the general conditions of employment experienced by workers in the SAWP, which include long hours and low wages, as well as exemptions from many basic labour standards. While primary attention is given to the ways in which the program constructs relations of "unfree labour" and exploitation, the chapter also briefly touches upon how these relations are contested through forms of labour organizing. It concludes by situating the SAWP within the broader context of the expansion of temporary foreign worker programs, arguing that the principles established in the SAWP have served as a model for this more general expansion of "unfree labour."

Global Capitalism, "Unfree Labour," and Labour Migration

While conditions of "free" wage labour were central to Marx's (1967) understanding of the uniqueness of capitalism, and despite free wage labour being the predominant condition of labour within capitalist economies, free wage labour may coexist with conditions of "unfree" wage labour in contemporary capitalist labour markets (Miles 1987). As this chapter outlines, "unfree" wage labour is particularly present through the organization of temporary labour migration programs.

Contemporary manifestations of unfree wage labour emerge through the political economy of global migration, which is organized in relation to the uneven geographic development of global capitalism (Stasiulis 1997; M. Thomas 2010). Currently, there is a global crisis of employment. By 2012 the International Labour Organization (ILO) estimated that approximately two hundred million people were unemployed (ILO 2013). In this context, migration patterns are often driven by the search for employment, with half of the world's 214 million people who live outside their country of origin being economically active (ILO 2012). Patterns of labour migration are also driven by demands for both "high-skilled" and "low-skilled" workers, particularly though not exclusively, in high-income labour markets. Moreover, since the 1990s, as nation-states have sought to tighten the connection between immigration policies and labour market needs, bilateral agreements that regulate the entry and labour market incorporation of labour migrants have proliferated. There has been dramatic growth in forms of temporary labour migration, with the numbers of temporary foreign workers entering OECD countries increasing by 4 to 5 percent a year since 2000 (D. Thomas 2010).

Contemporary dynamics of "unfree labour" are often conceptualized through the framework of the International Labour Organization's (ILO) definition of "forced labour," as articulated in its Forced Labour Convention, 1930 (No. 29), which includes "all work or service which is exacted from any person under the menace of any penalty and for which the said person has not offered himself [sic] voluntarily" (Article 2(1)) (see also ILO 2005). This conceptualization directs attention toward what are perhaps the most egregious forms of "unfreedom" in the organization of labour; for example, forms of trafficking, indentured/bonded labour ("modern slavery"), and child labour (Lerche 2007; Strauss 2012). However, the ILO definition of forced labour that frames many current debates is actually a subset of much broader conditions of "unfreedom," which rather than being anomalous, are in fact systemic to the organization of capitalist labour markets. For example, Phillips (2011) argues that conditions of freedom/unfreedom should not be understood as a simple dichotomy, as this binary approach occludes many of the conditions of "adverse incorporation" experienced by workers in the global economy. Rather, as Strauss (2012, 141) argues, unfreedom occurs "as a continuum of exploitation to which any worker might be subject, but to which particular groups and individuals have particular vulnerabilities." "Unfreedom" more broadly conceived and understood in the context of capitalist labour markets thus needs to be seen in relation to a wide range of conditions that may restrict or constrain one's capacity to sell one's labour power.

Within this framework, Phillips (2011, 13) argues that contemporary conditions of "unfreedom" often involve the exchange of labour for money through "varied forms of coercion and manipulation designed to make workers work harder, for longer [hours] and for less money." This may be established through a range of employer practices and government policies, which themselves vary by spatial context and reflect the uneven geographic development of global capitalism (Rogaly 2008). In the context of labour migration, conditions of "unfreedom" are often established through the denial of citizenship and residence rights, thereby maintaining connections between labour migrants and their home country (Burawoy 1976). More specifically, the political economy of migration directs attention to processes of incorporation, the term used to refer to the manner in which migrants are integrated into the dominant relations of production of the host society. Satzewich (1991) argues that there are at least four primary forms of incorporation of foreign-born labourers, the specifics of each being reliant upon: (i) the ability of the workers to circulate in the labour market; and (ii) the nature of their citizenship status. Migrant workers (noncitizens) constitute a form of unfree wage labour as their ability to circulate in a labour market is limited by the temporary labour contract, which curtails their right to seek alternate employment.

In addition to these dynamics of labour incorporation, the organization of unfree labour in the migration context is also connected to the discursive construction of nationalism and national identity, the regulation of borders and citizenship rights, and the normalization of the differential treatment of citizens and foreigners that stems from these processes (Sharma 2012). The production of borders is key to the organization of unfree labour in this context. Sharma (2012) argues that borders are sets of institutional relationships shaped by the law, government policies, the market, and social relations. They regulate how people can move across space defined as "national territory" and, moreover, are connected to the construction of different levels of status that have profound impacts on peoples' lives. With regards to the organization of labour, borders are connected to class relations in that not all are equally affected by the laws and regulations that govern mobility. Borders are also connected to discourses of race and racialized hierarchies, which are reflected in immigration policies that have historically restricted entry on racial grounds. Thus, borders are not so much absolute barriers to mobility as they are mechanisms of social, political, and economic control. Thus they play a key role in securing and reproducing low-wage and "unfree" labour.

Nationalist discourses are central to these processes. Specifically, nationalist discourses legitimize differential treatment and rights between those constructed as "citizens" and those who are "noncitizens." Sharma (2012, 323) states, "the result is not necessarily the exclusion of all those who are seen as being 'foreign,' but rather their subordination in Canada." Thus, these discourses are directly linked to the production of the "other," understood in relation to membership in a national community. Moreover, as Sharma (2012) argues, these discourses construct an understanding of "national" versus "foreigner" that normalizes different sets of rights.

While nationalist discourses are constructed in relation to notions of membership in a national community, they may not necessarily take the form of constructing simple dichotomies of inclusion and exclusion. Instead, they may be framed around notions of desirability, with the "other" deemed "undesirable" in terms of their potential membership in the national community and then defined as a threat that must be regulated, policed, and contained, even as they live and work within the respective nation-state (Sharma 2012). "Outsiders" who are defined as threats that need to be regulated are then subject to forms of incorporation that construct differential treatment. As will be discussed below, in this way "outsider" groups are contained politically and at the same time integrated into a labour market in ways that address the imperatives of capital accumulation.

These discourses are often constructed in racial/ethnic terms, producing racialized hierarchies of inclusion, exclusion, desirability, and undesirability. In Canadian immigration policy, which historically was developed to promote white (Anglo/British) settlement of Canada, nonwhite immigrants were categorized as "nonpreferred races" or from "nonpreferred nations" prior to 1967. Before the late 1960s, there was a great deal of public opposition to the granting of Canadian citizenship to those applying for entry to Canada from nontraditional (i.e., non-Western/European) source countries (Satzewich 1991). Underlying this sentiment was the belief that non-Western European and particularly nonwhite immigrant populations were incompatible or inassimilable with the Canadian population as it existed at that time. As immigration policy changed to allow for much greater diversity, there began to be a shift toward the increased emphasis on temporary labour permits, something that has grown significantly in recent years, indicating that the framing of "desirable citizen" in racialized forms is still a powerful organizing force in constructing the national community and legitimizing the subordination of racialized "foreigners" within it.

Returning to questions of political economy, nationalist discourses are institutionalized through the regulation of citizenship, as citizens hold a privileged standing within the nation-state in relation to noncitizens. The regulation of citizenship is supported by nationalist discourses that legitimize the subordination of those who are "foreigners" to the nation-state; "denying the rights, entitlements, and protections that citizens have to those made into noncitizens is a crucial feature of how dominant ideas of nations-as-homes operate within today's world" (Sharma 2012, 332). These discourses then both legitimize and contribute to the reproduction of relations of unfree labour. The chapter now turns to examine the ways in which the temporary status of workers in the SAWP shapes dynamics of unfree labour.

The Seasonal Agricultural Worker Program

The prevalence of labour shortages in Canadian agriculture has historically placed pressure on the Canadian state to undertake initiatives to ensure an adequate supply of agricultural labour (Thomas 2009). As one solution to agricultural labour shortages, the state has sought to make use of racialized immigrant and migrant labour. Through much of the twentieth century, difficulty in ensuring a continuous supply of seasonal labour persisted due to the tendency of agricultural workers to leave agricultural production for industries that offered more permanent employment. The solution to these labour shortages came in the form of the SAWP and the incorporation of workers from Mexico and the Caribbean as unfree migrant labour.

The use of foreign labour became a primary means to compensate for shortages of domestic labour following World War II. Between 1946 and 1966, 89,680 immigrants entered Canada destined for seasonal agricultural production in Ontario (Satzewich 1991). These were primarily immigrants from European countries, many of whom were leaving Europe as a result of the war. Three of the major groups of immigrants destined to agricultural production in Ontario were Polish war veterans, displaced persons (as a result of the war), and Dutch farmers. All three groups were accorded the right to apply for permanent residence and citizenship. While providing temporary relief to the employment shortages faced by agricultural growers, none offered the potential for a permanent source of seasonal agricultural labour, as they tended to seek forms of employment that would provide greater security and monetary benefits than provided by seasonal agricultural labour, which was viewed as a stepping-stone to employment in other industries or as a means to lead to the establishment of one's own farm (Haythorne 1960). This meant that growers continued to face labour shortages.

The solution came in the form of the SAWP, a federal government program that facilitates the entry of foreign workers for temporary employment in the agricultural industry. In 1966, following intense lobbying pressure from growers, the federal government established an agreement with the Commonwealth Caribbean to import farm labourers on a seasonal basis. In its initial year, the program brought 264 Jamaican workers into Canada. In 1967, Trinidad-Tobago and Barbados became participants in the program. It expanded rapidly in ensuing years, and within a decade it was incorporating approximately 5,000 workers. In 1974, Mexico negotiated a similar agreement to allow Mexican workers into Canada on a temporary basis. In 1976, the program expanded again to facilitate entry of workers from Grenada, Antigua, Dominica, St. Christopher-Nevis-Anguilla, St. Lucia, St. Vincent, and Monserrat. By 2012, the SAWP employed over 20,000 workers a year (Faraday 2012).

The workers' period of employment ranges from six to forty weeks, with a minimum of forty hours of work per week, though this can exceed sixty hours. Under the employment agreements that govern the program, farm labourers are paid at an hourly wage just over Canadian minimum wage levels and are provided with health care coverage throughout their period of employment. Employers are responsible for covering transportation costs for their employees to and from their home country and for providing accommodation.

Essentially, the program facilitates the incorporation of migrant workers from the Caribbean and Mexico into seasonal agricultural production as unfree migrant labour. SAWP workers are not permitted to seek employment outside their specified contract or establish permanent residence within Canada via the program. Through these restrictions, the state is able to continually secure a labour force that is both seasonal in nature and static in terms of upward mobility. Further, through these processes it can secure a labour force that accepts the physically demanding and low-paying work that is subject to labour standards abuses without effective mechanisms of appeal (Suen 2000; Sharma 2001; Faraday 2012).

While provided access to housing and health care coverage, workers often experience substandard housing and heightened health and safety risks while at work, encounter barriers to accessing the health care system, and are exempt from some key legislated minimum employment standards (Thomas 2009; Hennebry 2012). For example, under Ontario's Employment Standards Act (ESA), there are two primary categories of employees that relate to SAWP workers: "farmworkers" and "harvesters" (Ontario 2011, 2). A farmworker is "a person employed on a farm whose work is directly related to the primary production of certain agricultural products" (ibid.), which could include planting, cultivating, pruning, and caring for livestock. A harvester is someone employed to harvest crops of fruit, vegetables, or tobacco for marketing or storage. In both cases, there are exemptions from key standards in the ESA (Commission for Labor Cooperation 2002; Verma 2003). Farmworkers are exempt from the standards regulating hours of work, daily and weekly rest periods, eating periods, overtime pay, minimum wage, public holidays, and vacation pay. Harvesters are covered by minimum wage provisions and public holiday and vacation pay (if employed for thirteen weeks). But like farmworkers, harvesters are exempt from hours of work, daily and weekly rest periods, eating periods, and overtime pay standards. These exemptions are justified based on the seasonal nature of the work, the argument being that the application of the minimum standards would jeopardize the completion of the seasonal harvests.

"Unfree Labour" and "Reliable Workers"

Due to the perception that migrant workers from the Caribbean were incompatible with Canadian culture, national identity, and even climate, policy makers were able to deny workers entering Canada under the SAWP the right to apply for citizenship (Satzewich 1991; Sharma 2001). This then enabled the enactment of a number of entrance restrictions when the program was initially established to ensure that the foreign workers remain in agricultural production and do not attempt to move to industries offering longer-term employment and better wages and working conditions.

As discussed above, temporary foreign worker programs such as the SAWP are framed through nationalist discourses that legitimize the differential treatment experienced by migrant workers. The SAWP itself and the very poor labour standards associated with the work are legitimized through a discourse that constructs these workers as "reliable" workers. For example, the Government of Canada (HRSDC 2004) describes the program as being designed to "provide a supplementary source of reliable and qualified seasonal labour in order to improve Canada's prosperity by ensuring that crops are planted and harvested in a timely fashion." (The employer association Foreign Agricultural Resource Management Services (FARMS) utilizes a similar discourse when explaining the program. A FARMS publication, *The Quest for a Reliable Workforce in the Horticulture Industry: Reliable Workers, Regardless of Source*, was commissioned to detail the importance of offshore workers to Ontario agriculture (FARMS 1995a)). The report stated that agricultural producers would much prefer to hire Canadian workers; however, there was a shortage of "reliable" Canadian workers. Former human resources minister Doug Young attributed this shortage to a "malaise" in Canada "fueled by unreal expectations" of Canadians of all ages; conversely, "workers in other countries around the world see opportunities created by hard work" and are "not afraid to do the dirty jobs" (C. Thomas 1996). The FARMS (1995b: 5) report argued that "seasonal offshore workers constitute a safety valve that assures a successful harvest," and that the SAWP "has a record of delivering workers that are 98% RELIABLE, i.e., [have] completed the harvest" (see also FARMS (2012), which reiterates this claim). Beyond the SAWP, Canadian employers accessing the expanded TFWP characterize foreign workers in similar terms (Gollom 2014). This discourse of reliability illustrates the multidimensional, contradictory nature of the use of temporary foreign workers. Growers argue that the foreign labourers are needed because they make good agricultural workers. The importance of foreign workers is proclaimed in federal and provincial government reports. But it is because they are foreign workers, and not recognized as deserving of the political rights of Canadian citizens, that makes them so desirable. The discourse of reliability obscures the conditions within the program that ensure that the workers remain "reliable," conditions that are themselves contingent upon the denial of citizenship rights. In other words, it masks the relations that create the conditions for the reproduction of the seasonal workforce. Moreover, this discourse of reliability works in conjunction with nationalist discourses that designate the "insiders" and "outsiders" of the Canadian nation. Specifically, it unites the imperatives of capital accumulation ("reliable"/unfree labour) with the containment of "outsider threats" ("undesirable" immigrant groups) by simultaneously justifying the employment of temporary migrant workers *and* legitimating their differential treatment within the Canadian labour market.

SAWP workers are under contractual obligation to work for a specific period of time. If they fail to do so, they will be deported and prevented from working within the program in the future. Workers are not permitted to settle permanently in Canada and their families are not permitted entry at all, thereby preventing any alternative economic security for the workers within Canada. Further, the program is structured so that farmers may request specific workers that have been previously employed if their work is considered satisfactory. Given that wages and working conditions are superior to those found in their home countries, this creates further incentive for the workers to perform in a "reliable" manner, despite long hours of work, pay that is low relative to other sectors in the Canadian labour market, and an inability to exercise many basic labour rights. Although liaison officers from the consular offices of the participating governments are charged with assisting workers in dealing with problems, they are also responsible for promoting the program and increasing the number of workers employed from their respective countries. This can result in situations where disputes between farmers and workers may be settled in ways that might not represent the workers' best interests, as the liaison officers must ensure that Ontario farmers are provided with a "reliable" labour force (Brem 2006). In sum, it is these conditions—which are obscured through the discourse of reliability—that produce "reliable" workers and provide the underlying rationale for the program.

Contesting "Unfree Labour"

Despite these overarching conditions of labour exploitation, the conditions of "unfree labour" are highly contested (see chapters by Ramsaroop, and Paz Ramirez and Chun, this volume). Unionization is one means through which agricultural workers have attempted to improve conditions of work. In Ontario, farmworkers have historically been exempt from labour relations legislation that facilitates freedom of association and collective bargaining. Since the 1990s, the United Food and Commercial Workers union (UFCW) has spearheaded a campaign through the legal system to win the legal right to organize and bargain collectively for agricultural workers in Ontario. While the campaign takes place within the courts, it is accompanied by efforts to organize agricultural workers into certified bargaining units and to negotiate collective agreements with employers if and when certification is achieved. Table 1 outlines the recent trajectory of legislative developments regarding farmworker unionization in Ontario.

Table 1. Legal Developments in Farmworker Unionization, Ontario

Year	Legal Development	Result
1943	Ontario Collective Bargaining Act	Excluded agricultural workers from collective association and collective bargaining
1994	Ontario Agricultural Labour Relations Act (ALRA)	Established the right to unionize for nonseasonal agricultural workers
1995	Labour Relations and Employment Statute Law Amendment Act (Bill 7)	Overturned the ALRA
2001	*Dunmore v. Ontario*, Supreme Court of Canada	Agricultural workers have association rights
2002	Ontario Agricultural Employees Protection Act	Agricultural workers may form associations; no collective bargaining rights
2008	Ontario Court of Appeal	Collective bargaining for agricultural workers to be established by Nov. 2009
2011	*Ontario v. Fraser*, Supreme Court of Canada	Charter requires "good faith" negotiation but not collective bargaining

Source: Choudry and Thomas (2012)

In conjunction with pursuing the legal challenge in Ontario (which has not been successful in establishing collective bargaining rights for agricultural workers in that province), the UFCW has undertaken organizing campaigns on farms in Quebec, Manitoba, and British Columbia (UFCW 2007; Preibisch 2010). These have produced collective agreements that include: a grievance procedure; the right to be recalled (named) each season based on seniority; workplace health and safety committees and training; and provision of contracts and other workplace documents in the worker's language. Most importantly, they provide the right to collective bargaining, giving workers' representatives a seat at the table in negotiating working conditions. On some worksites, collective agreements "also oblige the employer to assist the workers in application for permanent status under the Provincial Nominees Program" (UFCW 2011, 21).

In addition, a number of migrant worker justice initiatives have emerged in the absence of unionization. Justicia for Migrant Workers is a grassroots activist collective based in Toronto and Vancouver that promotes the rights of migrant farmworkers, including those in the SAWP. The Migrant Workers Alliance for Change includes advocacy and community groups working in alliance to pressure the federal and provincial governments to eliminate the differential treatment experienced by migrant workers. The Agricultural Workers Alliance is associated with the UFCW and maintains advocacy and information centres for migrant workers across Canada. The Immigrant Workers Centre in Montreal provides education on labour rights for migrant and immigrant workers, and engages in organizing campaigns to pressure governments and employers to improve their conditions of work. Finally, the Independent Workers Association, formed through cooperation between the United Steelworkers of America (Canada) and MIGRANTE-Ontario, pressures the federal government to improve conditions of workers in the TFWP, and provides education and advocacy services for those workers. These and ongoing initiatives such as those discussed in this volume demonstrate the ways in which relations of "unfreedom" as constructed through temporary foreign worker programs in Canada are highly contested. As they unfold, a key challenge for movements and organizations seeking justice for migrant workers will be to construct strategies of resistance that do not succumb to the insider/outsider dichotomies contained in nationalist discourses (for example, see Ramsaroop, this volume). Instead, strategies are needed that seek to eliminate differential treatment that is constructed in relation to citizenship status.

Conclusion: Expanding the TFWP

The SAWP is characterized by policy makers as a migration program of best practices, providing not only economic benefits for the participating countries, but also a model for other states and other economic sectors. The "best practices" element of the program—and thus its characterization as a model migration program—stems from its capacities to ensure a permanent cycle of temporary migration. A representative from the Mexican consulate said that it is "a tangible, positive example of what can happen when two parties agree to administer migration, given the need of one party for labour, and the need of the other party to provide jobs" (Amuchastegui 2006).

The SAWP provided a model for the Canadian federal government's 2002 expansion of the TFWP (M. Thomas 2010). In July 2002, the federal government developed the Low-Skilled Pilot Project for occupations requiring either a high school diploma or a maximum of two years of job-specific training. As part of the program, employers are expected to assist the foreign workers in finding accommodation, must pay full airfares to and from the home country, and have to provide medical coverage until the worker is eligible for provincial health insurance. The Low-Skilled Pilot Project initially placed a twelve-month time limit on employment contracts for foreign workers, with the requirement that the worker must return home for a minimum period of four months before applying for another work permit. This was subsequently increased to periods of up to twenty-four months (HRSDC 2007), and in April 2011 to a maximum of four years. Under the newest regulations, once they have reached the four-year limit, workers must wait four years before they can reapply to the program. This expanded program extends the principles established by the SAWP to a wide range of low-skilled occupational categories. As with the SAWP, workers are employed under conditions of unfree wage labour as they are not permitted to circulate in the labour market. Nor can they apply for per-manent residence through the program. Thus these workers become effec-tively tied to and marginalized within a stratum of lower-tier employment, without regulatory mechanisms to enforce basic labour rights. Moreover, the program creates a high degree of labour flexibility for employers, as it is based solely on short-term labour demands. The TFWP's expansion con-stitutes another growing example of the ways in which racialized migrant workers are constructed as highly exploited labour in the contemporary labour market. More generally, the spread of such programs reveals a key contradiction of early twenty-first century capitalism—one that holds clear ties to the past—namely that in the so-called "era of globalization" there remain many constraints placed on the free movement of labour. It also reveals the ways in which the contemporary state may act to support and secure capitalist interests through new strategies to regulate and control labour that originates outside its borders.

In conclusion, the growth of temporary foreign worker programs exhibits two common features: first, foreign migrant workers provide a source of inexpensive and temporary labour in cases of shortages of domes-tic labour; and second, the nation-state, through its control over citizenship and residence rights, specifically in the denial of these rights to foreign migrant workers, plays a crucial role in the reproduction of the respective systems of migrant labour. These processes produce what Sharma (2012, 338) defines as global apartheid, "the organization of an ever-widening differentiation between people in either wealthy or impoverished nation-states through restrictive immigration policies that imprison impoverished people within zones of poverty." The employment of migrant workers through the SAWP and the expanded TFWP, legitimated by national-ist discourses that occlude conditions of "unfreedom," constitutes the Canadian example of these wider global processes.

References

Amuchastegui, Maria. 2006. "Farming It Out." *This Magazine* (May–June).

Balibar, Etienne. 2004. *We, the People of Europe? Reflections on Transnational Citizenship*. Trans. James Swenson. Princeton: Princeton University Press.

Brem, Maxwell. 2006. *Migrant Workers in Canada: A Review of the Seasonal Agricultural Worker Program*. Ottawa: North-South Institute.

Burawoy, Michael. 1976. "The Functions and Reproduction of Migrant Labour: Comparative Material from Southern Africa and the United States." *American Journal of Sociology* 81, no. 5.

Canadian Broadcasting Corporation (CBC). April 12, 2013. "Temporary Foreign Worker Impacts Felt Far Beyond RBC." <cbc.ca/news/canada/british-columbia/story/2013/04/12/bc-rbc-apology-union-business-reaction.html>.

Castles, Stephen, and Mark J. Miller. 2003. *The Age of Migration: International Population Movements in the Modern World*. New York: Guilford Press.

Choudry, Aziz, and Mark Thomas. 2012. "Organizing Migrant and Immigrant Workers in Canada." In Stephanie Ross and Larry Savage (eds.) *Rethinking the Politics of Labour in Canada*. Halifax and Winnipeg: Fernwood.

Chun, Jennifer, Mark Thomas, and Leah Vosko. 2013. "Organizing Precariously Employed Workers in Canada." *Experiences Organizing Informal Workers—Canada Inventory*. Unpublished report.

Commission for Labor Cooperation. 2002. *Protection of Migrant Agricultural Workers in Canada, Mexico and the United States*. Washington: Commission for Labor Cooperation.

Faraday, Fay. 2012. *Made in Canada: How the Law Constructs Migrant Workers' Insecurity*. Toronto: Metcalf Foundation.

Foreign Agricultural Resource Management Services (FARMS). 2012. "Seasonal Farm Worker Program Prepares for Labour Influx: Seasonal Agricultural Workers Program Eyed as a Model Around the World." News release, May 22.<http://www.farmsontario.ca/media_centre/labourinflux>.

_____. 1995a. *Horticulture Industry Launches Quest to Secure Reliable Labour Force*. News release, September 19. Mississauga: FARMS.

_____. 1995b. *The Quest for a Reliable Workforce in the Horticulture Industry: "Reliable Workers, Regardless of Source."* Mississauga: FARMS.

Freeman, Gary. 2004. "Immigrant Incorporation in Western Democracies." *International Migration Review* 38, no. 3.

Gollom, Mark. April 8, 2014. "Temporary Foreign Workers Have Better Work Ethic, Some Employers Believe." *CBC News*. <cbc.ca/news/temporary-foreign-workers-have-better-work-ethic-some-employers-believe-1.2600864>.

Haythorne, George. 1960. *Labour in Canadian Agriculture*. Cambridge: Harvard University Press.

Hennebry, Jenna. 2012. *Permanently Temporary? Agricultural Migrant Workers and Their Integration in Canada*. Montreal: Institute for Research on Public Policy.

Hollifield, John. 2004. "The Emerging Migration State." *International Migration Review* 38, no. 3.

Human Resources and Skills Development Canada (HRSDC). 2007. *Pilot Project for Occupations Requiring Lower Levels of Formal Training (NOC C and D): Changes to the Pilot Project as of February 23, 2007*. Ottawa: HRSDC.

_____. 2004. *Agriculture Programs and Services: Overview*. Ottawa: HRSDC.

International Labour Organization. 2013. *Global Employment Trends 2013*. Geneva: International Labour Office.

_____. 2012. *Labour Migration*. Governing Body, 316 Session, November. Geneva: International Labour Office.

_____. 2005. *A Global Alliance Against Forced Labour: Global Report Under the Follow-Up to the ILO Declaration on Fundamental Principles and Rights at Work*. Geneva: International Labour Office.

Lerche, Jens. 2007. "A Global Alliance against Forced Labour? Unfree Labour, Neo-Liberal Globalization and the International Labour Organization." *Journal of Agrarian Change* 7, no. 4.

Marx, Karl. 1976. *Capital: A Critique of Political Economy*, vol. 1. Trans. Ben Fowkes. Harmondsworth: Penguin.

Miles, Robert. 1987. *Capitalism and Unfree Labour: Anomaly or Necessity?* London and New York: Tavistock.

Ontario Ministry of Labour. 2011. *Agricultural Workers Employment Standards Fact Sheet*. Toronto: Ontario Ministry of Labour.

Phillips, Nicola. 2011. *Unfree Labour and Adverse Incorporation in Global Production Networks: Comparative Perspectives on Brazil and India*. Chronic Poverty Research Centre working paper 176. Manchester: Chronic Poverty Research Centre.

Preibisch, Kerry. 2010. "Pick-Your-Own Labor: Migrant Workers and Flexibility in Canadian Agriculture." *International Migration Review* 44, no. 2.

Rogaly, Ben. 2008. "Migrant Workers in the ILOs Global Alliance Against Forced Labour Report: A Critical Appraisal." *Third World Quarterly* 29, no. 7.

Satzewich, Vic. 1991. *Racism and the Incorporation of Foreign Labour: Farm Labour Migration to Canada Since 1945*. London and New York: Routledge.

_____. 1990. "Rethinking Post-1945 Migration to Canada: Towards a Political Economy of Labour Migration." *International Migration* 28, no. 3.

Schuster, Liza, and John Solomos. 2002. "Rights and Wrongs across European Borders: Migrants, Minorities, and Citizenship." *Citizenship Studies* 6, no. 1.

Sharma, Nandita. 2012. "Nation States, Borders, Citizenship, and the Making of 'National' Difference." In Deborah Brock, Rebecca Raby, and Mark Thomas (eds.), *Power and Everyday Practices*. Toronto: Nelson Education Ltd.

_____. 2006. *Home Economics: Nationalism and the Making of 'Migrant Workers' in Canada*. Toronto: University of Toronto Press.

_____. 2001. "On Being *Not* Canadian: The Social Organization of 'Migrant Workers' in Canada." *Canadian Review of Sociology and Anthropology* 38, no. 4.

Stasiulis, Daiva. 1997. "The Political Economy of Race, Ethnicity, and Migration." In Wallace Clement (ed.), *Understanding Canada: Building on the New Canadian Political Economy*. Kingston and Montreal: McGill–Queen's University Press.

Strauss, Kendra. 2012. "Coerced, Forced and Unfree Labour; Geographies of Exploitation in Contemporary Labour Markets." *Geography Compass* 6, no. 3.

Suen, Rachel Li Wai. 2000. "You Sure Know How to Pick 'Em: Human Rights and Migrant Farm Workers in Canada." *Georgetown Immigration Law Journal* 15, no. 1.

Thomas, Chris. 1996. "Minister Assures Farmers Offshore Labour Will Continue." *Simcoe Reformer* (April 22).

Thomas, Derrick. 2010. *Foreign Nationals Working Temporarily in Canada*. Ottawa: Statistics Canada.

Thomas, Mark. 2010. "Labour Migration and Temporary Work: Canada's Foreign Worker Programs in the 'New Economy'." In Norene Pupo and Mark Thomas (eds.), *Interrogating the New Economy: Restructuring Work in the 21st Century*. Toronto: University of Toronto Press.

_____. 2009. *Regulating Flexibility: The Political Economy of Employment Standards*. Montreal and Kingston: McGill–Queen's University Press.

United Food and Commercial Workers (UFCW). 2011. *The Status of Migrant Farm Workers in Canada, 2010–2011*. Toronto: UFCW.

_____. 2007. *The Status of Migrant Farmworkers in Canada, 2006–07*. Toronto: UFCW.

Valiani, Salimah. 2007. *Briefing Note: The Temporary Foreign Worker Program and Its Intersection with Canadian Immigration Policy*. Ottawa: Canadian Labour Congress.

Verma, Veena. 2003. *The Mexican and Caribbean Seasonal Agricultural Workers Program: Regulatory and Policy Framework, Farm Industry Level Employment Practices, and the Future of the Program under Unionization*. Ottawa: North-South Institute.

Migrant Live-In Caregivers: Control, Consensus, and Resistance in the Workplace and the Community

Jah-Hon Koo and Jill Hanley

DOMESTIC WORK AND CAREGIVING HAS BEEN PART OF CANADA'S FABRIC SINCE its colonial founding and has long represented one of the most easily accessible routes for migration available to women in economically less developed regions or countries (Cohen 1994). Whether rural or urban, north or south, women have turned to domestic work and caregiving to earn income when their home communities were unable or unwilling to support them. This form of labour has always been gendered and racialized, reliant on the existence of inequalities of wealth (Parreñas 2000). Within the unstructured work setting of a private home, domestic workers' labour process and employment relationships are ambiguous.

The Live-in Caregiver Program (LCP)—jointly managed by Citizenship and Immigration Canada (CIC) and Employment and Skills Development Canada (ESDC)—channelled international migration for private-home domestic and caregiving work, framing LCP workers' living and working conditions. The program was designed to import and maintain docile, low-cost labour through severe restrictions of their choices and mobility (Arat-Koç 1993; Choudry et al. 2009; Valiani 2009; Brickner and Straehle 2010; see also Bakan, this volume). LCP workers must complete 3,900 hours or twenty-four months of full-time live-in caregiving work in a private home if they hope to apply for permanent residence for themselves and their families, many workers' primary motivation in coming to Canada. While the LCP was replaced by the Caregiver Program in November 2014, introducing changes that may have significant impact on the rate of participants staying in Canada permanently, the empirical research presented here was collected prior to this change and the basic conditions of the day-to-day work and precarious immigration status remain the same.

The difficult situation in which LCP workers find themselves has not, however, completely stifled their efforts to defend their rights. LCP workers grapple with ways to increase their sense of autonomy, respect, and control. Of particular importance within the context of this book, workers in the LCP (and its preceding programs) are arguably the temporary foreign workers with the longest, most autonomous, and most diverse organizing history in Canada. Ethnic-specific, self-organized groups of domestic workers have for decades been organizing social events, social networking opportunities, and—on occasion—individual advocacy for members who run into trouble. Central to these efforts is the hard work undertaken by informal social networks, religious congregations, and ethnic associations often on the "front line" of informing migrants and motivating them to defend their rights with confidence.

Caribbean women, the first wave of women who came on the programs preceding the LCP, pioneered the recent forms of organizing for domestic workers' rights in Canada. Among Filipina workers in Canada, such groups have been active since the late 1980s and early 1990s. Although far from achieving all their goals, LCP organizers have managed to win important policy improvements in the past twenty years, something that can perhaps offer some inspiration for organizing among other categories of so-called low-skilled migrant workers.

While recognizing the long history of LCP workers' precariousness and vulnerabilities as well as their triumph of self-organizing and social change, it is important to consider the interplay of their community involvement and their workplace labour processes. We draw on recent research on Montreal-based Filipina live-in caregivers' experiences,[1] with a particular focus on the patterns of power relations behind the closed doors of private LCP workplaces. We then explore the context in which LCP workers wrestle in the public sphere—with echoes of the same power dynamics—for control over their situations through social networks, ethnic and community associations, and, increasingly, community-labour initiatives.

---

1   Koo's doctoral research (twenty-five interviews with sixteen participants) and Hanley's FQRSC project (interviews with ten LCP workers plus LCP community organizations); also drawing on Hanley's fifteen years of research (interviews with more than twenty LCP workers, surveying nearly two hundred and fifty) and alliance work with LCP and other Filipino organizations.

LCP workers are acutely aware of the unequal power relations within their workplace and in broader society in general and make difficult choices about whether and how to challenge them. With the LCP as a clear example of how labour can be made "unfree," we argue that despite divergent power dynamics, workers' individual efforts to challenge unequal power relations in the workplace have limited consequences so long as the LCP's overarching structure keeps the threat of losing livelihood and immigration status over their heads. We conclude with some reflections on the long road to justice for migrant domestic workers in consideration of the challenge to connecting unfree labour to public resistance.

"Unfree Labour"? Power Dynamics behind the Closed Doors of the LCP Workplace

The LCP is about as controlling of labour as you can get. With the requirement of these foreign workers to live in their employer's private residence, it is notoriously difficult for workers to have any control over their living and working conditions (Oxman-Martinez et al. 2004). Critics have documented the ways in which the LCP structures labour vulnerabilities for over twenty years but behind the closed doors of the private homes that are LCP workplaces, to what extent are LCP workers really "unfree"? How do LCP workers respond to their restrictive and exploitative working conditions? In this section, we aim to identify and explain diverse power dynamics in the LCP workplace from a labour process perspective—ranging from control to consensus to resistance (Thompson and Newsome 2004; Thompson 2010).

Here we present the ways in which control is exercised over workers within the workplace (overtly by employers and more subtly by policy constraints related to their immigration status); how in some settings, employers and workers reach some form of consensus about the work arrangement; and finally, the various ways in which LCP workers resist difficult conditions, from simple noncompliance to overt challenge of the employer's power.[2]

Control over LCP Workers

Through the investigation of LCP workers' detailed labour processes, we found there was minimal worker control in most workplaces. However,

---

2   It remains difficult to document the conditions across all LCP workplaces, with samples subject to self-selection bias. We cannot estimate the relative frequency of these various power dynamics.

workers were aware of their vulnerable positions and poor working conditions; some asserted that they were modern slaves and that "living-in" is like being a prisoner. The most common responses to excessive control of LCP workers in their workplaces were silence and endurance, despite their dissatisfaction with their working conditions. LCP workers tended to emphasize that they are in Canada "just to work," not to make any trouble. They typically portrayed themselves as extraordinarily responsible and hardworking and regarded the LCP as a "stepping-stone," hoping that making it through the program would lead to better work opportunities after they became permanent residents.

Restrictive government regulations, particularly with respect to workers' mobility, motivate LCP workers' silence and endurance. The twenty-four-month live-in requirement as a path to permanent residence for LCP workers was both carrot (the chance to establish themselves in Canada permanently with their families) and stick (restrictions of the program with deportation an enduring risk). LCP workers commonly complained about CIC or ESDC's processing times, particularly during transition periods between employers, which in one case lasted eight months. They perceived this long processing period as a crucial barrier to deciding to leave an undesirable workplace. Subsequently, it seemed that in some workplaces employers did not necessarily need to put much effort to harness the labour of LCP workers due to state bureaucratic control.

But a closer look at the labour process of LCP workers reveals that their employers exercise a variety of controls, echoing the employers' strategies described by Pratt (1999). In addition to employers' preliminary decisions over basic working conditions such as wages, working hours, and the types of duties, many employers exercised arbitrary control over the details of their ambiguous home-setting labour processes through persuasion, prohibitions, subcontracting, threat, lay-off, and delay or refusal in immigration paperwork.

Rather than risk losing their employment—and potentially their immigration status—by complaining or resisting, we found that many LCP workers would prefer to accept unfair, disrespectful, or abusive treatment. Apart from potential violations of rights, there is the difficult reality of the LCP: isolation within the employer's home; family separation; and tiring, difficult work for low pay. Enduring such work conditions has a heavy psychological toll.

Workplace Consensus

Despite the overwhelming control of LCP workers, workplace consensus can be found around particular issues. As Stasiulis and Bakan (1997) noted, we observed that LCP workers' decisions related to "living-out" (mostly during the weekend) were generally based on negotiation and mutual agreement between LCP workers and employers—in direct contravention of government rules.

More importantly, we found that the ambiguous LCP workplace of the private home presents very distinct labour processes and relations. A couple of LCP workers expressed exceptional satisfaction with their current autonomous labour process and harmonious relationships. One said that she was like her employer's older sister and even the boss of the house. As LCP workers tend to build strong mutual attachment with care-recipients, workplace consensus seemed more likely when the care-recipient was their employer, particularly when the care-recipient was a senior who wanted a companion rather than a housekeeper. The LCP workers under these exceptional conditions could determine their duties, their schedule, and when to have breaks—for example, taking a day off for a hospital appointment without having any concern or trouble.

Although unstructured work settings may sometimes allow the workers to enjoy more autonomy and enhanced personal relations, these so-called "family-like" workplaces sometimes go hand-in-hand with blurred duties and work hours and lead to the justification of irregular working conditions. However, we found that LCP workers with exceptional workplace satisfaction experienced fewer ambiguities in terms of their conditions; their employers actually provided more favourable working conditions than other LCP workplaces, treated them fairly (as workers rather than as family members), and ensured more privacy. Their satisfaction was not only based on their subjective perceptions or feelings, but can be supported by measurable work-related indicators (e.g., number of work hours, paid overtime).

Another notable case challenging traditional antagonistic worker-employer relations was that collaborative processes were found between one LCP worker and her current employer when she was encouraged and supported in fighting against unjust treatment by her former employer through a lawsuit. This leads us to the next form of power dynamic: resistance.

Worker Resistance

Although most LCP workers in this study were silent and a few enjoyed exceptionally favourable working conditions, others were able to express their grievances and resist against their employers in order to improve conditions. There was a high level of acceptance among LCP workers with respect to their basic working conditions, such as wages and work hours, particularly when these conditions were written in the contract. It seemed that they took it for granted that they received the minimum wage and worked intensively more than eight hours a day as no one seriously attempted to demand higher wages or fewer working hours. However, many workers raised their voices when other aspects of their contract were violated, particularly when there were arbitrary schedule changes.

Thus the issues leading to explicit conflicts and/or their resistance were not necessarily monetary or material. One worker challenged her employer only when her weekend social and community involvement was denied, despite the employer's placation by offering overtime payment. For her and some others, opportunities for engagement with her (extended) family, friends, and other LCP workers or in religious activities were absolutely essential and not to be denied, despite the power imbalance. The cases of several other workers also prove that excessive control over their living conditions, such as restriction of certain foods within the workplace where they also live, was a major factor in their resistance. As Choudry et al. (2009) point out, a denial of dignity often triggers resistance.

We have identified various strategies, networks, and resources the workers in our study employed in order to resist. At the individual level, this included both passive resistance (simply quitting and looking for another job at great personal sacrifice) and soft demands, such as formally requesting that the employer respect their responsibility to notify ESDC that their contract is terminated. One successful individual strategy used by several workers was keeping records (e.g., daily schedule, journals, or written duty orders) of their labour process, which were or would potentially be used as a legal proof should conflicts arise.

Almost all the study participants used both formal and informal social networks—connections with family members, friends, other LCP workers, and/or community organizations—to deal with workplace problems. One worker was offered a place to stay with some financial support by a Filipina stranger she met on the street right after she was laid off and lost her residence. A strong sense of community among Filipinas led the new acquaintance to offer help. Other LCP workers began their relationships with community groups through rather innocuous participation in a French language course, a social event such as apple picking, or a Christmas party. Becoming comfortable with the organizations in these nonthreatening contexts made LCP workers more open to dedicating their precious time off to such things as popular education about labour or immigration rights.

These organizations eventually accompanied the few LCP workers who filed labour complaints against their previous employers. Through such support, certain workers were able to win their legal complaints. Some government bodies, namely the Commission des Normes de Travail (Quebec Labour Standards Commission) and the Human Rights Commission, were perceived as worker allies, actually facilitating their defence of labour rights; CIC and ESDC were seen to maintain the status quo through bureaucratic control. Some workers were informed of community resources through the Quebec immigration package issued to incoming LCP workers and thus felt the Quebec immigration authority (MICC) played a positive role in providing information for their initial community involvement. In contrast, workers condemned recruitment agencies not only for excessive fees and irresponsible services (e.g., some workers found themselves unemployed upon arrival) but also for an allegation that agencies removed community resource information from the immigration package to prevent workers from connecting with these organizations and demanding their labour rights.

LCP workers' attempts to gain control over their working lives are not limited to the boundaries of their workplaces. Community engagement can be both the motivation for and the medium of their resistance in the workplace. We turn to explore diverse ways that LCP workers engage in the wider community beyond their isolated workplaces.

LCP Workers "Breaking Free" of the Workplace?
Engagement in the Community

In the past decade, LCP workers have emerged from the private sphere into public consciousness. Ongoing organizing and media engagement have made the LCP familiar to people beyond those directly concerned. With the growing numbers who have finished the program and who often, along with their spouses and children, become immigrants, LCP workers have emerged from the isolated workplace into the general community.

As we have analyzed elsewhere (Hanley et al. 2012), several factors have facilitated LCP organizing since the early 1990s. First, LCP workers have been overwhelmingly Filipina, giving them a common language and cultural references when they leave their workplaces to seek companionship and services on their days off; they meet each other in stores, in churches, and at parties. Second, in many Canadian cities, the LCP has been the major vehicle for Filipino immigration, removing some of the stigma related to doing domestic work that has been noted in previous studies on domestic work (Hanley et al. 2010) and allowing Filipinas to feel comfortable coming together *as* domestic workers. Third, Filipina LCP workers are on average more highly educated than other categories of "low-skilled" TFWs and are generally quite comfortable in English, giving them an easier sense of entitlement in Canada and making it easier for them to engage in public debate. Finally, some LCP workers come to Canada with prior activist involvement with the Philippines' wide-reaching people's movements. Over the years, these workers have built ties with a transnational Filipino movement to defend migrant workers' rights.

Community support for LCP workers corresponds in many ways to the diverging workplace power relations discussed above. Workers are often encouraged to be silent and endure control; they may be supported in negotiating consensus with their employers; and/or they sometimes resist their conditions through directly challenging either their employers or the LCP's very structure. For the purpose of clarity, here we identify three different approaches, without suggesting that either organizations or LCP workers stick to just one.

Keeping Things under Control: Learning to Endure

The most common attitude expressed by LCP workers is that they would prefer to just be able to endure their time under the LCP. In their effort to make it through the LCP, workers rely on social support from a number of sources. Informal social support is usually available from family and friends—near and far—via phone, Skype, or text message to share daily news, to seek advice, or just to vent. More formal sources of social support include Filipino fraternities, mixed-gender organizations of college alumni, and cultural associations that can be pan-Filipino, for regional ethnic groups or Indigenous Filipino. Finally, religious organizations ranging from Catholic to evangelical to the Philippine Independent Church to Muslim ones are also very present within Filipino communities in Canada.

Apart from the basic sense of belonging such organizations can give LCP workers, they offer activities such as social events (cultural festivals, dance parties, meals, outings); professional or peer counselling for distressed workers; material support for personal emergencies (illness, unemployment, death in the family) or for major life events (marriage, birth of a child); and language classes to get through immigration requirements. Some LCP workers may be passive recipients of such support or services, but others become actively engaged in providing such support or organizing events for others.

The actors included in this category recognize that the LCP is very difficult but the overall message is, "You can make it" or "It gets better." LCP workers are reminded that their personal sacrifice will help their family in the long run. The LCP is understood to be a long-term investment, particularly for their children's education and future employment. Workers are also reminded that they don't want to give the community a bad name. There is a fear that if Filipinas begin to be perceived as too contentious, Canadians may no longer want to hire them as caregivers, thereby closing the door of immigration to others. Finally, many workers do not share their hardships or the reality of the LCP work with their family and friends back home in order to avoid worrying them and so as not to discourage the next wave of prospective LCP workers. In this sense, the culture of silence and endurance is reinforced within the Filipina community.

In recent years, on the more extreme end, there has been a rise of evangelical churches in the Filipino community that explicitly discourage any form of labour resistance as being against God's will. Women are told by such churches that the suffering and personal sacrifice they endure under the LCP are a sign of their religious devotion.

In sum, LCP workers in these communities are advised to sacrifice their current labour for their own future, their family, the Filipino community, and even God. In their efforts to help LCP workers endure the program, such organizations are contributing to keeping them "under control."

Informed Engagement: LCP Workers Moving toward Consensus with Employers

While endurance remains the strategy for most LCP workers, some are exposed to rights education by happening to be in the right place at the right time. For example, a community organization may come to do a workshop in their language class or they may receive a rights booklet from an acquaintance at a community party. This unsought information may lead to subtle changes in an LCP worker's relations with her employer. But sometimes endurance is just not possible; LCP workers may feel a need to try to change their work conditions. Whether due to personal values, personalities, or simply the extreme nature of their situation, some simply can't take it anymore.

With the fear of losing the job still paramount, such LCP workers often begin by simply seeking information, hoping to be able to better communicate with their employers and reach a consensus with them. Many workers felt that knowing their rights was empowering. Simply knowing that their employer was breaking the rules allowed workers to feel somewhat morally superior, even if they never directly confronted them.

Family and friends are often a first—if sometimes inexpert—source of information about workers' rights. While experienced LCP workers, including those who have "graduated" from the program to settle in Canada permanently, are a wealth of knowledge about living through the LCP, they are not always up-to-date on the law. Labour and immigration regulations change and people may simply be ill informed. More formal sources of such information are labour and immigration rights organizations (both Filipino and general). Less often, LCP workers turn to a union for information.

Information on rights gets transmitted to LCP workers in a wide variety of ways. Many organizations offer "Know Your Rights" workshops, offering factual information as well as a chance to exchange about the reality on the ground and the difficulty of enforcing such rights. These organizations believe that preventive education allows LCP workers to better cope with their difficulties and be on a more equal footing in negotiations with employers. LCP workers are advised to be proud of their care work and expect their employers to respect the value of their labour.

Individual rights counselling is also a commonly offered service. If a worker wants to confront her employer about a bad situation but feels unable to do so alone, certain organizations will mediate with the employers, trying to persuade them to respect the worker's rights. Thus, providing information to employers to ensure compliance with labour standards is sometimes another role of these organizations. Some of these organizations will help those in particularly bad situations to find new employers who respect workers' rights and offer more desirable working conditions.

In recognition of the risk that formal complaints pose for LCP workers, the approach under this perspective is to begin by seeking consensus. These organizations believe that LCP workers can be respected and loved by the employer and their family members—again, a somewhat ambiguous position in worker-employer relations. LCP workers engaging in these organizations learn to work in harmony with their employer without necessarily challenging structural inequalities embedded in the LCP.

Public Resistance: From Fighting for Individual Rights to Challenging the Structure of the LCP

Public resistance to individual work conditions, it is important to recognize, is often a last resort for LCP workers when they have nothing left to lose. They have often already lost their jobs or had their applications for permanent residence refused. On the other hand, organizing for changes to the LCP program itself is less individually risky. For politically or community-minded LCP workers, participation in meetings or peaceful demonstrations is relatively risk-free. Acting as a spokesperson or appearing in the news can create friction with employers, however.

The same organizations offering rights education are often involved in individual rights advocacy when LCP workers make official complaints about their labour or immigration situations. Community-based organizations, whether specifically Filipino or with general labour or immigration rights mandates, offer accompaniment to LCP workers going this route. A few unions, such as Ontario Steelworkers or Montreal's Service Employees Union, Local 800, also offer such support to LCP workers. These organizations can offer individual rights accompaniment or professional advocacy with government officials to reform LCP rules and eligibility for social benefits (e.g., Medicare, employment insurance), encouraging LCP workers to defend their rights both for their individual interests and for others who follow.

Finally, a minority of LCP workers engage in community organizing, the process of mobilizing the people most affected by a social problem and building power to challenge the status quo. These workers and their organizations are dedicated and vocal, often those who have experienced serious difficulties or who have finished the program and feel safe to take action. These activist organizations are dominated by Filipinas with allies in the labour and immigrant rights sector. They engage in direct action casework (bringing individual cases to the media, organizing delegations to government offices, "rescuing" workers from abusive employers' homes) and policy organizing to increase legal rights around social benefits and the very structure of the LCP. These organizations contend that the LCP is unjust, racist, and sexist, and that workers must fight back. There is a deep critique of the global inequality and international division of reproductive labour that underpin Filipinos' need to migrate for work in the first place, the structure of the LCP, and today the general shift away from permanent to temporary immigration programs. These organizations tend to operate with awareness of or direct links to transnational migrant organizing efforts.

In recent years, this type of organizing has led to limited reforms. Due in part to LCP workers' collective efforts, recent policy changes include: mandatory private insurance offered by employers if LCP workers are excluded from public health insurance or workers' compensation; extension of the LCP time limit for completing the required live-in service from three to four years and counting hours worked (now a total of 3,900 hours) rather than simply months (previously twenty-four months);[3] and exemption of LCP workers from a health screening between the end of their LCP service and their acceptance as a permanent resident (Juana Tejada Law).[4] There have also been campaigns to fight the deportation of specific workers who ran into extenuating circumstances that impeded their ability to complete the program (e.g., pregnancy, stroke, cancer, a series of bad employers). The tactics used by LCP organizations include popular education, media pressure, lobbying by grassroots members, public demonstrations, and alliance-building with unions and women's organizations.

Without being exhaustive, the following table presents an overview of some of the LCP-dominated labour and immigration-oriented organizations across Canada. We have excluded the numerous informal groups and more "control-" or "endurance-" oriented social, cultural, and religious organizations that do not directly address labour and immigration issues as part of their mandates. It is hard to categorize groups as firmly located in

---

3   In many provinces, LCP workers are excluded from Medicare if their contract is shorter than six months or in the first three months if their contract is longer (e.g., Quebec, Ontario, BC).

4   Juana Tejada was an LCP worker who arrived in Canada in good health but was diagnosed with cancer during her contract, leading to the refusal of her permanent residence application because she was deemed an "undue burden" on the health care system. This led to a successful grassroots campaign to grant Tejada permanent residence and change the rules that required all LCP workers to undergo a second medical exam before accessing permanent residence.

the control, consensus, or resistance modus operandi. More often, groups offer a range of activities, and LCP workers get involved at the level at which they feel comfortable.

Table 2. Organizations Focused on Addressing Labour and Immigration Issues of LCP Workers in Canada

Region	Organizations	Dates	Resistance — Organizing	Resistance — Advocacy	Consensus — Rights Education	Consensus — Services	Control — Language Courses	Control — Social Events
British Columbia	Philippine Women Centre of British Columbia	1986–	✓	✓	✓	✓		✓
	West Coast Domestic Workers Association	1986–		✓	✓	✓		
	Vancouver Committee for Domestic Workers' and Caregivers' Rights	1992–		✓	✓	✓		✓
Ontario	Intercede	1979–2011		✓	✓	✓	✓	✓
	Caregivers' Action Centre	2007–	✓	✓	✓	✓		✓
	Philippine Women Centre of Ontario	2000–	✓	✓	✓	✓		
	iWorkers (Independent Workers Association)—Home Workers Section	2008–		✓		✓		
	GABRIELA Ontario	2009–	✓	✓	✓	✓	✓	✓
Quebec	Association des aides familiales du Québec (AAFQ)	1975–		✓	✓	✓		✓
	PINAY	1991–	✓	✓	✓	✓		✓
	PWC of Quebec	2006–	✓	✓	✓	✓		✓

Nearly all of the groups include simple social events as part of their repertoire. LCP workers join them for activities such as apple picking, Christmas parties, monthly birthday celebrations, or yoga classes. For rights-oriented organizations, however, these social activities serve two purposes. First, they attract new members who are interested in social activities but might not be comfortable with the idea of more political engagement. Their presence at social events allows the organization to build relationships with them in a context in which the workers feel safe. As they hear information about their rights and observe and exchange with other LCP workers engaged in political action, they may or may not decide to get more involved. Second, even for those already engaged in the political or advocacy work, a sense of belonging within the organization, of caring for other members, builds dedication and commitment.

There is also a distinction between organizations offering only professional advocacy services and those engaging LCP workers in direct political action. The more organizing-oriented groups tend to have an ethnic-specific mandate and lack a professional staff. In many cities, there is a political and ideological tension between these different groups. However, they are often able to come together around specific campaigns, and individual LCP workers may be members in more than one organization.

Connecting the "Unfree" LCP Workplace to Community

In talking with LCP workers and community organizers, there is a continuum of power relations among workplaces and in the community. Most LCP workers seem to learn to endure control in an effort to protect their long-term goals. A few learn about their rights and manage to arrive at working conditions that are mutually acceptable. A small minority resist poor conditions either directly with their employer or on a structural level through action-oriented community organizations. However, we suggest that this continuum does not necessarily mean that they exercise any significant control over their labour process.

To begin with, when we consider the issue of "control" of LCP workers, it ranges from being directly controlled by the employer (i.e., overt exercise of power) to self-discipline shaped by policy constraints (i.e., covert exercise of power). While some LCP workers have a little wiggle room for consent or resistance, power inequality and the absence of worker control are the dominant pattern among LCP workplaces. The patterns of power relations may diverge over time, but almost all LCP workers begin their work experience in Canada under the least desirable work conditions, characterized as severe control over their life and labour.

Consensus and (exceptionally) satisfaction in LCP workplaces do not necessarily mean that these conditions were achieved through workers' resistance, through control of their labour process, or through their becoming more assertive over time in Canada. While the majority of those with undesirable workplaces remain in their jobs, few manage to improve existing conditions. Rather, a select and limited number of workers who escape or are kicked out of negative workplaces manage to enter a better segment of the already peripheral caregiving labour market. Thus, consensus is available only for those at later stages of their LCP trajectory and/or who have built existing Canadian social ties.

We have identified some resistance and subsequent victories within workplaces, yet LCP workers' struggles usually only result in minor work condition improvements under the same unequal power relations (e.g., achieving the employer's permission to use a heater in the worker's room in the basement). Although we also identified some significant legal victories assisted by rights-based community organizations, the challenges were retrospective, occurring after the termination of employment in the problematic workplace. In addition, some of the legal cases were more related to LCP workers' immigration status rather than working conditions. Workers' resistance in LCP workplaces thus does not necessarily show that they built sufficient power to control and improve their existing working conditions.

A final observation is that of a striking limitation of LCP collective organizing. Unlike groups such as Montreal's Immigrant Workers Centre or Toronto's Workers' Action Centre featured elsewhere in this book, LCP organizations rarely if ever publicly target actual workplaces. They are overwhelmingly focused on structural changes, largely due to their analysis—one we share—that the very structure of the LCP creates and enables vulnerability and abuse in the workplace. Paradoxically, an individual LCP worker can be an active member of such structural resistance, effectively challenging the state in the wider community, without ever confronting her employer and possibly enduring terrible work conditions. Tactics such as media exposure, workplace demonstrations, or assertive delegation visits to the employer's home are nearly unheard of. An obvious reason for this is that, unless a worker has already left or been fired from her job, it seems nearly impossible for her to handle the repercussions of living within the home of the person targeted.

Even with the long history of LCP worker organizing, it remains difficult to treat the private home of the employer as a workplace, to separate the personal relationships of caring from the formal employment relationship. As long as LCP workers are held within their "unfree" private workplaces by structural immigration measures, it seems unlikely the problems encountered within their workplaces will diminish. However, while the pressure to abolish or fundamentally reform the LCP must continue, a little less squeamishness about using public pressure to affect the behaviour of private employers—perhaps targeting those whose LCP employees have already left the home—might raise awareness among other employers about the problem of a lack of respect for LCP workers' legal and moral rights.

In conclusion, our research confirms that LCP workers' lives and labour are under control as the LCP imposes a condition of "unfree labour." There are complex power relations within LCP workplaces, however, and these dynamics are affected by workers' engagement with a variety of actors, strategies, and assumptions in the community. LCP workers find ways to increase control over their lives and labour and to exercise resistance within their isolated workplaces and beyond. Our challenge is to illuminate a way to connect the majority of "unfree" migrant domestic workers in the workplace to collective organizing in the wider community.

References

Arat-Koç, Sedef. 1993. "Politics of the Family and Politics of Immigration in the Subordination of Domestic Workers in Canada." In Bonnie. J. Fox (ed.), *Family Patterns, Gender Relations,* 2nd ed. Toronto: Oxford University Press.

Bakan, Abigail Bess, and Daiva K. Stasiulis. 1997. *Not One of the Family: Foreign Domestic Workers in Canada.* Toronto: University of Toronto Press.

Brickner, Rachel K., and Christine Straehle. 2010. "The Missing Link: Gender, Immigration Policy and the Live-in Caregiver Program in Canada." *Policy and Society* 29, no. 4. doi: 10.1016/j.polsoc.2010.09.004.

Choudry, Aziz, Jill Hanley, Steve Jordan, Eric Shragge, and Martha Stiegman. 2009. *Fight Back: Work Place Justice for Immigrants.* Black Point, NS: Fernwood Publishing.

Cohen, Rina. 1994. "A Brief History of Racism in Immigration Policies for Recruiting Domestics." *Canadian Woman Studies* 4, no. 2.

Hanley, Jill, Stephanie Premji, Karen Messing, and Katherine Lippel. 2010. "Action Research for the Health and Safety of Domestic Workers in Montreal: Using Numbers to Tell Stories and Effect Change." *New Solutions* 20, no. 4. doi: 10.2190/NS.20.4.c.

Hanley, Jill, and Eric Shragge. 2010. "Organizing Temporary Foreign Workers: Rights and Resistance as Canada Shifts Towards the Use of Guestworkers." *Social Policy* 40, no. 3.

Hanley, Jill, Eric Shragge, André Rivard, and Jah-Hon Koo. 2012. "'Good Enough to Work? Good Enough to Stay!' Organizing Temporary Foreign Workers." In Patti Tamara Lenard and Christine Straehle (eds.), *Legislated Inequality: Temporary Labour Migration in Canada*. Montreal: McGill–Queen's University Press.

Oxman-Marinez, Jacqueline, Jill Hanley, and Leslie Cheung. 2004. "Another Look at the Live-in-Caregivers Program." *Publication IM* 24. Montreal, QC: Centre de recherche interuniversitaire de Montreal sur l'immigration, l'integration et la dynamique urbaine.

Parreñas, Rhacel Salazar. 2000. "Migrant Filipina Domestic Workers and the International Division of Reproductive Labor." *Gender and Society* 14, no. 4.

Pratt, Geraldine. 1999. "Is This Canada? Domestic Workers' Experiences in Vancouver, BC." In Janet Henshall Momsen (ed.), *Gender, Migration, and Domestic Service*. London: Routledge.

Ramirez, Judith. 1982. "Domestic Workers Organize!" *Canadian Woman Studies* 4, no. 2.

Stasiulis, Daiva K., and Abigail Bess Bakan. 1997. "Negotiating Citizenship: The Case of Foreign Domestic Workers in Canada." *Feminist Review* 57.

Thompson, Paul. 2010. "The Capitalist Labour Process: Concepts and Connections." *Capital & Class* 34, no. 1.

Thompson, Paul, and Kirsty Newsome. 2004. "Labor Process Theory, Work, and the Employment Relation." In Bruce E. Kaufman (ed.), *Theoretical Perspectives on Work and the Employment Relationship*. Champaign, IL: Industrial Relations Research Association.

Valiani, Salimah. 2009. "The Shift in Canadian Immigration Policy and Unheeded Lessons of the Live-in Caregiver Program." Ottawa: Ontario Council of Agencies Serving Immigrants. <http://celarc.ca/cppc/217/217538.pdf>.

"Systemic Discrimination" in the Canadian Context: Live-in Domestic Care, Employment Equity, and the Challenge of Unfree Labour Markets

Abigail B. Bakan

Systemic Discrimination: Introducing the Problem

SYSTEMIC DISCRIMINATION IS A WIDELY RECOGNIZED BUT LITTLE UNDERSTOOD concept.[1] Liberal democratic states are grounded in notions of universal equality, specifically assuming rights guaranteed in the United Nations Universal Declaration of Human Rights that has grounded liberal state principles in the postwar era (Ariye et al. 2012). The right of women and minorities to be free from discrimination in political, economic, and social spheres is presumed to be a default; acts of discrimination are considered an aberration, and as the acts of individuals. Yet the sheer persistence of identifiable, systemic patterns of discrimination that deny equal rights to specific groups continues to pose a challenge, not only in terms of the impact of this experience for marginalized groups, but also for theory and policy in liberal democratic state formations.

Canada offers no exception. For the purposes of this discussion, systemic discrimination can be understood to be apparent when there is a demonstrable pattern of group-based inequality—notable over time, across institutions and/or geographic space—resulting in ideological and/or material group deficits relative to general social, economic, and political norms. It is significant that, although it resisted such a specific definition, the Canadian state has formally acknowledged and named the existence of systemic discrimination

---

[1] This chapter refers to the Live-in Caregiver Program, which was replaced by the Caregiver Program in November 2014. While a number of changes were made, including the removal of the live-in requirement, we feel that the analysis here makes important contributions to theorizing unfree labour and ongoing migrant workers' struggles in Canada.

in one area of federal labour policy oriented to its redress: the policy and legislation associated with employment equity (Bakan and Kobayashi 2000). At the same time, other federal policies perpetuate discriminatory policies. The paradigmatic case, arguably, is the Live-in Caregiver Program (LCP).

This chapter argues that systemic discrimination, as embedded in the LCP, has been increasingly centred in state policy and employment practices and normalized unfree labour markets. An alternative approach to systemic discrimination, exemplified in a different policy—employment equity and the related federal Employment Equity Act (EEA)—is simultaneously increasingly decentred. While the EEA calls for proactive measures to counter the persistence of systemic discrimination in employment as part of management practices, such an approach has not been generalized beyond the limited remit of the EEA. Moreover, even in its limited effect the policy has been the subject of ongoing opposition and backlash.

The LCP was formally silent regarding the concept of systemic discrimination. In practice, however, the legislation was clearly and explicitly market centred, unhindered by proactive mechanisms and structured to ensure a "captured" labour market subject to exceptional conditions. The LCP was once considered to be exceptional in its extreme restrictions on labour mobility, but in the face of unfree labour markets the policy now actually indicates greater rights than the increasingly common trends in temporary migrant labour. In the latter programs, temporary migrant workers are not permitted to apply for permanent residence status following a certain period of restriction, as in the case of the LCP (Citizenship and Immigration Canada 2009). In addition to the LCP, other temporary worker programs in Canada have grown dramatically in the 2000s, as noted elsewhere in this volume. The trend challenges the principles regarding systemic discrimination as forwarded in employment equity. Rather than working to ameliorate systemic discrimination in the workplace, the model of exploitation of temporary foreign workers normatively entrenches systemic discrimination.

How can we explain this pattern? How and why does systemic discrimination continue unabated despite policy such as that associated with the EEA, designed specifically for its redress? I suggest four distinct but related explanatory factors: (i) the centring of temporary migrant labour employment practices, such as those forwarded by the LCP, that embed systemic discrimination, particularly against women of colour migrant labourers; (ii) the limited effectiveness of the EEA on its own terms, decentring the potential impact of policy that challenges systemic discrimination; (iii) the particularly sharp ineffectiveness of the EEA regarding systemic discrimination that affects visible minority workers, or racism; and (iv) the wider, structural impact of what I term *unfree labour markets*, which support systemic discrimination even in conditions of apparently "free" labour mobility. Each of these points is elaborated below.

Centring Systemic Discrimination: The Live-in Caregiver Program

The LCP embeds systemic discrimination on grounds that combine racialized and gendered discrimination against a vulnerable migrant population. Canada's domestic worker policy has historically relied on foreign recruitment of private caregivers rather than comprehensive social policy geared specifically to childcare, where the greatest demand has been indicated (Bakan and Stasiulis 1997; Stasiulis and Bakan 2005); the LCP, established in 1992, continues this pattern. The LCP is a separate piece of federal legislation that governs the recruitment, placement, and terms of immigration of private live-in domestic workers. The work and care provided usually services families with very young children or, increasingly, with elderly adults.

To be accepted to come to Canada under the LCP, an applicant must meet a series of qualifications. These include: the equivalent of a Canadian grade twelve education; six months of full-time training or twelve months of experience in paid work in an area related to live-in caregiving; and competence in English or French. The criteria for qualifying for the program have been challenged, as there is incongruence between the relatively high level of skills required and the low level of status associated with paid, live-in domestic labour. However, the LCP is simultaneously an immigration policy and a means to screen, hire, place, and regulate foreign domestic workers, a majority of whom are female, in an area of high demand. The LCP therefore addresses a demand for childcare, and increasingly, elder care, through private employment of vulnerable foreign workers. Although officially an immigration policy, in practice the LCP acts simultaneously as a labour policy of a special type.

The LCP falls under federal jurisdiction associated with recruitment and migration to Canada. But once in Canada, employees' working conditions and rights are subject to regulation through provincial labour law; there is no consistency regarding live-in paid work across the provinces. Moreover, work in the private home, which has traditionally been performed overwhelmingly by women, is notoriously difficult to monitor regardless of regulatory measures that may be applicable (Brooks 2005). Enforceability of foreign domestic workers' rights to fair employment practices is therefore structurally challenging, as it is complaints-driven, and subject to contest from the employer. The site of employment is the private home, usually the property of citizens with considerably greater social and political capital than the employees. And private placement agencies, also largely unregulated, figure highly in the original entry of workers on the LCP to Canada. The LCP

> acts as a mediating instrument linking the interests of the Canadian state and the private domestic placement agencies. The agencies can operate in a formally legal manner, within the confines of the legislation, and at the same time enforce overtly discriminatory practices that violate the norms of liberal democracy. The compulsory live-in requirement and the enforced temporary residential status of the domestic worker, embedded in the program, create an unequal relationship of citizen employer/noncitizen employee at the outset. (Stasiulis and Bakan 2005, 64)

The LCP is an example of a piece of legislation and a policy package based on decades of past practices that presume and perpetuate patterns of systemic discrimination. The employing families are overwhelmingly white, two-income professional earners, male and female heterosexual couples with two or more children, and Canadian citizens (Belleau and Langevin 2000; Stasiulis and Bakan 2005). The employees are overwhelming female, recent, racialized migrants originating from poor Third World countries—historically principally the English Caribbean and the Philippines. Those who enter Canada on this program are therefore vulnerable to numerous forms of abuse—from lack of privacy and nonpayment of overtime, to sexual and physical assault. Documented cases of abuse are common (Bakan and Stasiulis 1997; Stasiulis and Bakan 2005).

While the LCP's compulsory live-in feature has been repeatedly challenged, this structural element in foreign domestic worker policy has continued. The program has been widely criticized, sometimes on grounds that the conditions are comparable to a form of indentured labour or serfdom, considered unacceptable in other sectors of employment in Canada (Belleau and Langevin 2000; Bakan and Stasiulis 2012). However, live-in labour is generally treated as a unique sector and the Canadian policy is considered to compare favourably with live-in care in other countries (Bakan and Stasiulis 1997; Oxman-Martinez et al. 2004). Such a comparison embeds the assumption of exceptionality for paid domestic service. The separation of paid domestic service from the general labour market constructs distinct criteria of comparison, lowering the bar regarding what is or is not considered an acceptable standard. A policy such as the EEA, for example, would simply not apply to this sector. A 2010 *Globe and Mail* editorial reflecting this view noted that Canada's Live-in Caregiver Program is "a flawed model" but "better than none at all" and compared it favourably against "many countries that host foreign domestic workers—including Hong Kong, Israel, and other nations in Europe and the Middle East" (*Globe and Mail* 2010).

When reforms have been made, these have been the result of considerable organizing among domestic worker advocacy groups, largely reliant on the activities and direction of foreign domestic workers themselves (see Citizenship and Immigration Canada 2010b, and Koo and Hanley, this volume). But the LCP's fundamental elements have remained unchanged; conditions of vulnerability through enforced temporary immigration status combined with the compulsory live-in condition continue to be embedded. These conditions combine to generate a structural relationship of dependence upon individual employers and placement agencies, including risks of what has been summarized as a condition of general "financial, psychological, and sexual abuse" (Oxman-Martinez et al. 2004, 14). These conditions collectively enforce and reproduce a pattern of systemic discrimination. Meanwhile, policies designed, at least ostensibly, to challenge systemic discrimination, notably through employment equity policy, have been increasingly decentred.

Decentring Equity: The EEA on Its Own Terms

Canada's employment equity policy can be understood as a limited effort to offset deeply embedded, systemic features of discrimination in some workplaces (Bakan and Kobayashi 2007a). Systemic discrimination against specific groups in public service employment practices was acknowledged in the findings of the Royal Commission on Equality in Employment, struck by the federal government on June 27, 1983. In the report *Equality in Employment: A Royal Commission Report*, the one-person commissioner,

Rosalie Abella suggested that "employment equity is a strategy designed to obliterate the present and residual effects of discrimination and to open equitably the competition for employment opportunities to those arbitrarily excluded" (Abella 1984, 214). The Abella Report (as it has come to be known) noted statistical evidence of a gap between specific populations available for employment in the public service, defined according to four designated groups (women, visible minorities, Aboriginal Peoples, and persons with disabilities), and patterns of hiring. The report drew from this evidence sufficient grounds to advance a plan—pathbreaking for its time— for employment policies that actively sought to remove barriers faced by "those arbitrarily excluded" and therefore to ensure equitable competition for employment. These barriers are not easily defined and may not be the result of conscious motivation, but are revealed in outcomes in employment patterns, argued the commission findings, throughout the public service.

The commission's recommendations found their way into legislation when the EEA was passed in 1986 and then revised with augmented authority in 1995. The legislation was presented as a necessary, minimal step to correct imbalances resulting from historic patterns of bias and exclusion that were documented to be so widespread as to constitute "systemic" discrimination against the designated groups. Abella recognized in the report that attaining equitable conditions of access and promotion in the workplace posed a challenge. Moreover, the report deemed the status quo unfair and found that, without intervention, recurrent patterns of discrimination would continue. Employment equity policy is aimed, therefore, to eliminate barriers that otherwise violate the principles of equality upon which Canadian democratic law, particularly as expressed in the Canadian Charter of Rights and Freedoms, is formally based.

The EEA, though far from comprehensive, is nonetheless designed to address a wide swath of Canadian employers of a certain size if they are subject to federal regulation. Its mandate currently includes "500 federally regulated private sector employers of 100 or more employees in banking, communication, transportation, and various other industries, as well as in grain elevators, uranium mines, and nuclear power operations.... It also covers approximately 90 federally regulated public sector departments and agencies" (CHRC 2010a). When amended in 1995, the Canadian Human Rights Commission (CHRC) became responsible for ensuring compliance with the EEA conducting periodic audits to this end (CHRC 2004).

It is significant that the Abella Report adopted the notion of systemic discrimination explicitly and challenged its salience. It is further significant that this policy has been entrenched in a body of legislation and is recognized to be consistent with the Charter (Abella 1984, 12–13). In particular, the report stressed the right to equality in employment as inherent in Canadian public policy rather than contingent on market factors (Abella 1984, 17). To emphasize the report's significance is not however to minimize its limitations. Those facing discrimination due to sexual orientation, for example, are not covered by the EEA (Bakan and Kobayashi 2007b). And there traditionally have been limited enforcement mechanisms associated with employer noncompliance (Bakan and Kobayashi 2000, 2007; Government of Canada 2007). But the notion of systemic discrimination as something that merits intervention and challenge, and stands contrary to the Canadian Charter, suggests a contradiction in state policy that is important strategically and analytically.

Employment equity policy then, from its origins, has not been grounded on a stable foundation. Employment equity has also been subjected to extreme backlash from provincial governments, particularly in Ontario (Bakan and Kobayashi 2007a) and in British Columbia (Bakan and Kobayashi 2004). And it was barely tolerated by Canada's recent Conservative government (Friesen 2010). The trajectory is therefore moving toward even more limited enforceability of the EEA. The EEA continues in the context of policies that "sell diversity" (Abu-Laban and Gabriel 2008) in terms that are good for business, rather than centring the principle of equity in labour and society generally (Agocs 2002; Bakan and Kobayashi 2007a). For example, the Conservative government omnibus budget amendment legislation passed in June 2012, Bill C-38, included the removal of an EEA clause requiring contractors under the Federal Contractors Program to comply with employment equity provisions. Thus even the rhetorical pressure to comply has now been eliminated (about one hundred compliance reviews were conducted each year) (Hervieux-Payette 2012).

One of the greatest challenges to employment equity as a means to redress systemic discrimination has occurred more covertly, with the elimination of the mandatory long-form census in 2011 (Cormack, Cosgrave, and Stalker 2012, 234). This backlash is an indication of the instability of the limited commitment within the Canadian state regarding principles that underlie employment equity (i.e., redress of systemic discrimination).[2] And as noted above, the policy has proven particularly limited in addressing one of its four targeted areas, visible minorities.

Systemic, Racialized Discrimination

Findings regarding Canadian employment equity policy in the federal public service and related sectors continue to indicate that, without enforcement, barriers to the achievement of equity in employment persist. However, among the four designated groups identified in the EEA, various "barriers," in Abella's terms, have been more or less resistant to elimination. Most resistant to reform have been barriers faced by visible minorities, where systemic discrimination takes the form of racialized discrimination or racism. According to the CHRC's 2010 report, some gains have been made for representation in employment sectors covered by the Act among women, Aboriginal Peoples, and persons with disabilities, but the gap between availability and employment for visible minorities continues (CHRC 2010b). A June 2012 brief submitted by the Public Service Alliance of Canada (PSAC) confirmed a similar pattern, noting that racialized groups continue to face particularly resistant barriers to employment equity practices in hiring in the public service (PSAC 2012, 1–3).

This persistent pattern has become obvious even to members of the Conservative Party in the Canadian government. According to Conservative senator Donald Oliver, a longstanding advocate for federal employment equity policy, there are no grounds to support the view that the EEA has successfully accomplished its goals and therefore outlived its mandate (regarding a debate raised by the minority Harper Tories in 2010). In Oliver's words, responding to questions in a media interview, "Of the four groups, visible minorities are at the bottom of the heap" (Friesen 2010). When pressed to explain why, he replied, "I think it's because of racism. I think it's because of discrimination. I think it's because of barriers that are ethnic based" (ibid.). Indeed, racialized discrimination is highly resistant to amelioration within and beyond the workplace, a finding supported by numerous other studies in Canada (Galabuzi 2005; Stasiulis and Bakan 2005; Fernando 2006).

Racialized minorities can be understood to be associated with a kind of noncitizen "otherness" in the context of Canada's white settler state colonial

---

2   The incoming Liberal government reinstated the long-form census in 2016.

formation (Stasiulis and Yuval-Davis 1995; Thobani 2007). This "otherness" is not a characteristic of the skills or capacities of the worker but of the labour market in which certain workers find themselves competing for jobs and encountering barriers to equitable opportunities. In a 2009 research study conducted by economist Philip Oreopoulos, six thousand employment résumés were sent randomly to employers in Toronto, Canada's most multicultural city. The report on findings identified discrimination on the basis of last names and foreign experience as determinant in employer callbacks (Oreopoulos 2009). My own research with Audrey Kobayashi, based on an analysis of provincial governments in Canada regarding employment equity practices, came to a similar finding but noted combined systemic factors associated with both race and gender to be significant. Visible minority women were the least represented (Bakan and Kobayashi 2000, 46). These limitations point to the weaknesses of employment equity policy even on its own terms within the narrow purview of the EEA. Deep barriers that enforce discrimination effectively decentre the normative analysis of the Abella Report regarding systemic discrimination more generally in Canadian labour markets. And further, other policies that embed systemic discrimination, notably the LCP, have rendered redress even more remote.

Unfree Labour Markets: Diminishing Employment Equity, Rising Temporary Precarious Labour

A structural pattern has developed in labour market practices that decentres policies that serve to redress systemic discrimination (EEA), while centring policies that entrench such discrimination (LCP). This pattern of centring/decentring regarding social policy can be understood as a reflection of ongoing tensions in state/civil society relationships, where hegemonic policies that have been historically adopted, or centred, are gradually rendered marginal and minimized, or decentred. In the case of the EEA and LCP, barriers facing visible minorities are key, with the neglect of effective challenges to systemic discrimination in the former, and the embedding of racialized and gendered barriers in the latter. Collectively, these two examples signal wider trajectories. They effectively foreground attitudinal biases that are discriminatory, generating what could be termed *unfree labour markets*. There is an inherent contradiction in the discursive acceptance of equality principles that oppose systemic discrimination (EEA), while other legislative and policy packages (such as the LCP) actively promote such discrimination. To address the more general issue of systemic discrimination, it is useful to consider not only the spectrum of free versus unfree labour but to move to a global scale and consider a spectrum of labour mobility where free versus unfree labour markets function along a spectrum of rights and restrictions.

This is a concept that links political economy and citizenship rights. As Harald Bauder (2006, 26) notes, "Noncitizenship is a condition for labor to be 'unfree', as exemplified not only by the slaves of ancient Greece and the nineteenth-century southern United States, but also by contemporary foreign migrant harvesters and seasonal workers in North America and Europe."

Even in conditions that might appear "free," as in the case of workers with full citizenship status employed in Canada's public sector, labour market stereotypes and systemic barriers can and do alter the accessibility to equity in employment. Both the LCP and the EEA assume specific types of labour markets. In the case of the LCP, the link between migration and temporary residence status is tied to compulsory living-in, "capturing" a workforce to reside in the home of the employer and direct supervisor.

The LCP addresses a chronic labour shortage associated with live-in domestic care. Live-in domestic service is considered such an oppressive option for employment that it is spurned by those with other options. It is constructed as a distinct sector of the labour market, associated with foreign workers with few employment options in their home countries. The LCP specifically assigns exceptional restrictions to foreign workers arriving in Canada in a high-demand employment sector. Rather than enticing workers to come to Canada with benefits associated with permanent resident status, these workers face restrictions that are not commonly applied in the broader Canadian labour force. They arrive as "visitors" of a special type, temporary workers required to live in the homes of their employers for two years within a consecutive period of years after their arrival date. If a migrant worker meets the program requirements, an incentive accompanies the extreme restrictions: satisfactory completion of the live-in home service allows the opportunity to apply for permanent residence from inside the country. In the case of the EEA, managers are pressed to consider labour force availability in terms of defined equity-seeking groups,[3]

---

3   This term is associated with those groups identified in employment equity policy who are recognized to suffer from systemic discrimination: women, visible minorities, Aboriginal Peoples, and people with a disability. In some contexts, sexual minorities—those who identify

which are based on features of difference recognized to be the subject of ubiquitous, systemic patterns of discrimination.

We generally consider the employing side of the pattern of inequity to be essentially "free" and issues of "unfreedom" to rest with the worker. With the LCP, there are clearly conditions of an unfree labour force but this would not apply to the workers employed in the public sector associated with the EEA. A notion of an unfree labour market as suggested here, however, enables consideration of these policies along a spectrum, where the weakness of employment equity policy works to reinforce the more blatant discriminatory practices of foreign domestic worker policy.

Unfree labour markets are the product of relationships between the two sides of the market relationship, the "buyers" and the "sellers" of labour power. It is this process that is arguably restricted by systemic factors, bounded by historic and recurrent patterns of discriminatory behaviour such as racism, sexism, etc. The subjects who suffer most from the systemic discrimination institutionalized in a program such as the LCP are people commonly removed or rendered invisible from any notions of equity—the poor who are also people of colour and disproportionately women. Moreover, they are in a global situation of highly limited mobility where they suffer from restrictions of "unfreedom." Policies such as the EEA are weak instruments to redress such patterns. This is not only in terms of legislative authority but also regarding discursive analysis. While Abella integrated an assessment of systemic discrimination into commission findings and recommendations, the account is descriptive rather than analytical. The notion of *systemic* used in the report is equivalent to *ubiquitous*; there are discernible and widespread patterns of labour force availability in four designated groups that fall short of proportional hiring targets, indicating a gap based on discrimination. But a deeper explanation is called for. As Carol Geller (1984, 20) has noted, Abella's challenge to systemic discrimination is thin, limited by a failure to address both root causes of and systemic remedies to discrimination.

As the flow of temporary migratory labour increases generally in Canada—in labour sectors that have historically relied on citizen-labour with mobility rights within Canada—considering a precarious global labour market of unfree workers and a competitive market of neoliberal employers can serve as a useful frame. Systemic discrimination, particularly toward

---

as lesbian, gay, bisexual, transgendered/transsexual, or queer (LGBTQ)—are also included among "equity-seeking groups."

those who are denied citizenship status and face racist and sexist barriers to equity, is therefore embedded in unfree labour markets on a global scale. While the EEA and the LCP appear to be differentiated regarding systemic discrimination in the labour market, these policies can be understood to demonstrate complementary dimensions of the dilemma of systemic discrimination. If there is in fact an embedded discriminatory practice in unfree labour markets, then policy challenging systemic discrimination would have to be far more robust than anything that has been set in place in the Canadian context.

Conclusion: Deeply Systemic

In this chapter, employment equity and foreign domestic worker policy are considered in relationship to one another, from the perspective of systemic discrimination. There is evidence to indicate that the precarious and temporary conditions associated with the LCP are becoming more generalized, while the approach to systemic discrimination that calls for redress, inscribed in the EEA, is diminishing. Not only are the numbers of workers with temporary status increasing, but the limitations of and backlash against employment equity are on the rise. The effects are particularly notable regarding the visible minority category among the equity-seeking groups delineated in employment equity policy. Relatedly, the notion of "unfree labour" can be extended to consider restrictions that generate more limited opportunities for labour equity among certain groups, and attendant ideological patterns conducive to conditions of systemic discrimination. This pattern is suggestive of the idea of unfree labour markets. Understood in this way, it is clear that the discrimination in patterns of employment is deeply systemic, demanding of deeply systemic transformation.

References

Abella, Rosalie Silberman. 1984. *Equality in Employment*. Ottawa: Minister of Supply and Services (October).

Abu-Laban, Yasmeen, and Christina Gabriel. 2008. *Selling Diversity: Immigration, Multiculturalism, Employment Equity and Globalization*. Toronto: University of Toronto Press.

Agocs, Carol. 2002. "Canada's Employment Equity Legislation and Policy, 1987–2000: The Gap Between Policy and Practice." *International Journal of Manpower* 23, no. 3.

Bakan, Abigail B. 2008. "Marxism and Anti-Racism: Rethinking the Politics of Difference." *Rethinking Marxism: A Journal of Economics, Culture and Society* 20, no. 2 (April).

Bakan, Abigail B., and Audrey Kobayashi. 2007a. "Affirmative Action and Employment Equity: Policy, Ideology, and Backlash in Canadian Context." *Studies in Political Economy* 79 (Spring).

_____. 2007b. "'The Sky Didn't Fall': Organizing to Combat Racism in the Workplace: The Case of the Alliance for Employment Equity." In Genevieve Fuji Johnson and Randy Enomoto (eds.), *Conversations on the Edge: Race, Racialization, and Anti-Racism*. Toronto: University of Toronto Press.

_____. 2004. "Backlash Against Employment Equity: The British Columbia Experience." *Atlantis: A Women's Studies Journal* 29, no. 1 (Fall).

_____. 2003. "Nunavut: Lessons of an Equity Conversation for Anti-Racist Activists." *Canadian Race Relations Foundation Reports* (March).

_____. 2000. *Employment Equity Policy in Canada: An Interprovincial Comparison*. Ottawa: Status of Women Canada.

Bakan, Abigail B., and Daiva Stasiulis. 2012. "The Political Economy of Migrant Live-in Caregivers: A Case of Unfree Labour?" In Patti Tamara Lenard and Christine Straehle (eds.), *Legislated Inequality: Temporary Labour Migration in Canada*. Montreal: McGill–Queen's University Press.

_____ (eds.). 1997. *Not One of the Family: Foreign Domestic Workers in Canada*. Toronto: University of Toronto Press.

Banaji, Jairus. 2010. *Theory as History: Essays on Modes of Production and Exploitation*. The Netherlands: Brill Academic Publishers; (rpt. 2011) Chicago: Haymarket Books.

Bauder, Harald. 2006. *Labor Movement*. New York: Oxford University Press.

Belleau, Marie-Claire, and Louise Langevin. 2000. *Trafficking in Women in Canada: A Critical Analysis of the Legal Framework Governing Immigrant Live-in Caregivers and Mail-Order Brides*. Quebec City: Status of Women in Canada.

Brooks, Kim. 2005. "Valuing Women's Work in the Home: A Defining Moment." *Canadian Journal of Women and the Law* 17.

Canadian Human Rights Commission (CHRC). 2010a. "Fact Sheet: Employment Equity Compliance Program." <chrc-ccdp.ca/publications/eecp_sheet_pceme-en.asp>.

_____. 2010b. "Impact of the *Employment Equity Act* and of the CHRC Employment Equity Program over the Years." <chrc-ccdp.ca/publications/eeprogram_program-meee/toc_tdm-en.asp>.

_____. 2004. "Legislative Review of the Employment Equity Act: A Discussion Paper." <chrc-ccdp.ca/publications/ee_eme/discussion-en.asp#2en>.

Canadian Political Science Association (CPSA). 2009. "New Section at CPSA." Circular from Michelle Hopkins for CPSA.

Citizenship and Immigration Canada (CIC). 2013. "Live-in Caregivers." <cic.gc.ca/english/work/caregiver/>.

_____. 2010a. "Regulatory and Administrative Changes to the Live-in Caregiver Program." Operational Bulletin 192, April 1. <cic.gc.ca/english/resources/manuals/bulletins/2010/ob192.asp>.

_____. 2010b. "Backgrounders: Improvements in the Live-in Caregiver Program." August 18. <cic.gc.ca/english/department/media/backgrounders/2010/2010-08-18a.asp>.

_____. 2009. *Facts and Figures 2008: Immigration Overview—Permanent and Temporary Residents*. <cic.gc.ca/english/pdf/research-stats/facts2008.pdf>.

Coates, Rodney D. (ed.). 2004. *Race and Ethnicity: Across Time, Space and Discipline*. Chicago: Haymarket Books.

Cohen, Marjorie Griffin. 1984. "Employment Equity Is Not Affirmative Action." *Canadian Woman Studies* 6, no. 4. <sfu.ca/~mcohen/publications/women/employment%20equity.pdf>.

Cormack, Patricia, James F. Cosgrave, and Lynda Harling Stalker. 2012. "Who Counts Now? Re-making the Canadian Citizen." *Canadian Journal of Sociology* 37, no. 3.

Dei, George J. Sefa. 2007. "Speaking Race: Silence, Salience, and the Politics of Anti-Racist Scholarship." In Sean P. Hier and B. Singh Bolaria (eds.), *Race and Racism in 21st Century Canada: Continuity, Complexity, and Change*. Toronto: Broadview Press.

Feigen, Joe R. 2006. *Systemic Racism: A Theory of Oppression*. New York: Routledge.

Fernando, Shanti. 2006. *Race and the City: Chinese Canadian and Chinese American Political Mobilization*. Vancouver: UBC Press.

Friesen, Joe. 2010. "Senator Who Fought for Employment Equity Defends Tories." *Globe and Mail*, July 26. <theglobeandmail.com/news/national/senator-who-fought-for-employment-equity-defends-tories/article1651635/?cmpid=rss1>.

Galabuzi, Grace-Edward. 2005. *Canada's Economic Apartheid: The Socialization of Racialized Groups in the New Century*. Toronto: Canadian Scholars Press.

Geller, Carole. 1984. "A Critique of the Abella Report." *Canadian Woman Studies* 6, no. 4. <sfu.ca/~mcohen/publications/women/employment%20equity.pdf>.

Globe and Mail. August 22, 2010. "Helping the Nannies Live In." <theglobeandmail.com/news/opinions/editorials/helping-the-nannies-live-in/article1680626/>.

Government of Canada, Minister of Public Works and Government Services. 2007. *Human Rights Commission Report 2006*. <chrc-ccdp.ca/publications/ar_2006_ra/page9-en.asp#52>.

Hervieux-Payette, Céline. 2012. "Goodbye Equity: Conservatives Eliminate Employment Equity Obligations for Federal Government Contractors." Press release, June 5. <http://eurekablog.ca/en/parliamentary-activities/press-releases/goodbye-equity-conservatives-eliminate-employment-equity-obligations-federal-government-contractors/>.

Hier, Sean P. 2007. "Studying Race and Racism in 21st Century Canada." In Sean P. Hier and B. Singh Bolaria (eds.), *Race and Racism in 21st Century Canada: Continuity, Complexity, and Change*. Toronto: Broadview Press.

Ontario Ministry of Labour. 2010. "Employment Protection for Foreign Nationals Act (Live-in Caregivers and Others)." <labour.gov.on.ca/english/es/faqs/epfna.php>.

Oreopoulos, Philip. 2009. "Why Do Skilled Immigrants Struggle in the Labor Market? A Field Experiment with Six Thousand Résumés." Vancouver: Metropolis British Columbia Working Paper Series.

Orsini, Michael, and Miriam Smith (eds.). 2007. *Critical Policy Studies*. Vancouver: UBC Press.

Oxman-Martinez, Jacqueline, Jill Hanley, and Leslie Cheung. 2004. "Another Look at the Live-in Caregiver Program." *Centre de recherché interuniversitaire de Montréal sure l'immigration, l'intégration et la dynamique urbaine* 24. <im.metropolis.net/research-policy/research_content/doc/oxman-marinez%20LCP.pdf>.

Public Service Alliance of Canada (PSAC). 2012. "Brief to the Senate Standing Committee on Human Rights on the Hiring Practices and Employment Equity in the Federal Public Service." <psacunion.ca/brief-senate-standing-committee-human-rights-0>.

Roediger, David. 2002. *Colored White: Transcending the Racial Past.* Berkeley and London: University of California Press.

_____. 1999. *The Wages of Whiteness.* New York: Verso.

Stasiulis, Daiva, and Abigail B. Bakan. 2005. *Negotiating Citizenship: Migrant Women in Canada and the Global System.* Toronto: University of Toronto Press.

Stasiulis, Daiva, and Nira Yuval-Davis (eds.). 1995. *Unsettling Settler Societies: Articulations of Gender, Race, Ethnicity and Class.* UK: Sage Publications.

Stepan, Nancy Leys. 2007. "Science and Race: Before and After the Human Genome Project." In Leo Panitch and Colin Leys (eds.), *Fighting Identities: Race, Religion and Ethno-Nationalism.* Socialist Register 2003. London: Merlin Press.

Thobani, Sunera. 2007. *Exalted Subjects: Studies in the Making of Race and Nation in Canada.* Toronto: University of Toronto Press.

Globalizing "Immobile" Worksites: Fast Food under Canada's Temporary Foreign Worker Program

Geraldina Polanco

MOST PEOPLE THINK THAT ALMOST ANYONE CAN WORK BEHIND THE COUNTER of a fast food restaurant. After all, how difficult can it be to flip burgers and serve coffees? Surely employers are just happy to have bodies behind the counter! While these ideas enjoy widespread currency in North America, they oversimplify hiring preferences and the nature of the work. Fast food employers, like all employers, have their version of the "best" worker, which is tied to occupational tasks. These workers combine "low-skilled" and "high-skilled" traits in one package—people with coveted skills and a strong commitment to the work in spite of poverty-level wages. The problem is employers don't want to pay more to access this workforce locally. Serendipitously, they gained access to their desired workforce through the Temporary Foreign Worker Program (TFWP).

On April 24, 2014, Jason Kenney, Canada's former minister of employment and social development, placed an immediate moratorium on the fast food sector's access to temporary foreign workers. This decision followed allegations that a McDonald's franchise owner in Victoria, British Columbia (BC), was sidelining Canadians in favour of temporary foreign workers. Additional claims featured prominently in the media included the case of Sandy Nelson, a fifty-eight-year-old Saskatchewan waitress who was reportedly discharged after almost thirty years on the job, while temporary foreign workers were retained in the same restaurant (CBC News 2014). The controversy surrounding such cases, and the moratorium imposed on the sector, marks a setback for corporations such as McDonald's and Tim Hortons, who have enjoyed quiet and uninterrupted access to migrant workers through the TFWP since 2002. While the future of this employment practice is unclear (Kenney initiated an ongoing review of the TFWP following a wave of criticism), fast food employers have clearly latched onto the TFWP to address their staffing needs. Freedom of Information requests show that from 2005 to 2010 franchise owners of Tim Hortons restaurants in Alberta and BC received positive labour market opinions for 3,575 workers. This indicates their intent to recruit 3,575 temporary foreign workers. Of those, 78 percent were from the Philippines.

The recent globalization in worksites has led many to question why fast food employers ever "went global" in their recruitment strategies. Franchise owners and their business associations bemoan crisis-level labour shortages, which they claim are impacting their ability to operate restaurants. Unions and labour activists emphasize employers' desire to access a "cheap" and "disposable" workforce. I suggest an additional dimension: fast food employers such as Tim Hortons prefer the social qualities of workers available abroad when compared transnationally with domestic workers. Moreover, "going global" gave them access to segments of workers unavailable locally at prevailing wages, to the detriment of domestic workers.

This chapter explores the social organization of low-wage service sector worksites and how the ability to recruit workers beyond domestic labour markets for occupations such as food services negatively impacts marginalized segments of the domestic workforce. Drawing from my research on the recruitment and employment of Filipino temporary foreign workers in western Canadian Tim Hortons restaurants, I show how the ability to select workers from abroad is causing a further social devaluing of already disenfranchised segments of the domestic workforce, namely aging, racialized, immigrant women of colour. This is accomplished in part through the vulnerability of temporary foreign workers. Research into the quick service restaurant industry shows that given the low-status, low-wage nature of the work, fast food employers have generally been confined to hiring workers with few other options available to them in local labour markets such as recent immigrants, single mothers, youth, and aging segments of the population (Reiter 1996, 2002; Tannock 2001; Royles and Towers 2002). However, with the TFWP's expansion, employers have been able to figuratively "relocate" to other destinations and draw workers with qualities beyond those available in local labour markets, in effect globalizing previously "immobile" worksites. Aside from foreclosing already limited opportunities available to socially undervalued segments of the domestic workforce, this raises questions about the social dimensions upon which labour markets are being transnationally organized under the TFWP, and in turn, the broader implications for social (in)equality in Canada. It also draws attention to another trend: the conditions under which residents of Canada respond to downward pressures in worksites and labour markets, and the implications for vulnerable workers (domestic and foreign).

Methodology

This chapter is part of a larger study on the Canadian fast food sector's turn to migrant labour. This was an inductive, transnational, and multisited ethnographic case study of a Canadian-Filipino fast food labour chain. From August 2010 to December 2011, I conducted sixty-two semistructured interviews with stakeholders involved at multiple levels with the TFWP and ethnographic field research in Canada and the Philippines. Interviews included Tim Hortons franchise owners in Canada; labour consultants and recruiters in both countries; government employees; frontline settlement workers and supporters of migrant workers including grassroots organizers, church-affiliated supporters, and union staff; and Tim Hortons food counter attendants (past and present domestic and temporary foreign workers). Ethnographic research included participant observation in government and industry conferences; in grassroots organizing spaces in both countries; and in the Philippines, community visits to migrant communities, recruitment fairs, and government-required "Pre-Departure Orientation Seminars." To learn specific details about Tim Hortons recruitment practices in western Canada (including whether a third-party labour recruiter was used, source country, gender of the workers, and destination in Canada), I filed Freedom of Information requests with Human Resources and Skills Development Canada (HRSDC). Through these, I was able to track important details about the social characteristics of Tim Hortons migrant worker flows.

While this research takes fast food and Tim Hortons as the industry and case study, there is considerable overlap and consistency in the franchising industry. This study also involved participant observation and interviews with other labour recruiters and consultants who supply workers for other Canadian fast food chains and it can be used to suggest similar processes in other corporations. Additional research in other regions, sectors, and sending countries would help advance our knowledge of service sector labour migration and transnational labour market regulation under migrant worker schemes.

Migrant Worker Programs and the Social Regulation of Labour Markets

Labour markets are socially regulated spaces. They are contradictory, complex social institutions wherein patterns of social inequality are magnified (Peck 1996). Labour market segmentation theory is one of a number of theoretical approaches increasingly emphasizing the socially organized nature of labour markets. Empirically, it advances analysis of how a labour force of socially disadvantaged and privileged sets of workers is mutually produced (Humphries and Rubery 1984), stressing production, reproduction, and state processes (Peck 1996). As a framework, labour market segmentation theory is analytically useful given that it highlights the creation of social inequalities and increasingly emphasizes how power and social (dis)advantage operate in labour market organization across time and space (Bauder 2001). It also sheds light on the fact that labour markets offer employers distinct sets of workers; qualities that present employers with unique benefits and challenges.

Given the locally situated nature of labour markets, research shows that employers will often target geographical regions and are often willing to physically relocate in order to gain access to their desired workforce(s). Indeed, "employers prove to be astute social geographers, keenly aware of local variations in the residential landscape, locating their firms to win proximity to a local labor force having the particular characteristics deemed desirable" (Hanson and Pratt 1992, 373). On a global scale this same principle applies—employers will often seek out geographical regions in search of desired workforces. In the manufacturing sector, employers have taken advantage of increased global connections and technological innovations and relocated production sites to the global South in pursuit of lower wages, laxer labour laws, and a desired workforce (Collins 2003; Salzinger 2003). Given the spatial confines of much interactive work, employers in less mobile industries such as restaurants and grocery stores have generally been considered incapable of relying on a strategy of relocation to attain their desired workforce. However, migrant worker programs allow employers to globalize their worksites without physically relocating, through the mechanism of global labour importation.

With the expansion of the TFWP, employers in low-wage sectors in Canada are increasingly looking to migrant workers to address supposed labour market pressures in a range of occupations previously identified as immobile and "low-skilled." With no set quotas for the TFWP Stream for Lower-Skilled Occupations (SLSO), the number of temporary foreign workers recruited under the program increased dramatically, from 1,578 to 30,267 between 2003 and 2012 (CIC 2012). The majority of the "low-skilled" migrant workforce employed in Canada are female (CIC 2012). While employers can draw this (primarily feminized and racialized) workforce from any source country, the Philippines quickly became the primary sending country of "low-skilled" migrant labour to western Canada (CIC 2011). Like many other employers, Tim Hortons has a preference for Filipino workers when recruiting transnationally.

The practice of recruiting workers transnationally is altering employer perceptions of domestic workforces, and contributing to new preferences in the fast food sector. When employers can look beyond domestic labour pools, they can be significantly more choosy about their desired workforce and select those with the social qualities they prefer, to the detriment of already marginalized domestic workers. In the fast food sector, these preferred workers combine low-wage and high-wage qualifications in one package—people with coveted qualities including high skills willing to work for less. This feature of transnational labour market organization highlights the need to explicitly consider dimensions of social location such as age, gender, and citizenship status when organizing for better employment conditions in transnationally supplied worksites.

Racialized, Immigrant Women of Colour and Western Canada's Fast Food Sector

On April 24, 2011, I travelled to a Vancouver suburb to meet with Sara [pseudonym], a domestically hired fast food worker. At the time Sara was fifty, married, with two children, and employed at a Tim Hortons. Sara recounted the process through which she came to be employed behind the counter of a fast food restaurant. As she explained, she immigrated to Canada eight years previously with her family from China. Upon arriving in the Greater Vancouver area she tried to attain professional employment in her previous field of work (accounting) but after many disheartening attempts concluded that it was unlikely she would secure comparable employment. Committed to finding "at least office work" she tried to upgrade her skills by taking diploma courses but continued to face difficulties securing what she considered "OK" employment. After four years in Canada, she and her family had spent most of their savings and she could no longer postpone entering the formal labour market. In tears, she recalled the day she had to "swallow pride" and accept a "teenager job" at the only place that would hire her, a Tim Hortons restaurant.[1]

Given Sara's migration history, foreign credentials, English as a second language status, and other socially devalued qualities, her segmentation into fast food work and associated downward social mobility is perhaps not surprising. Many have analyzed work and employment conditions in the quick service restaurant industry, emphasizing the low status of the sector and its reliance on marginalized workers. Fast food work offers low-status, low-wage part-time work with few employment benefits or opportunities for upward mobility and significant insecurity (Newman 2000; Royle and Towers 2002; Williams 2006). The monotonous, routinized nature of the work renders employment in the industry boring and "unskilled," a justification for the poverty-level wages. Given these conditions, the sector tends to draw workers with few other options available to them in local labour markets including racialized immigrant women. In short, the quick service restaurant industry offers a lack of job security, poor working conditions, minimal employment benefits, and few opportunities for upward mobility (Leidner 1993, 2002; Reiter 1996, 2002; Newman 2000; Tannock 2001; Royle and Towers 2002; Talwar 2002).

Like Sara, other aging immigrant women of colour in my study were similarly segmented into fast food work due to social valuing processes that limited their employment options despite their professional credentials and work experience. Beyond a Canadian context of reception that marginalizes feminized and racialized newcomers into secondary segments of the labour market, what was also informative about my interview with Sara was her emphasis on the physical, bodily demands of fast food work and her struggle to keep up with employer and industry expectations. Sociological literature on fast food has largely overlooked the bodily

---

1   Domestic Tim Hortons employee, April 24, 2011.

demands associated with the work. In the pursuit of profits, fast food employers and corporations expect employees to work at an unreasonably fast pace, a significant challenge to the aging body (Polanco 2013).

Fast Food Work and the Temporary Foreign Worker Advantage

Fast food work is fast paced and physically demanding. Considerable physical effort has to be exerted to ensure the smooth running of restaurants. Workers don't "just" pour coffees and flip burgers. They also stock freezers, mop floors, and take out the garbage. This work is physically taxing. When asked to describe the qualities that make for ideal Tim Hortons workers, a franchise owner in BC responded "energy level... you've been in a Tim Hortons, you've seen how much is going on behind the counter. There's a lot of movement. The good workers are [physically] able to keep up."[2] Fast food work is also customer-service oriented, making English language skills important for hiring decisions. An abundant supply of preferred workers are available for import from the Philippines, compared to other labour-sending countries such as India and Mexico, and locally. The Philippines is an important detail in Tim Hortons' global quest for the "best" worker.

Since 1974, the Philippines has exported labour throughout the world to alleviate high unemployment rates, and address excessive levels of national debt and a failing economy (Battistella 1999). It has gained a reputation for being a model labour-sending state through the workings of its migration apparatus. Guevarra (2010) and Rodriguez (2010) show that compared to other labour-sending states, the Philippines is touted for having a "comparative advantage" because it can deliver supposedly docile, hardworking, English-speaking, and loyal workers. Also, compared to other labour-sending countries it is the best equipped to deliver employers their desired workforce. This includes preferences about education, gender, and work experience, and subtler criteria such as height and religious orientation. This Philippines context facilitates employers' ability to be highly selective along occupationally relevant dimensions. It is said to accomplish the delivery of this coveted workforce through the workings of the Philippines' highly regulated labour brokerage state (Rodriguez 2010).

---

2   Tim Hortons franchise owner, October 27, 2010.

In Canada, fast food work is an employment niche of last resort for those with few other options or first-time job seekers. Those who are college educated, aged between twenty-five and forty, and fluent in English generally gravitate to segments of the labour market that offer higher wages and better working conditions. But employers want their ideal worker. Moreover, by recruiting transnationally, fast food employers gain access to a global workforce possessing a range of desirable social characteristics including being eager and motivated to work hard for low wages, a workforce in comparatively short supply domestically. I found that Tim Hortons franchise owners in Alberta and BC have sought to recruit primarily young, educated, English-speaking, eager, and able-bodied Filipina/o migrant workers when recruiting workers transnationally for food counter attendant positions.

Access to global labour pools allow employers to be highly selective and recruit workers along dimensions such as nationality, "race," and sex (Preibisch 2010) but also qualities deemed particularly advantageous for the industry and occupation in question. Fast food employers can recruit young, eager, and able-bodied workers to meet the physical and interactive demands of fast food work, in turn circumventing aging segments of the population (Polanco 2013). With fierce competition on the part of migrant-sending countries to supply their "best" to global employers, this transnational labour market organization comes at the expense of people like Sara and through the vulnerability of temporary foreign workers. In an interview, an employment counsellor in BC recounted working at a settlement agency and receiving job advertisements for Tim Hortons food counter attendant positions. He recalled encouraging his clients, all recent immigrants, to apply and remembers they would generally secure these jobs. However, since the introduction of the Low-Skilled Pilot Project (now the SLSO) he had observed that his clients were no longer necessarily getting these jobs, in spite of continued job advertisements and the growth of the TFWP.[3] Moreover, while employers in western Canada bemoan an inability to staff their worksites due to labour shortages, perhaps what is actually in short supply domestically is their preferred workforce. Employers want more control to select their desired workforce, while local workers are (unintentionally) devalued and displaced by migrant workers who can satisfy

3   Settlement worker, October 12, 2010.

employer demands along a host of dimensions. Migrant worker vulnerability is also an important factor that makes TFWs so appealing to employers.

Temporary foreign workers face significant vulnerability as a result of their temporary citizenship status and through the regulatory system of the TFWP. For example, I met Neil in the summer of 2011 in the Philippines. At the time, Neil was in his midthirties and had been back in the Philippines for only a few months following almost three years of employment in an Alberta-based Tim Hortons as a food counter attendant. It was immediately clear that Neil possessed many of the qualities esteemed by fast food employers. First, his English language skills were extremely strong. He was college educated, physically fit, and funny. Moreover, he had all the qualities that would make for an excellent customer service worker in a physically demanding worksite. Neil recalled how he came to be employed at Tim Hortons. As he explained, he had always dreamed of immigrating to the United States but lacked the necessary capital to do so. So he decided that he would work temporary contracts in other regions and save up, to eventually immigrate to North America. In his midtwenties he migrated to Dubai, and for the next ten years worked consecutive contracts in the food and services industries, first in a coffee shop and eventually working his way up the service sector ladder into a managerial position in a midlevel restaurant. But the work was starting to take a toll on his personal life; he found it hard to stay connected with his wife during long separations and his children were growing quickly. He therefore took it as a sign when one day he saw an advertisement for a "service sector job" in Canada. Believing that this would lead to permanent residence, he went through a competitive recruitment process and was eventually selected and deployed to Canada. What he later experienced was a rude awakening.

In the Philippines, migrating to Canada on a temporary work contract is associated with permanent migration, given Canada's longstanding Live-in Caregiver Program (LCP). Under the LCP, workers were often treated as would-be immigrants, streamed through what Hennebry (2010) describes as a "two-step" system of migration: initial entry as a temporary foreign worker with a direct and permanent pathway toward permanent residence following the meeting of certain criteria. What Neil did not know was that Canada had expanded its TFWP and the legal context of reception for migrant workers had changed. Workers recruited under the TFWP Stream for Lower Skilled Occupations (SLSO) do not enjoy a direct pathway to permanent residence. Instead, those who aspire toward permanent residence under this program require an employer nomination under a Provincial Nominee Program (PNP). Unlike the LCP, workers cannot initiate the process. It is up to the employer to decide whether or not to nominate a worker. This context lends itself to a host of violations as migrant workers compete for a nomination. As Neil explained, "First point of the first day, I am working hard… we were all, we were even extending hours … for them, for free! Because… everybody [each of the temporary foreign workers at the restaurant] was saying, I want to be nominated. I want the company to nominate me, help me bring my family over." For a time Neil thought that he had attained his objective. Shortly before the termination of his contract, his employer told Neil to return to the Philippines, get some rest, and be ready to collect his family; he was going to nominate him under the PNP. He recalled being thrilled! Before returning to the Philippines, Neil went out and bought furniture as well as a car with his hard-earned money in anticipation of this. However, once back in the Philippines he could not reach his employer. After several months, he realized he had been misled; his employer was not going to nominate him. Last we spoke, Neil was trying to arrange for a friend in Alberta to sell his new furniture and car (at a loss) and send him back the remaining money.

Beyond the perceived social qualities of (Filipino) migrant workers that make them appear preferable to fast food employers over various segments of the domestic workforce, employers can also rely on the vulnerability of temporary foreign workers to attain a disciplined, committed, and in turn desired workforce through global labour importation. Fast food has long struggled with high turnover rates given the difficulty in securing a workforce willing to work hard for low wages. A Vancouver labour consultant explained, "It's tough to buy loyalty with eight dollars an hour"[4] or rather the minimum wage. While temporary foreign workers technically enjoy the same employment rights as other workers in Canada, they are disproportionately vulnerable to exploitative working conditions in part because their "temporary" immigration status vis-a-vis the state disempowers them from accessing these rights (Preibisch 2010; Goldring and Landolt 2012, 2013). This makes it difficult for migrant workers to resist or reject harsh working conditions and employment violations, especially since

---

4   Labour consultant, October 6, 2010.

their right to work and live in Canada is tied to their employment contract. Thus migrant workers are unlikely to exit the employment relationship and are seemingly willing to work hard for low wages, to the benefit of Canadian employers.

Often, the social dimensions that make migrant workers appear "preferable" to employers are in fact not objective differences but rather rooted in subjective assessments and social valuing processes. Perceived evaluations of language skills are one such example. Given the interactive nature of fast food work, employment in the quick service restaurant industry requires knowledge of the dominant language. In western Canada, this limits opportunities for non-English-speaking segments of the local and global workforce but also forecloses opportunities for those perceived to lack English language skills domestically. Sara described at length how her "bad English" had acted as a significant barrier to attaining employment beyond fast food. Other racialized workers I interviewed expressed parallel struggles, though they (like Sara) also spoke English. Moreover, what is often at stake with racialized populations is as Creese (2002) describes, the "colour" of people's English, or rather low assessments of English language competence among racialized people even when there is evidence to the contrary. This makes Filipino migrant workers especially desirable compared to other sending countries such as Mexico (Polanco and Zell 2013), as well as by comparison with those regarded as "nonfluent" in the Canadian labour market. Moreover, transnational labour market organization is both about concrete qualities that socially distinguish workers—such as gender and age—and also social processes of assessing traits and ascribing value to socially situated subjects, locally and globally.

Migrant Workers and the New Transnational Worksite

The global availability of different labour pools from which low-wage employers can draw their workforces changes the social characteristics of local worksites and redefines what constitutes the "desirable" worker. Research on the quick service restaurant industry has tended to emphasize the "unskilled" nature of fast food work, and the sector's reliance on marginalized workers. However, with the globalization of service sector worksites as a result of the expansion of the TFWP, employers can now move beyond those with few other options available to them in local labour markets through importing their desired workforce. In so doing, they can select a workforce well suited to the nature of the work without having to improve work and employment conditions in the sector to attain this coveted workforce.

Beyond a transnational labour market organization rooted in comparatively ascribing value onto different sets of workers, the shift toward migrant workers and other employer-friendly policies has also been associated with the rise in precarious work and employment conditions. There is an explicit link between temporary migration and labour market flexibilization (Preibisch 2007). Jobs staffed by low-wage migrant workers offer the worst working conditions and lowest levels of compensation (Sharma 2006; Anderson 2010). Such conditions benefit capital at the expense of workers, while promoting a downgrading in work and employment conditions and a general devolution of risks from capital onto workers. There are also long-term, negative consequences associated with these processes.

Goldring and Landolt (2012, 2013) have introduced the concept of precarious legal status as a way to empirically examine the effects of immigrant and noncitizenship status on work and labour market outcomes. Precarious legal status includes all individuals without permanent residence status. Their research with Latin American and Caribbean workers in the Greater Toronto Area suggests that initial entry into the labour market with a precarious legal status is linked to long-term negative economic outcomes, even after transition to a more permanent status. Pathways to precarious status are also gendered and racialized (Goldring et al. 2007). Far from being politically neutral, the expansion of the TFWP and related diversification in legal status categories through which newcomers can enter Canada is introducing new systems of social inequalities and of regulating labour market performance. The more individuals enter Canada on temporary worker statuses—especially for "low-skilled" occupations through programs such as the SLSO—the worse work and employment outcomes we can expect for these primarily feminized and racialized people from the global South. It also appears to suggest a general race to the bottom in worksites staffed by both domestic and migrant workers alike given that people like Sara are also impacted and devalued in the process. They are further marginalized by exploited global inequalities that promote South-North labour migration in the first place, and the vulnerabilities of those such as Neil generated through shortcomings in the TFWP.

Toward an Appreciation of the Aging Immigrant Worker

Work and labour markets organize numerous aspects of people's lives and shape broader conditions of privilege and inequality. The move toward normalizing the presence of those with precarious legal status raises important questions about recent changes to immigration policies and the social fabric that is being weaved through programs such as the TFWP. As I have shown, Canada is institutionalizing the transnational segmentation of primarily racialized and feminized workers into the bottom tiers of Canadian labour markets, with negative impacts on domestic workers. A large body of literature has shown the negative effects of migrant worker programs on temporary foreign workers (e.g., Basok 2004; Sharma 2006; Hennebry 2010; Thomas 2010). Such programs promote vulnerability and employment precarity among transnational workers primarily from the global South. As these programs expand in Canada, we also need to consider how other sets of (domestic) workers are being impacted through the globalization of Canadian worksites and labour markets.

While different processes of producing vulnerability regulate the experiences of workers within labour markets, the expansion of the TFWP has had negative effects for both domestic and migrant workers in western Canada. Rather than encouraging employers to improve work and employment conditions that might resolve purported labour shortages in the fast food sector, the Canadian federal government was until recently facilitating the ability of employers to circumvent vulnerable segments of the domestic workforce and recruit workers from abroad. The result was the displacement of more vulnerable and socially undervalued segments of the domestic labour market, including aging, racialized, and immigrant women of colour.

While there are numerous challenges associated with organizing workers in the bottom rungs of the labour market, I suggest that we should more centrally consider how the diversification of labour markets through programs such as the TFWP impacts employer preferences and worksite hierarchies. This dimension of labour market organization takes us beyond the realm of employment contracts and working conditions, and into the micro and social world of ideas. Indeed, some like Sara are being rendered "undesirable" through the introduction of a new set of workers like Neil who are in their own right differently vulnerable; workers with different social qualities along dimensions like age and immigrant status.

Comparatively, these young and able-bodied workers are valued for their physical characteristics and vulnerabilities (including ability to work fast and "commitment" to the employment contract), putting Sara's value as an aging immigrant worker into question. We see initial signs of domestic workers being displaced through the TFWP, as media cases have sensationalized. It remains to be seen how other sets of workers in different sectors will be comparatively assessed and potentially displaced through the globalization and diversification of Canadian worksites and labour markets.

Thus, as we work toward organizing with workers on the bottom rungs of Canadian labour markets we must pay greater attention to these social dimensions of (transnational) labour market organization. For the fast food sector, this might pragmatically mean that we need to reject and organize around the low value associated with the aging, immigrant body while also organizing against vulnerabilities associated with precarious legal status. Workers like Sara may have many advantages over migrant workers (including permanent residence) but they also have relative disadvantages.

While labour markets are spaces in which actors buy and sell labour power, they are also primary institutions involved in the organization of societies where social inequalities are both created and magnified. In the case of fast food, we must collectively reject the low value ascribed to the social characteristics of marginalized workers, whether locally or globally, as one step toward resisting worker disenfranchisement in worksites such as Tim Hortons in spite of citizenship status.

References

Anderson, Bridget. 2010. "Migration, Immigration Controls and the Fashioning of Precarious Workers." *Work, Employment and Society* 24, no. 2.

Basok, Tanya. 2004. "Post-National Citizenship, Social Exclusion and Migrants Rights: Mexican Seasonal Workers in Canada." *Citizenship Studies* 8, no. 1.

Battistella, Graziano. 1999. "Philippine Migration Policy: Dilemmas of a Crisis." *SOJOURN: Journal of Social Issues in Southeast Asia* 14, no. 1.

Bauder, Harald. 2001. "Culture in the Labor Market: Segmentation and Perspectives of Place." *Progress in Human Geography* 25, no. 1.

Bourette, Susan. 2007. "Welcome to Canada: Hope You Weren't Planning on Staying." *Globe and Mail,* September 26. <theglobeandmail.com/report-on-business/article783502.ece>.

CBC News. 2014. "Weyburn Restaurant Defends Staffing Moves and Use of Foreign Temps." April 23. <cbc.ca/news/canada/saskatchewan/weyburn-restaurant-defends-staffing-moves-and-use-of-foreign-temps-1.2619644>.

Citizenship and Immigration Canada (CIC). 2012. *Facts and Figures 2011: Immigration Overview—Permanent and Temporary Residents.* <cic.gc.ca/english/resources/statistics/facts2011/>.

Collins, Jane. 2003. *Threads: Gender, Labor and Power in the Global Apparel Industry.* Chicago: University of Chicago Press.

Goldring, Luin, and Patricia Landolt (eds.). 2013. *Producing and Negotiating Non-Citizenship: Precarious Legal Status in Canada.* Toronto: University of Toronto Press.

_____. 2012. "The Impact of Precarious Legal Status on Immigrants' Economic Outcomes." Institute for Research on Public Policy study 35. Montreal, QC: IRPP.

Goodine, Isaac. 2007. "On Reinventing Oneself." *The North American Filipino Star* 25, no. 9b.

Guevarra, Anna Romina. 2010. *Marketing Dreams, Manufacturing Heroes: The Transnational Labor Brokering of Filipino Workers.* New Jersey: Rutgers University Press.

Hanson, Susan, and Geraldine Pratt. 1992. "Dynamic Dependencies: A Geographic Investigation of Local Labor Markets." *Economic Geography* 68, no. 4.

Hennebry, Jenna. 2010. "Who Has Their Eye on the Ball? 'Jurisdictional Fútbol' and Canada's Temporary Foreign Worker Program." *Policy Options.*

Humphries, Jane, and Jill Rubery. 1984. "The Reconstitution of the Supply Side of the Labour Market: The Relative Autonomy of Social Reproduction." *Cambridge Journal of Economics* 8, no. 4.

Nakache, Delphine, and Paula J. Kinoshita. 2010. "The Canadian Temporary Foreign Worker Program: Do Short-Term Economic Needs Prevail over Human Rights Concerns?" Institute for Research on Public Policy study 5. Montreal, QC: IRPP.

Newman, Katherine. 2000. *No Shame in My Game: The Working Poor in the Inner City.* New York: Vintage Press.

Peck, Jamie. 1996. *Work-Place: The Social Regulation of Labor Markets.* New York: Guilford Press.

Polanco, Geraldina. 2013. "Behind the Counter: Migration, Labour Policy and Temporary Work in a Global Fast Food Chain." Doctoral thesis, University of British Columbia.

Polanco, Geraldina, and Sarah Zell. 2013. "Migrant Workers in Labour Markets Gone Global: English Language Capital and the Production of Global Hierarchies." Unpublished paper.

Reiter, Ester. 2002. "Fast Food in Canada: Working Conditions, Labour Law and Unionization." In Tony Royle and Brian Towers (eds.), *Labour Relations in the Global Fast Food Industry.* New York: Routledge.

_____. 1996. *Making Fast Food: From the Frying Pan into the Fryer.* Montreal: McGill–Queen's University Press.

Rodriguez, Robyn. 2010. *Migrants for Export: How the Philippine Brokers Labor to the World.* Minneapolis: University of Minnesota Press.

Royle, Tony, and Brian Towers. 2002. "Summary and Conclusions: MNCs, Regulatory Systems and Employment Rights." In Tony Royle and Brian Towers (eds.), *Labour Relations in the Global Fast Food Industry.* New York: Routledge.

Salzinger, Leslie. 2003. *Genders in Production: Making Workers in Mexico's Global Factories.* Berkeley and Los Angeles: University of California Press.

Sharma, Nandita. 2006. *Home Economics: Nationalism and the Making of 'Migrant Workers' in Canada.* Toronto: University of Toronto Press.

_____. 2002. "Immigrant and Migrant Workers in Canada: Labour Movements, Racism and the Expansion of Globalization." *Canadian Woman Studies* 22, no. 4 (Summer).

Talwar, Jennifer Parker. 2002. *Fast Food, Fast Track: Immigrants, Big Business and the American Dream.* Boulder: Westview Press.

Tannock, Stuart. 2001. *Youth at Work: The Unionized Fast Food and Grocery Workplace.* Philadelphia: Temple University Press.

Tomlinson, Kathy. 2013. "RBC Replaces Canadian Staff with Foreign Workers." *CBC*, April 6. <cbc.ca/news/canada/british-columbia/story/2013/04/05/bc-rbc-foreign-workers.html>.

Valiani, Salimah. 2009. "The Shift in Canadian Immigration Policy and Unheeded Lessons of the Live-in Caregiver Program." *MRZine*. New York: Monthly Review.

Williams, Christine. 2006. *Inside Toyland: Working, Shopping, and Social Inequality.* Berkeley and Los Angeles: University of California Press.

Struggling against History: Migrant Farmworker Organizing in British Columbia

Adriana Paz Ramirez and Jennifer Jihye Chun

ON JULY 26, 2006, THE BRITISH COLUMBIA (BC) CHAPTER OF THE GRASS-roots collective Justicia for Migrant Workers (J4MW) hosted a film screening of *El Contrato* about the plight of migrant farmworkers under Canada's Seasonal Agricultural Worker Program (SAWP).[1] J4MW activists sought to raise money for Mexican workers facing deportation and a potential lifetime ban from SAWP after walking off their jobs. Although Canadian labour laws protect workers' right to strike, these workers faced immediate retaliation from employers and the Mexican consulate for openly challenging their unjust living and working conditions. At the time there was little public understanding of the restrictive and dehumanizing conditions of guest worker programs in BC, which joined SAWP in 2004, nearly five decades after Ontario, as part of the province's aggressive expansion of the Temporary Foreign Worker Program (TFWP) in a variety of low-paid occupations. Much to the surprise of the J4MW activists, the event was packed, including people from Abbotsford, Delta, Chilliwack, and other Fraser Valley farming towns located over seventy kilometres from Vancouver.

Former leaders of the Canadian Farmworkers Union (CFU), the first farmworker union, which was established in Canada in 1980, also attended. Few people knew about the CFU's history. According to local historian Sadhu Binning (1986, 14–15), the CFU was not just "another union"; it was a "moral" force that galvanized a broad base of unions, community organizations,

---

1   J4MW, which has chapters in BC and Ontario, organizes and advocates for the rights of migrant farmworkers who come to Canada under temporary workers' programs. *El Contrato* (2003) was produced and directed by Minsook Lee.

religious leaders, women's groups, progressive lawyers, political party officials, artists, academics, and students to support BC farmworkers, who then
consisted primarily of South Asian immigrants from Punjab, India. Charan
Gill, who still serves as CFU secretary treasurer—an entirely symbolic position—and moved on to lead one of the largest immigrant-serving agencies
in BC's Lower Mainland, commended the "young people" of J4MW, yet
expressed deep pessimism. As passionate union organizers, he and other
CFU leaders rose up and fought, and tried many times and in different
ways, but they finally had to give up, unable to sustain the CFU's victories in
the face of employer backlash, a deepening economic recession, a complex
legal environment, and diminishing organizational resources. Gill and other
former CFU leaders told J4MW activists that if organizing farmworkers with
full citizenship rights was nearly impossible, organizing migrant farmworkers on temporary work permits was indeed an *impossibility*.

The encounters between former CFU leaders and J4MW activists raise
important questions about migrant farmworkers organizing in BC, as well
as the complex ways in which past struggles bear on the present. The CFU's
fight on the farms, on the streets, and in the legal arena garnered historic
victories for BC farmworkers. However, its gains were short-lived for BC's
farmworker communities and in the public memory. How do we make
sense of the contradictory messages of former CFU leaders, who recognize
the urgency of challenging the migrant farm labour system, yet view such
efforts as hopeless? What lessons can be learned from the CFU's historic
struggles, as a new generation of migrant farmworkers and their advocates
strive to challenge the unequal and unjust power relations in BC's agricultural industry? What impact do the histories of resistance and struggles by
racially subordinated groups of workers, histories that go unrecorded and
often exist as fleeting memories, have on current struggles to bring about
a more just and emancipatory world?

This chapter explores past and current organizing efforts in BC's farmworker movement. We examine the relationship between CFU's efforts
to organize the predominantly South Asian migrant workforce under the
farm labour contract system in the 1970s and 1980s and the current dilemmas of migrant farmworker organizing under temporary worker programs.
On the surface, this relationship can be understood in terms of capitalist
dynamics and the power of capital to perpetually thwart worker resistance. Faced with threats to capital accumulation by unions, farm owners

reorganized production relations and enacted classic "divide and conquer" tactics between two groups of racialized workers: South Asian immigrants with full residence and citizenship rights, and Mexican migrants with highly restrictive temporary work permits under SAWP. While employer backlash certainly explains the extreme difficulties that workers face in mounting resistance and sustaining victories over time, it provides little insight into the ongoing resistance of workers, especially racially subordinated groups, to ongoing commodification and exploitation.

Drawing upon Foucault's (1980) notion of subjugated knowledges—that is, entire histories of struggle against dominant ways of understandings that have been erased, masked, and disqualified as insufficient—we propose another starting point. We ask how such largely unrecorded acts of resistance waged from subordinated groups, often hidden and submerged, become reactivated at different historical moments by different social actors. We also examine the cultural and institutional context that influences how acts of resistance are expressed and formalized. By reflecting on the ways in which subjugated histories come in and out of focus, we seek to deepen understanding of the limits and possibilities of bringing structural transformation through seemingly impossible acts of worker resistance and collective action. Such interventions are rooted in our critical ethnographic approach to producing situated knowledge, but also informed by our commitment as activist-scholars and grassroots organizers.

First, we discuss CFU's struggles during the late 1970s and early 1980s, examining the CFU's efforts to challenge the exploitative and discriminatory conditions of farm work for a predominantly South Asian immigrant workforce. This section draws primarily from the extraordinary digital historical archive of over seven hundred CFU publications, documents, and records housed at Simon Fraser University's special library collections.[2] Second, we analyze the daily lives and struggles of migrant workers under the SAWP in BC, drawing upon in-depth qualitative interviews and participant observation conducted by Adriana Paz Ramirez (2013) and her work as a longtime J4MW organizer. We conclude by exploring the insights that analyzing worker resistance through the lens of subjugated histories has on current organizing efforts, and the political urgency and necessity of challenging both systemic racism and capitalist exploitation.

---

2   The Canadian Farmworkers Union Project can be found at: <lib.sfu.ca/special-collections/canadian-farmworkers-union>.

South Asian Farmworkers in BC's Agricultural Industry, 1970s and 1980s

The history of labour migration in BC's agricultural industry is tied to the history of racial exclusion and subordination in a newly forming white settler society. After early Chinese migrants were subject to an exorbitant head tax restricting entry into Canada in the late 1800s, white settlers' demands for cheap labour resulted in new flows of migrants from India, primarily from Punjab. Permitted entry to work in designated occupations such as farming, canning, and domestic services, the number of South Asians or "East Indians," as they were referred to at the time, increased from one hundred to forty-seven hundred persons in BC between 1904 and 1907 (Jhappan 1981, 23). Growing fears of a "Hindu invasion" and intensifying anti-Asian violence by white workers, however, quickly halted migration. The passage of the 1908 Continuous Journey Act, which remained in effect until 1947, imposed a de facto ban on all Indian immigrants. Immigrants from India who remained in BC were stripped of the right to vote in 1909, despite their legal status as British subjects, and faced pervasive discrimination regarding jobs, property ownership, family, marriage, intimate relationships, and the courts in the following decades.

The second wave of South Asian labour migration to BC occurred during the 1970s after the removal of race and national origins quotas in federal immigration and citizenship policies. The family preferences category, which allowed people to sponsor family members to immigrate, created a flow of South Asian immigrants to BC's sawmills, canneries, garment factories, and farms, the few sectors that hired racialized workers. A gendered pattern of employment emerged in many South Asian households during this period. Men tended to work in forestry, which provided union jobs, while women and children tended to work in lower-paid domestic work and farm work, sectors that were excluded from most provincial labour protections including the Minimum Wages Act, the Hours of Work Act, the Annual and General Holidays Act, and the Payment of Wages Act. In the Fraser Valley, just east of Vancouver, approximately 80 to 90 percent of all farmworkers were from Punjab and an estimated 60 to 70 percent were women (Binning 1986, 9).[3]

---

3   The BC Federation of Agriculture reported that approximately thirteen thousand farmworkers were employed in BC's agricultural sector during the 1970s and 1980s; the vast majority consisted of East Indian, Chinese, and Japanese workers (Jhappan 1981, 20).

The concentration of South Asian immigrants in the Fraser Valley was linked to an ethnic-dominated farm labour contract system that first appeared in 1969 and began to flourish in 1976 (Chouhan et al. 1983, 3). Fruit and vegetable growers, mostly family farms and some of which were owned by members of the Punjabi community, contracted out their labour needs to intermediary contractors that hired Sikh Punjabi workers through kinship networks, social ties, and foreign-language newspapers. Contractors paid farmworkers by the piece, often delayed compensation until the end of the season to ensure that workers would not quit midseason, and subtracted an additional 25 to 40 percent from workers' earnings.

The farm labour contract system was exploitative and dehumanizing on and off the fields. Many workers became physically ill after pesticide exposure. Few if any growers and contractors sought medical assistance for workers who fell ill. Substandard housing conditions resulted in high rates of sexual violence, injury, and sometimes death. Worker accommodation, often consisting of barns converted into living quarters, lacked running water, privacy, and security. Stories circulated about rampant sexual harassment and violence by contractors. Workers, who depended on labour contractors for transportation to as many as twenty different farms during the four to five month harvesting season, were also victims of traffic accidents due to the lack of auto safety on poorly maintained vehicles. Housing and transportation accidents were particularly lethal for workers and the many children who accompanied their mothers to the farms (CFU 1980).

Farmworkers had little recourse to improve working and living conditions as new immigrants with limited English skills and few social networks outside their ethnic community. Not only were farmworkers excluded from basic legal protections against employer abuse and workplace health and safety accidents, but labour contractors also designated themselves as interpreters for all matters pertaining to wages, housing, and unemployment contributions, leaving workers with extremely limited access to independent information and alternative sources of support. When a crisis occurred, be it a sexual assault or a tragic accident, workers tended to rely on trusted family and community members rather than the law or mainstream institutions. This began to change in the late 1970s when South Asian community members, including Raj Chouhan, Charan Gill, and Marinder Mahill, began to challenge the exploitation and injustice of BC's agricultural industry.

The Canadian Farmworkers Union (CFU)

> We are proud to be farmworkers
> we sweat like all the rest of the toilers
> as they do in the factories and mills
> yet you say in the eyes of your law
> we are not workers
> —Sadhu Binning, "Farmworkers Are Workers Too" (poem)

On April 6, 1980, around two hundred workers attended the CFU's founding convention in New Westminster, approximately two years after Chouhan and others began going door-to-door to workers' homes and Sikh temples. One of the first acts of business was the passage of a resolution demanding that the BC government recognize farmworkers as legitimate workers entitled to basic labour protections such as minimum wage standards and protection against wage theft, employer fraud, and dangerous working and living conditions. In his convention speech, Chouhan (1980, 3), who was elected CFU president, avowed: "As long as the provincial government does not extend labour laws to farm and domestic workers, it is guilty of discriminatory action through inaction. It is maintaining areas of oppression into which people can be driven through societal discrimination."

For Chouhan and the CFU, the legislative discrimination of farmworkers under provincial labour laws was tied to the long history of legal racism enacted against people from India and other colonized regions. Referencing the *Komagatu Maru*, a ship carrying 376 passengers from India who were refused entry in Vancouver for two consecutive months in 1914 and subjected to violent attacks by government officials and locals while on board, Chouhan called attention to the long history of "racial abuse" that people of South Asian descent faced in western Canada. Chouhan also acknowledged the histories of resistance waged by racially subordinated workers along the West Coast. Drawing parallels with the David and Goliath fight of the United Farm Workers (UFW), which represented highly exploited groups of Mexican and Chicano farmworkers in California, the CFU stated that it "regarded the struggle of farmworkers in California as its own."[4]

---

4   See information on CFU support of UFW boycott of Chiquita bananas (FWOC 1979, 3).

Cross-racial solidarity was a central principle of the CFU's political vision and organizing strategy. CFU leaders were keenly aware of the interconnections between labour exploitation and legal racism, and recognized the "divide and conquer" strategies that farm owners used to pit racially oppressed groups of workers against each other. In their first newsletter, the Farm Worker Organizing Committee (FWOC), the organizational predecessor of the CFU, publicly welcomed to Canada Vietnamese refugees who were displaced by the war, yet denounced owners' efforts "to reap profit from the misery of a people cast away from their own homeland" (FWOC 1979, 3) by recruiting them into exploitative and unregulated farm labour. FWOC rebuked owners' attempts to "stimulate hostility and suspicion between the two sections of the working class with racist ideas like: 'Immigrant workers take away jobs from Canadian workers'" (ibid., 11).

Through grassroots organizing and an antiracist platform, the CFU successfully unionized over one thousand farmworkers in under two years at some of BC's largest farms, and sparked a broader social movement. The union collected thousands of signatures petitioning the BC government to extend basic labour protections to farmworkers. It garnered the support of numerous unions and labour organizations, including financial contributions from the Canadian Labour Congress (CLC) and the BC Government Employees' Union (BCGEU). It established the BC Organization to Fight Racism (BCOFR), a multiracial coalition that brought together BC Indigenous communities with Chinese-, Filipino-, and Indo-Canadian communities to fight anti-Asian violence and white supremacy. It also mobilized community allies to attend public protests and solidarity events, volunteer as tutors for the union's "ESL Crusade" and legal clinics, and attend plays and documentary films about the plight of BC farmworkers, including *A Time to Rise*, produced by Anand Patwardhan and Jim Munro.

As the farmworkers' movement gained momentum, growers escalated their counterresponse, hiring external consultants and lawyers to challenge union certification campaigns, prolong strikes and collective bargaining negotiations, and dismantle the efficacy of union contracts. Growers also fought against legal gains that included farmworkers in provincial employment standards and health and safety protections, reversing the 1982 decision to extend the BC Workers Compensation Act to farmworkers and reinstating restrictions to farmworkers' ability to claim unemployment insurance in 1983. Their efforts to revise the provincial labour code in 1984 "created the biggest single legislative block to organizing new Canadians" (Boal 1987, 4–5). According to CFU's next president, Sarwan Boal, this measure gave employers "at least one week (between application and vote) to harass and intimidate the workers," which was particularly detrimental to "new Canadians" who feared the arbitrary power of white Canadian growers and male Punjabi labour contractors (ibid.).

The growers' intense counteroffensive took a tremendous toll on the CFU's ability to sustain and grow their organization. In reports issued during their sixth and seventh national conventions, the CFU described many obstacles and setbacks: "The year 1985 was especially a killer, when we had lost almost all the certified units except one, and our overall membership had dropped to only twenty" (CFU 1987). Although the CFU's renewed commitment to grassroots organizing and their new emphasis on "community unionism," a strategy that "organizes farmworkers in their communities around community and political issues" (Boal 1987, 6), helped rebuild its membership in the late 1980s, it faced an uphill battle to sustain its organizational activities in the context of limited legal victories, continued employer backlash, and a deepening economic recession (see also Binning 1986). Unable to pay full-time staff salaries, rent, and the publication of its *Farmworker* newsletter after 1991—the year the CFU lost funding support from the Canadian Labour Congress—the union gradually waned and CFU supporters redirected their attention toward advocacy, community service provision, and formal politics.

The Seasonal Agricultural Worker Program in British Columbia

Despite its attempts to collectively organize farmworkers, the CFU was unable to withstand the antiunion backlash. Provincial labour authorities supported employer counteroffensives by allowing labour contractors and growers to engage in ongoing worker abuse with little consequence. The provincial and federal governments took additional steps in the early 2000s to depress working conditions by enacting regressive revisions to employment standards protections (Fairey et al. 2008) and restricting entry through the family reunification provision of Citizenship and Immigration Canada (CIC), the main avenue of entry for South Asian immigrant farmworkers. The most decisive changes, however, took place in 2002 and 2004 when BC's powerful agribusiness lobby convinced the provincial government to authorize temporary visas to alleviate purported "labour shortages" under SAWP and the Stream for Lower-Skilled Occupations. SAWP on the West Coast started as a "pilot program" with forty-seven Mexican workers. The following year, two hundred workers were recruited to work in the Fraser Valley. SAWP now brings approximately six thousand workers annually to the Fraser Valley and Okanagan Valley (Employment and Social Development Canada 2012).

Migrant workers under the SAWP are regulated by a distinct set of labour and immigration rules that creates a two-tiered legal system for citizen and noncitizen workers (Basok 2004; Preibisch 2007). Temporary migrant workers do not enjoy the same political citizenship rights and social benefit programs afforded to Canadian citizens or permanent residents such as provincial employment standards legislation and unemployment insurance (UI) (see Ramsaroop chapter, this volume). SAWP does not grant or contain policies for family reunification or paths to regularization on an individual basis regardless of how many years workers have been coming to work in Canada and the ties they develop in local communities. As such, SAWP operates as a "forced rotation" program, dispensing temporary work permits that tie workers to a single employer for periods of up to eight months (Wong 1984). Before leaving their home countries, workers must sign a contract with their employer specifying wages and terms of employment, thereby signing away the right to seek better working and living conditions while in Canada. To ensure that migrant workers do not overstay their contracts, employers and government officers from CIC monitor the number of workers who overstay in Canada through mechanisms such as the absent without leave (AWOL) recourse (Verma 2003). SAWP participants from Mexico routinely emphasize that applicants are required to be married and have children—conditions that are not required for workers from the Caribbean—and give employers additional guarantees that workers will return home to their families (Basok 2004).

The SAWP has its own contractual and extralegal mechanisms of coercion, control, and discipline (Ramsaroop 2008; Preibisch and Encalada 2010). Workers must live on or nearby the places where they work, in accommodation provided by the employer, which are often cramped and substandard. These living arrangements enable employers to demand that work is performed outside regular hours, rarely with overtime compensation. As with South Asian immigrant workers under farm labour contractors, workers depend almost entirely on their employers for essential things such as visits to doctors, transportation to and from the farm, groceries, and banking (Basok 2002). Employers exercise control over workers' private and personal matters, including restrictions on socialization and spatial mobility. Employers decide when workers have time off, what they do in their time off, and what kind of social relationships they can establish (Paz Ramirez 2008). On some farms workers must abide by curfews and are not allowed to mingle across gender lines. They are required to inform employers of their whereabouts when off the farm. They are surveilled by their supervisors, and through peer-to-peer anonymous reporting behaviour mechanisms to the employer and to Mexican Ministry of Labour officers (Encalada and Preibisch 2010). These tactics are powerful forms of control and governance. Many workers have lost their places in the program for not complying with these rules. Once a worker has lost his or her employer in Canada it is difficult to become eligible again.

Programs such as the SAWP rely on the supply of an indentured migrant labour force that is reliable, dedicated, controlled, and disciplined. Workers from rural areas in Mexico devastated by NAFTA policies and who face extremely limited job prospects at home view programs such as the SAWP as a lifeline. Because workers know they can be replaced at any time at the employer's whim, they endure the harsh and exploitative conditions. Martin, a SAWP worker, explains:

> Basically, we [migrant farmworkers] are treated like machines, but machines that are not even allowed to break ... because if you do then they [employers] send you to Mexico. ... That is why many of us go to work even in pain or high fever so you are not sent back [to Mexico]. (Paz Ramirez 2013, 2)

SAWP workers commonly describe labour migration programs as "fear regimes" that compel workers to endure workplace abuses and violations to guarantee their spot in the program the following season. Workers' lack of labour mobility creates structural vulnerabilities for them, which are rooted in a structural framework of governance of how Canada manages its migrant labour regimes, and that are manifested in tangible forms such as vulnerabilities to health risks and widespread labour and human rights violations that are structural and endemic in the agricultural industry (Hennebry and McLaughlin 2012). Employers' ability to repatriate workers when no longer needed—if they fall sick or are injured, if they exhibit behaviour deemed undesirable, or if they are deemed to lack a disposition to work—extend their power to control and discipline. Consequently, workers experience a constant sense of disposability, displacement, anxiety, and uncertainty on the farms—feelings that permeate different aspects of their transient lives and travel with them as they move from their country of origin to Canada each year.

The restriction of workers' rights and mobility constitutes an apartheid-like system of labour control and domination built on "unfree labour" (Paz Ramirez 2013). Sharma (2006, 1250) writes "like past forms of apartheid, its global manifestation is not based on keeping differentiated people apart but instead on organizing two (or more) separate legal regimes and practices for differentiated collectivities within the name nationalized space." Conventionally, apartheid has been regarded as an intensification of race-based segregation policies; however, while the role of racial supremacy was a prominent element in the formation of apartheid, it cannot be reduced to racial domination alone. In the case of South African apartheid, Harold Wolpe (1972) argues that race operated as a political construct that enabled capital and the state to deny fundamental rights and freedoms to racially subordinated groups to guarantee the reproduction and maintenance of cheap labour power for capital accumulation. Although the SAWP does not explicitly contain race-based exclusions and restrictions, following a guiding policy in line with the de-racialization of the Canadian immigration system since 1960 (Shakir 2008), it enacts racialized forms of governing and disciplining of migrant labour through seemingly "raceless" mechanisms such as the denial of political and economic rights, the denial of citizenship, spatial segregation, restrictions on territorial movement and movement within the labour market, family separation, and prohibition of intimate sexual relations.

By subjecting temporary migrant workers to multiple forms of political, cultural, and spatial exclusion, state-sponsored migrant labour programs exercise racialized forms of labour discipline and control that seek to transform displaced groups of migrant workers into disposable populations of cheap labour. Just as growers and employers used ethnicity-based "divide and conquer" strategies in the 1980s with South Asian, white, and Vietnamese farmworkers, SAWP employers engage in similar "divide and conquer" tactics, hence preventing cross-racial alliances that can result in farmworkers organizing. The SAWP and the Agricultural Stream for Lower-Skilled Occupations can be seen as part of employers' and provincial government backlash to the organizing efforts of the CFU two decades ago that threatened to undermine the profit-making of the agricultural industry. If the CFU challenged what they called "legislated racism," temporary worker programs now operate through more covert and subtle expressions of racism under a system of labour apartheid.

Resisting Labour Apartheid through Everyday Acts of Resistance

While most studies suggest that migrant farmworkers in Canada consent to their own oppression and engage in "performances of subordination" as a survival strategy to succeed in the program (Basok 1999; McLaughlin 2010) and while that assertion is partially true from a liberal understanding of freedom under the rule of law, workers *do* resist against powers that oppress them. However, they do so in ways that are not commonly recognized. Resistance has typically been conceptualized in two ways: either as disengaging or not participating, or as participating in organized forms of collective opposition such as strikes and union campaigns. SAWP workers' resistance does not fall neatly into either category. It could be said that migrant farmworkers "choose" to return to Canada year after year through SAWP, mostly with the same employer, and thus consent to an oppressive system of labour control. Nonetheless, this does not imply nor should it mean that workers do not resist and push back against labour apartheid conditions. What it does mean is that we need to engage deeper into their everyday lives and reframe our notions and ways of measuring resistance.

Migrant farmworkers' acts of labour, resistance, courage, survival mechanisms, and expressions of political subjectivity speak directly to the kinds of oppressions and restrictions they face. Unlike acts of resistance that are open and loud manifestations of opposition to power, migrant farmworkers engage in "hidden transcripts"—veiled, disguised, and often unspoken forms of resistance that cannot be openly expressed or articulated because of the extreme imbalances in power between the dominant and oppressed (Scott 1990). Workers exercise subtle forms of resistance such as "stealing" products of the farm produce to give to friends or to exchange, filing workers' compensation claims or parental benefits, or even visiting a doctor against their employer's wishes. Workers also challenge employers' racially divisive strategies to pit workers of different racial and ethnic backgrounds against each other. A Mexican worker on a Chilliwack farm explained, "The supervisor is always finding ways to make us to compete with the South Asian [workers]. Since we found out and understood his strategy, we decided to slow down the pace and we agreed that none will 'run' anymore because that only benefits no one else than the *patron* [boss] while we break our backs."[5]

For racialized workers, class solidarity is often mediated and articulated through race, gender, and place of origin, opening the potential for cross-racial and multilingual alliances (see Lowe 1996). This was the case with the first Mexican workers' wildcat strike in 2005. South Asian farm coworkers shared chapatis with striking Mexican workers as a gesture of support, sympathy, and solidarity during the days of the conflict. Even though these solidarities are not expressed or articulated in terms of class identity and can be sporadic, they point to the recognition of intersections of class- and race-based economic exploitation. Based on practices and networks of solidarity mediated through aspects of their identities such as race, class, and nationality, workers develop ethics of community care for each other that become evident in cases of aggression or overt inhumane treatment from the employer.

How migrant farmworkers frame and make sense of their acts of resistance differs from typical "labour disputes" mediated through labour unions or political institutions. For racialized migrant farmworkers, these acts of resistance help workers regain control over the conditions of their lives and their relationships with one another, rather than wage an overarching "working-class struggle." Migrant workers rarely identify themselves as part of the Canadian working class because their struggles are specific to their conditions of "temporariness" and the intersections of race, gender, immigration, and employment status that prevent them from enjoying essential freedoms. Unlike unionized (white) workers' struggles, which often revolve around better wages and benefits under union collective agreements, for migrant farmworkers these are not the primary concerns. From their specific localities their salaries are actually good and are precisely the reason why they want to come to Canada. This was articulated by a group of workers who were invited to join Vancouver's "Living Wage

---

5   Migrant farmworkers' group interview conducted by Adriana Paz Ramirez, April 2011.

Campaign" led by the Hospital Employees Union (HEU).[6] According to Juan, who attended the meeting:

> It would be good to have higher wages but to begin with it would be good if employers would start by following the contract as it says that we [SAWP workers] enjoy same rights as Canadians; that we can refuse unsafe work, have vacations to visit family, and so on.... That is not true. Our contract is a dead letter, a dead paper. Nobody follows it. We are imposed under each employer's rules. (Paz Ramirez 2012, 74)

Because workers' immediate concerns generally have more to do with health and safety issues, living conditions, limited and insufficient access to health care, unpredictable work hours, and long periods of family separation, issues such as wage increases are often less salient.

For transnational migrant farmworkers, what ultimately matters is to preserve a sense of dignity and to regain their humanity as they struggle to support themselves and their families in an unjust global economic system. For example, as in the blueberry workers' wildcat strike, twenty workers ended up being deported to Mexico by their employer with the assent of the Mexican consulate. Workers' demands to improve housing and working conditions were not met; however, from the workers' point of view, this was considered neither a failure nor a victory. Daniel, one of the strike's main organizers, said, "We are going back to Mexico with broken illusions and with no money but we are leaving with our heads up and that is what we will tell to our families. We could not keep living [on the farm] as animals with no dignity" (Paz Ramirez 2012, 76).

In the same way that resistance must be reconceptualized from the specific location of temporary migrant workers, the notion and meaning of what constitutes victory and failure must also be reconceptualized. As Kelley (1994, 10) puts it, "Politics is not separated from lived experience or the imaginary world of what is possible; to the contrary, politics is about these things." For migrant farmworkers, resistance sometimes looks like open challenges to authority, but it more often looks like finding cracks

---

6   At the time of writing, the living wage for Metro Vancouver is $19.14 an hour. SAWP workers' wage is the minimum wage, $9.25 an hour before government deductions, housing, health insurance, and passport and visa fees.

and openings in a highly exploitative and dehumanizing system of unfree labour where resistance can be waged in both direct and indirect ways.

Rethinking the Politics of Organizing and Solidarity

Migrant farmworkers' political subjectivities and resistance strategies provide insight into the complex workings of power. We must be willing to delve beneath the surface to appreciate seemingly innocuous or futile acts of resistance. Challenging and transforming the current racial labour apartheid regime means first developing a language and vocabulary that ties the economic exploitation and sociopolitical marginalization of migrant farmworkers to the logics and practices of racial oppression. This necessitates demystifying the neoliberal discourse used by states, employers, and even academic literature that analyzes the program as purely a consequence of the rise of neoliberal hegemony. By creating a counternarrative that names the program as a form of de facto racial labour apartheid, we can begin to develop cultures of resistance that connect and speak to the particular concerns, needs, and demands of racialized migrant farmworkers. Second, we must be willing to reflect upon questions such as: Why after more than forty years in Canada do migrant farmworkers remain at the margins of established political movements and organized labour organizations? How do migrant farmworkers struggle outside of established organizations and social movements? What kind of impact do migrant workers' hidden struggles and daily concerns have on movements that claim (or attempt) to speak for the dispossessed? Workers' acts and strategies of daily resistance contain the seeds for a new political vision of social change. The challenge is how much *we* engage in understanding and making sense of *their* struggles and meet them where they are at, instead of trying to engage workers in our visions and perspectives of their struggles. Third, we need a multipronged strategy that tackles the multiple levels and fronts where workers face oppression, control, and domination. This was clear for the CFU that adopted a "community unionism" approach to organize farmworkers in their workplaces and communities where they faced racial and socioeconomic exclusions.

In contrast to the United States, the plight of farmworkers in Canada is less known, perhaps due to the absence of a civil rights or immigrant rights movement that mobilizes communities around racial justice issues. Yet radical left, Marxist working-class, environmental, and feminist struggles have had an impact on mobilizing marginalized sectors, and have created languages and cultures of resistance. Racialized communities have been (and still are) subjects of the creation of political and cultural organizations and have mobilized around their cultural, class, race, and gender identities. Examples include the Chinese community, who created the Coalition of Chinese Head Tax Payers to connect historic exclusions and ongoing injustices against Chinese immigrants. South Asian immigrant farmworkers in BC carried forward a momentous struggle over decades resulting in the founding of the CFU. Similar are the organizing efforts of the Filipino community that fight for a "genuine and just integration" stemming from their experiences as temporary workers under the Live-in Caregiver Program (LCP). Yet these narratives of resistance largely remain part of the "hidden history" or, in the language of Foucault, stay as part of subjugated narratives and knowledge.

Grassroots groups such as J4MW that seek to build their analyses and organizing efforts with migrant farmworkers draw from the sources of collective sites of memory rooted in working-class immigrant communities. Lisa Lowe (1996, 21) calls these experiences "sites of collective memory" that act as "collective critical consciousness" and remain sceptical of liberal democracies' values and notions of fairness, equality, and citizenship. J4MW links the histories of indentured servitude inflicted upon im/migrant communities, and emphasizes the need to stand in solidarity with migrant farmworkers at the intersection of class and antiracist struggles. J4MW organizers take the time to approach workers where they live, work, dance, shop, eat, pray, and have fun. Some organizers also visited workers' families and communities in their home countries and carry out small projects with migrant communities. By engaging with multiple dimensions of workers' lives and working across borders, J4MW members have learned multiple lessons together, especially that organizing and resisting, even when they "lose" a fight, can still make a difference.

Organizations and movements that start with the daily struggles, concerns, desires, and dreams of disenfranchised communities are the seeds of a new political vision. The building blocks of their vision are workers' everyday hidden transcripts of resistance, the subjugated narratives, the sites of collective memory, and the accumulated experiences found in the multifaceted lives of marginalized im/migrant workers. What to do next with these building blocks remains the question and the challenge that lies ahead.

References

Basok, Tanya. 2004. "Post-National Citizenship, Social Exclusion and Migrants Rights: Mexican Seasonal Workers in Canada." *Citizenship Studies* 8, no. 1.

_____. 1999. "Free to Be Unfree: Mexican Guest Workers in Canada." *Labour Capital and Society* 32, no. 2.

Binning, Sadhu. 1986. "The Canadian Farmworkers Union: A Case Study in Social Movements." MA thesis, Simon Fraser University. <content.lib.sfu.ca/cdm/compoundobject/collection/cfu_2/id/2354>.

Boal, Saran. 1987. "Discussion Paper on New Strategies for Organizing Canadians." <content.lib.sfu.ca/cdm/ref/collection/cfu_2/id/300>.

Canadian Farmworkers Union. 1982. "Canadian Farmworkers Union 1982 to June 1983 Plan of Action." <content.lib.sfu.ca/cdm/compoundobject/collection/cfu_2/id/5459>.

_____. 1980. "Canadian Farmworkers Union National Constitution." <content.lib.sfu.ca/cdm/compoundobject/collection/cfu_2/id/759/rec/1>.

Chouhan, Raj. 1980. [Canadian Farmworkers Union Public Meeting] Speech, Surrey, BC, May 31. <content.lib.sfu.ca/cdm/ref/collection/cfu_2/id/4671>.

Chouhan, Raj, Sarwan Boal, Judy Cavanagh, and David Lane. 1983. "1983 CFU Report—Draft 2." Canadian Farmworkers Union Internal Report. <content.lib.sfu.ca/cdm/ref/collection/cfu_2/id/2781>.

Fairey, David, et al. 2008. *Cultivating Farmworker Rights: Ending the Exploitation of Immigrant and Migrant Farmworkers in BC*. Vancouver: Canadian Centre for Policy Alternatives BC, Justicia for Migrant Workers, Progressive Intercultural Community Services, and the BC Federation of Labour.

Farm Worker Organizing Committee. 1979. "Press Release, August 3, 1979." *Farm Worker* 1, no. 1. p. 3. <content.lib.sfu.ca/cdm/ref/collection/cfu_2/id/3692>.

Foucault, Michel. 1980. *Power/Knowledge: Selected Interviews and Other Writings, 1972–1977*. Colin Gordon (ed.). New York: Pantheon Books.

Gill, Charan. 1980. *The Birth of the Farmworkers Organization Committee*. UBC School of Social Work. <content.lib.sfu.ca/cdm/compoundobject/collection/cfu_2/id/2648/rec/2>.

Hennebry, Jenna, and Janet McLaughlin. 2012. "The Exception that Proves the Rule: Structural Vulnerability, Health Risk and Consequences for Temporary Migrant Farm Workers in Canada." In Patti Tamara and Christine Straehle (eds.), *Legislated Inequality: Temporary Labour Migration in Canada*. Montreal: McGill–Queen's University Press.

Jhappan, Carol Rhada. 1981. "Resistance to Exploitation: East Indians and the Rise of the Canadian Farmworkers Union." MA thesis, University of British Columbia. <content.lib.sfu.ca/cdm/compoundobject/collection/cfu_2/id/4542/rec/6>.

Kelley, Robin D.G. 1994. *Race Rebels: Culture, Politics and the Black Working Class*. New York: Free Press.

Lowe, Lisa. 1996. *Immigrant Acts*. Durham and London: Duke University Press.

McLaughlin, Janet. 2010. "Classifying the 'Ideal Migrant Worker': Mexican and Jamaican Transnational Farm Workers in Canada." *Focaal—Journal of Global and Historical Anthropology* 57 (Summer).

Paz Ramirez, Adriana. 2013. "Embodying and Resisting Labour Apartheid: Racism and Mexican Farm Workers in Canada's Seasonal Agricultural Workers' Program." MA thesis, University of British Columbia. <hdl.handle.net/2429/45530>.

_____. 2008. "Harvest of Injustice: The Oppression of Migrant Workers on Canadian Farms." <globalresearch.ca/index.php?context=va&aid=9425>.

Preibisch, Kerry. 2010. "Pick Your Own Labour." *International Migration Review* 4, no. 2.

_____. 2007. "Local Produce, Foreign Labor: Labor Mobility Programs and Global Trade Competitiveness in Canada." *Rural Sociology* 72, no. 3.

Preibisch, Kerry, and Evelyn Encalada Grez. 2010. "The Other Side of El Otro Lado: Mexican Migrant Women and Labor Flexibility in Canadian Agriculture." *Signs: Journal of Women in Culture and Society* 35, no. 2.

Ramsaroop, Chris. 2008. "Why We March." Unpublished document.

Scott, James C. 1990. *Domination and the Arts of Resistance: Hidden Transcripts*. New Haven: Yale University Press.

Shakir, Uzma. 2007. "Demystifying Transnationalism: Canadian Immigration Policy and the Promise of Nation Building." In Luin Goldring and Sailaja Krishnamurti (eds.), *Organizing the Transnational: Labour, Politics, and Social Change*. Vancouver: UBC Press.

Sharma, Nandita. 2006. "White Nationalism, Illegality and Imperialism: Border Control as Ideology." In Krista Hunt and Kim Rygiel (eds.), *(En)Gendering the War on Terror: War Stories and Camouflaged Politics*. Burlington: Ashgate Publishing Ltd.

United Food and Commercial Workers (UFCW). 2011. *The Status of Migrant Farm Workers in Canada, 2010–2011*. Toronto: UFCW.

Wolpe, Harold. 1972. "Capitalism and Cheap Labour-Power in South Africa: From Segregation to Apartheid." *Economy and Society* 1, no. 4.

Wong, Lloyd T. 1984. "Canada's Guest Workers: Some Comparisons of Temporary Workers in Europe and North America." *International Migration Review* 18, no. 1.

The Case for Unemployment Insurance Benefits for Migrant Agricultural Workers in Canada

Chris Ramsaroop

IT IS WELL ESTABLISHED THAT SEASONAL AGRICULTURAL WORKERS IN CANADA pay into the employment insurance (EI) scheme but cannot access "regular" benefits (UFCW Canada 2006). In *Fraser v. Attorney General of Canada*,[1] a case addressing the accessibility of EI for seasonal agricultural workers, the United Food and Commercial Workers union (UFCW) argued that mandatory payments violated the Charter of Rights and Freedoms since the temporary work permit issued to workers and the Canadian residence requirement under the Employment Insurance Act (EIA) prevented them from accessing these benefits. Claiming to advocate on behalf of seasonal agricultural workers from the Caribbean and Mexico, the UFCW (2006) asserted that the ruling "potentially opens the door to others seeking justice for disadvantaged groups through the courts," arguing that seasonal agricultural workers should not pay into Canada's EI scheme.

Alternatively, I contend that the UFCW erred in its litigation because their position failed to challenge the legal structures that create the conditions whereby migrant farmworkers are denied EI benefits. Neither did the UFCW consider the historic role that racism has played in Canada's immigration system, nor its continuing role in denying racialized communities' access to EI, among other social entitlements and benefits. Instead of advancing or addressing the plight of migrant agricultural workers, the

---

[1] The UFCW initiated two separate cases named Fraser. *Fraser v. Canada (Attorney General)* 2005 O.J. No. 5580 focused on whether or not migrant workers should pay into employment insurance as opposed to the Fraser ruling issued by the Supreme Court on whether or not agricultural workers have the right to organize. The SCC ruling is referred to as *Ontario (Attorney General) v. Fraser*, 2011 SCC 20, [2011] 2 S.C.R. 3.

UFCW's legal challenge reaffirms the subordination and exploitation that workers face by not challenging the racially discriminatory practices embedded in the Canadian legal system. Hence the UFCW, perhaps inadvertently, has positioned itself in the role, well entrenched in Canadian history, of denying rights and benefits to workers from racialized communities.

This chapter is divided into three sections. First, I discuss the pivotal role that racism has played in the development of Canada's immigration system. Second, I argue that the failure to challenge the racialized exclusion of migrant workers from social benefits reinscribes the traditional role of Canadian unions in selectively protecting the interests of white working-class members. Specifically, in supporting a position based on differences (racial, ancestral, citizenship), the union movement reinforces a binary relationship between migrant and nonmigrant workers. Finally, I advocate a transnational solidarity approach to the provision of benefits to migrant workers. The basis of this approach rests on the political-economic effects of the Canadian state on the displacement and dislocation of peoples abroad. For instance, Thobani (1999) argues that Canadian economic policies have had a devastating impact on communities of the global South. Attributed to the increasing levels of inequality and poverty, this has intensified the influx of impoverished workers seeking employment in programs such as the Seasonal Agricultural Worker Program (SAWP). In Thobani's (1999, 94) words:

> The current phase of globalization has made increased international migration inevitable. The growing global polarization between the North and the South and the environmental devastation that is the fruit of the neoconservative "free trade" agenda promoted both within Canada and at the international levels are forcing people to migrate in increased numbers. And it is the very people who are forced to migrate as a result of the policies that the Canadian state is pursuing internationally that the Canadian state seeks to keep from entering Canada as permanent residents who can subsequently claim citizenship.[2]

While the intent of the EIA's architects may have been to meet the national interests of the Canadian state and its labour force, current social policies

---

2   See also Thobani 2001, 25.

incorporate neither the increasing global interdependence of national economies nor the role that migration plays in sustaining global capitalism. In my view, we must reexamine state policies to account for how migration and the increasing reliance of guest worker programs necessitate shifts in areas such as social entitlements.

Racism and Immigration: The Control and Denial of Entry to Asian Canadians

Over time, the Canadian state, through various political and legal strategies, has created a system that severely restricts or excludes the immigration of racialized communities while encouraging the permanent settlement of Europeans. Jakubowski (1997, 11) and others note that the emergence of Canada's immigration system was rooted in ensuring the continuation of the "British character of Canada." European settlers were viewed as superior due to their supposed ability to better adapt to harsh weather conditions whereby racial characteristics and features rendered them more assimilable than non-European immigrants. However, to address "low-skilled" labour shortages, Canada's immigration system permitted the entry of racialized workers when needed to meet the interests of capital, most notably in the construction of the Canadian Pacific Railway. While requiring their labour, the government ensured that these workers could not settle in Canada by denying them citizenship rights, and forcing workers to return to their home country after the termination of their work contract. Through these and related policies, racialized bodies became synonymous with cheap labour. Racialized immigrant workers were subjected to a differential standard of treatment that served to justify their exploitation. The assignment of racial characteristics coupled with ideological notions of superiority and inferiority meant that Chinese labourers, for example, were paid lower wages and subjected to dangerous working conditions. However, when their labour was no longer required by the state or employers, their status as noncitizens enabled exclusion from a range of social entitlements beginning with permanent residence (ibid.).

Over the last 150 years, racial discrimination has proven a central and formidable means of controlling immigration flows. Three separate but equally racist legal initiatives ensured that immigration from non-European countries was first tempered and later terminated to protect the interests both of the white labour movement and of capital (ibid.).

Enacted first in 1885, the Chinese Exclusion Act placed a heavy financial burden on male Chinese workers arriving in Canada. Upon arrival, each Chinese immigrant paid a head tax set in 1885 at $50. In 1903 the head tax was raised to $500. By 1923, following an amendment to the Act, Chinese immigration to Canada was halted. While not explicitly preventing Chinese immigration, the hefty fee and the application of differential immigration admission standards "virtually stopped any future immigration of Chinese to Canada until 1947" (Jakubowski 1997, 14). Chinese applicants were segregated from other groups of immigrants and subjected to differential standards of entry relative to other categories of immigrants (Li 1988). This served to perpetuate the inferior status associated with Chinese immigrants already residing in Canada.

The experiment of legislatively mandated treatment for Chinese workers heralded the development of a differential standard of admission for Japanese nationals to Canada. Under the 1908 Gentlemen's Agreement, Japanese immigration faced similar curtailment. By permitting the arrival of only four hundred Japanese men a year, the Japanese government reached an understanding with the Canadian government that if no discriminatory action was taken against Japanese immigrants, they would "voluntarily restrict the number of people permitted to emigrate to Canada" (Jakubowski 1997, 14–15).[3] The origins of these restrictions are attributed to the so-called Anti-Oriental Riots of 1907, which exemplified Vancouver residents' hostility to Chinese and Japanese immigrants, many of whom were physically attacked and their homes and businesses burnt to the ground. In response to these hostilities, the Japanese government opted to self-regulate emigration.

A third initiative, the Continuous Journey Stipulation, was introduced to curtail immigration of South Asians to Canada through continuous passage from their country of birth or nationality. Walia (2006) notes that the regulation, while appearing racially neutral, was in practice racist. Without explicitly discriminating against South Asians, the continuous journey requirement worked to limit immigration of South Asians to Canada while continuing amicable relations with other nations within the British Empire (Jakubowski 1997).

These examples capture the continuous role and legacy of Canada's racist immigration policies. While the introduction of the points system in

---

3   See also Walia 2006.

the mid-1960s and subsequent reforms to immigration legislation eliminated the overt use of race as a category of restriction, a number of critical
commentators have convincingly shown how that system continues to
produce racist outcomes (Jakubowski 1997). Through guest worker programs such as the SAWP, Canada has also continued the use of restrictive
and discriminatory policies and tactics (Satzewich 1991; Sharma 2006).
Through the SAWP, the state has created a process of differential treatment
and incorporation to render inferior a group of people temporarily admit-
ted into Canada. The Canadian state and capital are the architects and
beneficiaries of a system that prevents the mass migration of "low-skilled"
labourers from the global South (Smith 2013). The lessons of earlier colonial periods of racial exclusion have built the foundation for the exclusionary nature of contemporary approaches to temporary labour migration.

The creation of the category of SAWP workers permits the state to
import foreign workers while at the same time restricting these migrants
from securing permanent residence. This restrictive approach alleviated
certain fears of federal state officials and others concerning the negative
impact that racialized labourers would have on the composition of the
population of rural Ontario (see Satzewich 1991). Yet, as Sharma (2006, 133),
Smith (2013), and others maintain, home governments are "complicit" in
the racial segregation of "low-skilled workers from nonwhite countries of
the South."

The Labour Movement Has Not Fought
Hard Enough against Racism

In the face of the historical and ongoing racialized legal construction of
migrant labour, the labour movement has played a prominent role in
defending the rights of white labour and subordinating racialized workers,
including through support for exclusions from benefits provided by the
Canadian state. The perpetuation of Canada's exclusive immigration policies needed—and in fact received—the active participation of nonstate
actors such as labour unions to reaffirm the state's national (white) identity.

Sharma's (2006) account of the role that difference plays in subordinating racialized communities is exemplified by the labour movement's
historical and ongoing responses to racialized and immigrant communities. The historical example of Chinese, Japanese, and South Asian workers,
and of other groups of workers such as African Canadians, is instructive as

to how the labour movement "embraced" notions of difference to exclude these racialized workers from membership in both labour unions and social relations more generally. But as Sharma (2006, 150–51) asserts, "identities based on difference are imposed identities, imposed in order to realize gross disparities in wealth and power." The exclusion of migrant agricultural workers due to their migrant and nonresident status ensures that their poverty and vulnerability remain intact.

Hunt and Rayside (2000) note that scepticism toward racialized workers has been common among white labourers, which they attribute to the fear that workers of colour would undercut wages, reduce employment opportunities, break union solidarity, and threaten job security. Unions adopted policies to defend their membership from the threat posed by the racialized other. In this, according to Hunt and Rayside (2000, 434), the Canadian labour movement shares "much of the sordid history of their American counterparts in their treatment of racial difference and immigrant status."[4]

Labour Takes Its Challenge to Court

The UFCW has lobbied to "secure better working and living conditions" for migrant agricultural workers by exposing their plight through the courts. The UFCW argues that the SAWP's structure ensures that workers, as a result of the threat of repatriation, do not challenge exploitative working and living conditions for fear of losing their primary source of income. In the *Fraser* case, the factum of Michael Fraser, on behalf of the UFCW, is explicit that migrant worker disentitlement is based on their immigration status.[5] The factum also notes that when workers require access to regular benefits they are not permitted to receive them:

> Because SAWP workers are foreign nationals who lack Canadian citizenship, their right to enter and remain in Canada can be and is subject to narrowly defined conditions which have the force of law. SAWP workers' right to enter Canada is in fact strictly conditional on the requirements that they must promptly leave Canada and return to their country of origin upon becoming unemployed and that they cannot seek other work while in Canada. (Fraser 2005, 38)

---

4   On the historical role of racism in the labour movement, see Persaud and Lukas, Creese, and Li.
5   Factum of Michael Fraser, p. 38, paragraph 125. At the time that this case was heard, Michael Fraser was UFCW president.

Further, the UFCW acknowledges that the SAWP's very nature disqualifies workers from EI due to the indentured basis of their employment:

> The very condition upon which SAWP workers are admitted into the country as temporary guest workers from the outset precludes any possibility of them receiving regular unemployment benefits. Under the legal framework that structures their right to being in Canada, they are disentitled from regular benefits at the very point when they would have need of and might otherwise claim them. (ibid.)

Despite their acknowledgement of disentitlement and indentureship, the UFCW fails to contest the residence status restrictions on SAWP workers. Instead they advocate for the maintenance of a binary difference between migrant and nonmigrant workers. The failure to challenge the residence requirements shows a willingness to accept the subordinated position of SAWP workers in Canada. It also points to a disturbing unwillingness to rectify the constraints that limit SAWP workers' access to regular social benefits. As Sharma notes, "People named as migrant workers are the very embodiment of the foreigner in that they can legally be denied many of the protections and entitlements offered by the state to its citizens. Indeed, it has been with the production of the category of migrant worker that the existential meaning of foreigner has been fully materialized within Canadian society" (2006, 148).

The impact of the categorization of workers as "migrant workers" enables the devaluation of racialized noncitizens. The experiences of migrant workers in Canada are powerfully constrained through a process shaped by racialization, job type, and wage levels. By accepting the denial of benefits to workers due to the exclusionary nature of residence requirements, the UFCW perpetuates a system of differences that continues to reaffirm a racialized conception of belonging in Canada. This is undertaken without examining why and how migrant agricultural workers are deemed nonresidents and excluded from the benefits of membership in Canadian society. This approach fails to confront immigration policies that prevent guest workers from applying for regular benefits. For example, the Immigration and Refugee Protection Act (IRPA) closely regulates the presence of foreign workers in Canada. The Act states that "a temporary resident must leave Canada by the end of the period authorized for their stay and may reenter Canada only if their authorization provides for reentry" (IRPA section 29(2)).

The manner in which the UFCW has brought forward this legal action shows shortsightedness in their interpretation of how racialized communities are excluded from adequate EI coverage. The UFCW litigation addresses the vulnerability of migrant agricultural labourers without challenging the racist legal structures that perpetuate their vulnerability. Moreover, the union fails to address the sociohistorical conditions of racism that have facilitated the emergence of temporary labour migration programs. The legal challenge ought to have encouraged an examination of how the denial of residence requirements restricted the access of migrant agricultural workers to regular EI benefits, and how employment benefits could be extended to migrant workers when they return home.

Employment Insurance and Migrant Seasonal Agricultural Workers

EI was developed to meet several objectives. The first of these, as argued by Phillips (2003, 45), an economist and expert witness for the UFCW, is that EI was:

> designed to protect not only the individual from the misfortune of unemployment but also society generally from cumulative effects of involuntary unemployment, cumulative effects that undermine the welfare of all of society and not just the individuals directly affected.

While the EI scheme originated to address inequalities in the local labour market, a similar principle of protecting both the unemployed worker and his or her community can be extended to the plight of migrant agricultural workers and the communities in which they live. While boundaries currently deny migrant agricultural workers regular employment benefits, they also face chronic un/underemployment in the Caribbean and Mexico (André 1990; Basok 2000a). The reasons for this include both structural unemployment and the nature of seasonal labour markets. Global factors that lead to high unemployment rates and the seasonal nature of work in their home countries have created the necessary conditions that leave migrant farmworkers involuntarily unemployed through no fault of their own. Therefore, migrant workers and their communities are eligible for EI on the same basis that Phillips outlines above: to protect not only the individual but also the welfare of their community from the cumulative effects of involuntary unemployment.

For André (1990, 254–55), the persistent annual migration of Caribbean migrant workers results not from "an exercise of the workers' freedom of mobility" but is "the inevitable end product of the political economy of the islands." Neoliberal globalization has exacerbated this through the displacement of locally produced goods by cheaper foreign-imported products and the decline of local agriculture. Mexico has also experienced significant changes through the liberalization of its economy under NAFTA. As a result, over one million Mexican subsistence farmers have lost their jobs (Bacon 2008) with many becoming landless farmworkers who migrate to the United States or Canada. As Basok (2000a: 95) notes, "the shortage of rural employment and the low salaries paid to jornaleros (day labourers) make it necessary for many to leave their communities." As the affidavit of Michael Fraser shows, many of the workers who participate in the SAWP are from economically depressed regions and they undertake work in Canada for subsistence during periods of unemployment in the home country.

Phillips (2003, 51) argues that in the Canadian context, "the more redistributive the [EI] system is, the more it will prevent the growth of inequalities in disposable income due to unemployment and the more it will alleviate poverty." Since EI is meant to assist workers experiencing involuntary unemployment, it is only rational that its protective coverage extends beyond Canada, to encompass workers who migrate from countries with high rates of poverty. Although he accounts for the increasing contributions that migrant agricultural workers make to the Canadian agricultural industry, Phillips neglects the political-economic factors that lead to the migration of SAWP participants. And while he acknowledges the downloading of unemployment onto workers' countries of origin, he fails to provide possible alternatives. The consequences, as noted by Satzewich (1991, 116), are evident: "Unemployment is simply exported to the Caribbean where the workers are forced to reproduce their capacity to work in the next year's harvest from the wages they received during the previous year's harvest and any other activity they may engage in within the Caribbean."

Seasonal Unemployment

Excluded from the initial scheme of EI were seasonal workers who, according to Phillips (2003, 46), were "believed to be uninsurable under actuarial principles because of the virtual certainty that they would become unemployed during the off season every year." However, due to public pressure of groups such as fishery workers, benefits were extended to address the special circumstances of seasonal workers. Phillips (2003, 46–47) argues that it is essential (Canadian) seasonal workers are provided the benefits of EI so that during periods of unemployment they have "sufficient purchasing power to support a decent standard of living . . . or else many will be forced onto welfare or other needs based programs which are not only degrading to the worker but frequently leads to a deterioration of the workers' morale as well as their work skills and their ability to job search."

Migrant agricultural workers experience similar deterioration of morale and skills due to lack of employment in their home country. The high levels of unemployment indicate that work is not readily available for many migrant workers who provide for themselves and their families with the salaries earned in Canada. This, coupled with an absence of a social safety net, spirals workers into positions that deny them a "decent standard of living." Examining how the EI system was amended to include benefits for Canadian seasonal workers provides insight on how a similar program may be established to alleviate income disparities arising from the seasonal nature of the employment of migrant workers. For example, in his examination of the impact that EI had on the fishing industry, Schrank (1998, 79) notes that benefits assisted in not only supplementing the low income of fishermen in the Maritimes but also played "a crucial economic role as a mechanism for transferring many millions of dollars from the federal government to the Atlantic provinces." Similar to the role that these funds played in the economic well-being of the Maritimes, the dispersal of EI benefits to migrant workers would provide some stability to counter the consequences of migration such as brain drain, breakup of families, and loss of social and economic infrastructure (Phillips 2003).

Reciprocal Agreement between Canada and the United States

Residence requirements have not precluded thousands of Americans from receiving benefits from the Canadian government. By order of a reciprocal agreement signed in 1942, the US and Canadian governments permitted residents of either country who are "not living in the same country to which they had been paying premiums... to become eligible for benefits" (Kelley 1992, 97). Kelley notes that "in the event of that person being laid off they are eligible to make a claim for benefits in their resident jurisdiction even though they are residing outside the home state" (ibid.). As such, the Canadian EI scheme, from the beginning, has provided exemptions for nonresident workers to receive regular benefits. Canada's reciprocal agreement with the United States serves as a model for a similar such agreement between Canada and each government that participates in the SAWP.

Canada has already signed reciprocal agreements with Mexico and the countries of the Caribbean in areas of social insurance, such as the Canada Pension Plan. These allow for the provision of entitlements to workers in their home country. EI legislation in Canada also enables the creation of special regulations to exempt residence requirements for special categories of workers such as US workers. Exemptions are specified in the EIA: "*except as may otherwise be prescribed*, a claimant is not entitled to receive benefits for any period during which the claimant... is not in Canada" (EIA Section 37(b), emphasis added). The EIA states that "a claimant who resides outside Canada... is not disentitled from receiving benefits for the sole reason of their residence outside Canada if... the claimant resides temporarily or permanently in a state of the United States that is contiguous to Canada" (EIA Section 55(6)).

For the purposes of any agreement between Canada, the Caribbean states, and Mexico, the high rate of return of workers under the SAWP, whereby over 80 percent of workers return to work in Canada every year, is especially relevant (Faraday 2012). While the Canadian government continues to deem residence as the reason to exclude migrant workers from benefits, clearly the Canada-US reciprocal agreement provides a precedent for extending entitlements to migrant workers. The discrepancy between who is and who is not seen as deserving of benefits is ultimately the crux of the government's determination of legitimate beneficiaries. This contradicts "the very basis for the creation of social programs," which, as Thobani (1999, 90) notes, occurred out of "the recognition that individuals are not responsible for the conditions which create unemployment and poverty, and that they need protection from economic cycles through access" to such programs. However, as seen by the differing treatment of US residents and migrant workers from the Caribbean and Mexico, the refusal to grant benefits is a product of the normalized perception of migrants as undeserving of benefits because of the seasonal nature of their work and their temporary work status. Defining these workers as outsiders justifies denial of benefits to them, thereby legitimizing unequal treatment.

How Transnationalism Can Help Challenge the Exclusion of Migrant Workers from EI

In this final section I show how a conception of transnationalism can be used to support the provision of social entitlements in migrant agricultural workers' home countries. Following Mitchell (2004), transnationalism enables scholars to reconceptualize immigration policies with a view toward the multiplicity of im/migrant lives and how these lived experiences transcend national boundaries. Portes (1999) notes that transnationalism also provides agency to nonstate actors such as individual migrants whose lived experiences are defined by their mobility between spaces and places. It is evident that current forms of state legislation contradict the lived experiences of migrant agricultural workers in Canada. Thus, expanding the scope of how policies are implemented is critical to challenging disparities that exist between the lived experiences of workers and state policies that both contain and regulate migrant bodies.

Contradictory policies such as denying employment benefits to migrant workers in their home country can be alleviated through concerted efforts to address current legislative shortcomings. Deconstructing binaries between "them and us" is integral to the process of expanding benefits to those defined outside of the Canadian "community." Workers and community groups have attempted to counter these divisions through a process of challenging the exclusionary nature of denying migrant workers entitlements to EI. Starting with parental and maternity benefits, which do not deny recipients access to entitlements based on residence requirements, workers and advocates have fought to secure benefits when workers return to their home country. These transnational acts of solidarity—what has been termed *diasporic solidarity*—hold great potential as strategies for migrant justice (Farooq 2013, 5–6).

Transnational solidarity is exemplified by a 2002 incident where a migrant worker approached Consuelo Rubio, a lawyer with the Centre for Spanish Speaking People and an EI expert, concerning parental benefits under Canada's EI scheme. Rubio examined the EI rules and regulations and discovered a loophole concerning parental benefits that enabled migrant workers to access EI despite their temporary status. Rubio's successful challenge has resulted in over five hundred workers receiving EI parental benefits.[6] This victory has given worker advocacy groups the credibility and the necessary groundswell to mobilize large numbers of migrant workers in challenging the broader exclusion of migrant workers from general EI benefits.

While community organizations were successful in expanding parental/maternity benefits for migrant workers in their home countries, workers and their advocates have also seen success in applying political pressure on both host governments and those sending workers out to other countries, to address issues relating to EI. In Canada, Justicia for Migrant Workers and others have engaged with the legislative process to advocate for the expansion of benefits in the workers' home countries. For example, during consultations with the Ministry of Human Resources and Skills Development (HRSDC) in 2006, members of Justicia urged the federal government to change previous positions around migrant workers and EI so that a "progressive framework [is implemented] to ensure that employment insurance is extended to [the workers'] home countries as well" (Justicia for Migrant Workers 2006).

In the home countries, workers are also challenging structural barriers inherent in the SAWP. In Barbados, for example, farmworkers used ceremonies commemorating the fortieth anniversary of the SAWP to draw attention to working conditions in Canada. By organizing protests and worker delegations to address the minister of labour, Barbadian farmworkers demanded an end to double pay, a process whereby workers were paying into both the Barbadian and Canadian unemployment schemes without receiving entitlements in either country (Barbadian Advocate 2006; Barbados Nation 2006). Through political advocacy and activism, workers and their advocates are challenging the structures of the program in both migrant-sending and migrant-receiving countries to address exclusions in areas such as unemployment insurance.

The above challenges faced by migrant workers illustrate how resistance strategies are successfully implemented in response to blocked opportunities

---

6   Conversation with Consuelo Rubio; Factum of Michael Fraser.

present in both the recipient and sending countries. Denial of rights in Barbados and Canada has led to creative forms of resistance where different strategies are adopted in different sites of struggle. Fearing repatriation when working in Canada, workers employ strategic alliances with Canadian advocacy groups to address discriminatory practices, while in the home country workers directly confront and rectify injustices that result from inaction by their own government (Barbadian Advocate 2006; Barbados Nation 2006). Portes (1999, 474) notes that while source governments such as Barbados may attempt to bypass the concerns of migrant labourers, "the experience of political socialization leads migrant communities and organizations to resist playing by the old rules and demand higher political standards." As illustrated above, the isolation that workers once felt is alleviated through greater contact with advocacy organizations as well as with workers from other countries, thus demystifying previously held beliefs about the SAWP and the limitations to workers exerting their rights. Previous government-to-government interactions excluded workers from exerting their rights to demand benefits. Through the process of coalition-building with local residents and learning from the experiences of migrant workers from other countries, workers were able to counter unfair labour practices. Through their efforts to expand parental benefits and their activism to end unfair EI practices, workers themselves are reformulating the discussion on how funds that they are forced to pay into are disbursed. Examining entire lived experiences enables both theorists and activists to reconfigure social policies so as to better reflect migrant labourers' lives in their entirety.

Conclusion

This chapter has argued for the extension of EI benefits for migrant workers upon return to their home country. Current federal policy denies migrant workers access to regular benefits due to their temporary status in Canada. The UFCW's court challenge to these exclusions falls short in its failure to acknowledge the role that racism has played—and continues to play—in excluding racialized workers from the rights and entitlements of permanent residence in Canada. In Canada's long and sordid history of racism, the SAWP is simply another program that perpetuates difference through the denial of permanent status to tens of thousands of so-called "foreign" workers.

While the contemporary labour movement espouses the rhetoric of respecting diversity and difference, and tacit support for racialized people including migrant workers, the EI legal challenge shows an unwilling-ness to confront the pattern of racist discrimination based on citizen-ship. Any future employment insurance litigation "on behalf of workers" must contest the exclusionary nature of not only the current Employment Insurance Act but also the Immigration and Refugee Protection Act since both statutes work simultaneously to deny migrant workers regular ben-efits and permanent status.

Furthermore, any future litigation undertaken by labour organiza-tions such as the UFCW must also incorporate the lived experiences of workers. Transnationalism provides a framework whereby the entirety of the migration process is examined, thus providing a holistic view of the structural reasons why workers from the Caribbean and Mexico par-ticipate in programs such as the SAWP. Transnationalism also provides a means to incorporate the various strategies that workers undertake to resist the forms of oppression and exploitation that they endure in Canada and back home. The joint efforts of workers and advocates in pushing for special benefits under the EI scheme exemplify this. Through the lens of transnationalism, one can see how the EI scheme can be adapted to address certain needs of migrant labourers. By developing a framework based on the reciprocal agreement between the United States and Canada, a similar agreement can be created to address the high rates of unemploy-ment and underemployment that migrant workers face upon return to their home country.

Until steps are taken to reconceptualize employment insurance schemes along transnational lines, unions will continue to perpetuate their historic role of advocating for exclusions for those who are defined as existing outside of Canadian society. If the lessons of history are meant to inform the practices of the present, then it is imperative that we formu-late policies that break down the barriers of racialized exclusion that come to define the experience of migrant labourers in Canada. This means that we must acknowledge the role that racial difference continues to play in the development of policies and that we work to rupture these inequities through the implementation of policies that reflect the lived experiences of migrant workers in their entirety.

References

André, Irving. 1990. "The Genesis and Persistence of the Commonwealth Caribbean Seasonal Agricultural Workers Program in Canada." *Osgoode Hall Law Journal* 28.

Bacon, David. 2008. "Displaced People NAFTA's Most Important Product." *North American Congress of Latin America*, September 3. <nacla.org/article/displaced-people-nafta%E2%80%99s-most-important-product>.

Barclay-Smith, Petal. 2006. "Challenges Eroding Workers Wage." *Barbados Advocate*, December 5.

Basok, Tanya. 2003. "Mexican Seasonal Migration to Canada and Development: A Community-Based Comparison." *International* Migration 41, no. 2.

_____. 2000a. "He Came, He Saw, He Stayed: Guest Worker Programmes and the Issue of Non-Return." *International Migration* 38, no. 2.

_____. 2000b. "Migration of Mexican Seasonal Farm Workers to Canada and Development: Obstacles to Productive Investment." *International Migration Review* 34, no. 1.

_____. 2000c. *Tortillas and Tomatoes: Transmigrant Mexican Harvesters in Canada.* Montreal: McGill–Queen's University Press.

Dalley, Horace. 2005. "Sectoral Debate 2005 Presentation by Hon. Horace Dalley, Minister of Labour and Social Security on May 17, 2005." *Jamaica Information Service*. <jis.gov.jm/sectoral-debate-2005-presentation-by-hon-horace-dalley-minister-of-labour-and-social-security-on-may-17-2005-2/>.

Faraday, Fay. 2012. *Made in Canada, How the Law Constructs Migrant Workers*. Toronto: Metcalf Foundation.

"Farm Workers to Protest Today." 2006. *Barbados Nation*, December 4.

Farooq, Nihad M. 2013. "National Myths, Resistant Persons: Ethnographic Fictions of Haiti." *Journal of Transnational American Studies* 5, no. 1.

Fraser v. Canada (Attorney General) 2005 O.J. No. 5580.

Fraser v. Canada (Attorney General) 2005 O.J. No. 5580 (Affidavit of Michael Fraser).

Fraser v. Canada (Attorney General) 2005 O.J. No. 5580 (Affidavit of Paul Phillips).

Fraser v. Canada (Attorney General) 2005 O.J. No. 5580 (Expert Brief of Paul Phillips).

Fraser v. Canada (Attorney General) 2005 O.J. No. 5580 (Factum of Michael Fraser).

Fraser v. Canada (Attorney General) 2005 O.J. No. 5580 (Factum of the Attorney General).

Government of Canada. n.d. "Immigration and Refugee Protection Act." *Justice Laws Website*. <laws-lois.justice.gc.ca/eng/acts/I-2.5/>.

"Historical Background of Legislation-Outline of Administration of Unemployment Insurance Act, 1940–1943." 1943. *Labour Gazette* 43, no. 5.

Hunt, Gerald and David Rayside. 2000. "Labour Response to Diversity in Canada and the United States." *Industrial Relations* 39, no. 3.

Jakubowski, Lisa Marie. 1997. *Immigration and the Legalization of Racism*. Halifax: Fernwood.

Justicia for Migrant Workers. 2006. Oral Presentation to the Standing Committee on Human Resources and Development Canada. <parl.gc.ca/HousePublications/Publication.aspx?DocId=2446965&Language=E&Mode=1#Int-1730778>.

Kelley, John G. 1992a. *The Influence of the Canada-United States Free Trade Agreement on the Government of Canada's Labour Force Development Strategy and Bill C-21: An Act to Amend the Unemployment Insurance Act and the Employment and Immigration Department and Commission Act*. Toronto: J. Kelley.

_____. 1992b. *Unemployment Insurance and the Claimant Re-employment Strategy: An Historical Perspective with International Comparisons Between Canada, Germany,*

Sweden and the United States. Toronto: J. Kelley. <socserv.mcmaster.ca/oldlabourstudies/onlinelearning/article.php?id=704>.

Li, Peter S. 1988. *The Chinese in Canada*. Toronto: Oxford University Press.

Linder, Marc, and Norton E. Laurence. 1995. "Down and Out in Weslaco, Texas and Washington, DC: Race-Based Discrimination Against Farm Workers under Federal Unemployment Insurance." *University of Michigan Journal of Law Reform* 29, no. 1–2.

Mitchell, Katharyne. 2004. *Crossing the Neoliberal Line: Pacific Rim Migration and the Metropolis*. Philadelphia: Temple University Press.

Nadeau, Mary-Jo. 2002. "Who Is Canadian Now? Feminism and the Politics of Nation after September 11." *Atlantis* 27, no. 1.

National Union of Public and General Employees website. <nupge.ca>.

Ong, Aihwa. 1999. *Flexible Citizenship: The Cultural Logics of Transnationality*. Durham: Duke University Press.

Persad, Judy Vashti, and Lukas Salome. 2004. *Through the Eyes of Workers of Colour: Linking Struggles for Social Justice*. Toronto: Women Working with Immigrant Women.

Portes, Alejandro. 1999. "Conclusion: Towards a New World—The Origins and Effects of Transnational Activities." *Ethnic and Racial Studies* 22, no. 2.

Sassen, Saskia. 2005. "Regulating Immigration in a Global Age: A New Policy Landscape." *Parallax* 11, no. 1.

Satzewich, Victor. 1991. *Racism and the Incorporation of Foreign Labour: Farm Labour Migration to Canada since 1945*. New York: Routledge.

_____. 1988. "The Canadian State and the Racialization of Caribbean Migrant Farm Labour 1947–1966." *Ethnic and Racial Studies* 11, no. 3.

Schrank, William E. 1998. "Benefitting Fishermen: Origins of Fishermen's Unemployment Insurance in Canada, 1935–1957." *Journal of Canadian Studies* 33, no. 1 (Spring).

Service Canada. n.d. Employment Insurance: Workers and/or Residents Outside Canada. <servicecanada.gc.ca/eng/ei/publications/outsidecanada.pdf>.

Sharma, Nandita. 2006. *Home Economics: Nationalism and the Making of 'Migrant Workers' in Canada*. Toronto: University of Toronto Press.

Smith, Adrian A. 2013. "Pacifying the 'Armies of Offshore Labour' in Canada." *Socialist Studies* 9, no. 2.

Stephen, Lynn. 2001. "Globalization, the State and the Creation of Flexible Indigenous Workers: Mixtec Farmworkers in Oregon." Centre for Comparative Immigration Studies working paper 36, April.

Thobani, Sunera. 2001. "Benevolent State, Law-Breaking Smugglers, and Deportable and Expendable Women: An Analysis of the Canadian State's Strategy to Address Trafficking in Women." *Refuge* 19, no. 4.

_____. 1999. "Closing the Nation's Ranks: Canadian Immigration Policy in the 21st Century." In Somer Brodribb (ed.), *Reclaiming the Future: Women's Strategies for the 21st Century*. Charlottetown, PEI: Gynergy Books.

UFCW Canada. 2006. "UFCW Canada Wins Right to Represent Migrant Agricultural Workers in Charter Challenge." <ufcw.ca/index.php?option=com_multicategories&view=article&id=534&Itemid=&lang=en>.

_____. 2002a. "National Report: Status of Migrant Farm Workers in Canada, December 2002."

_____. 2002b. "Status of Migrant Farm Workers in Canada, 2002."

United States Department of Labour. 1951. "Agreement between the Government of Canada and the Government of the United States of America." <workforcesecurity. doleta.gov/unemploy/pdf/agree_us_and_canada.pdf>.

Walia, Harsha. 2006. "Colonialism, Capitalism and the Making of the Apartheid System of Migration in Canada." *Seven Oaks Magazine*, March 4. <sevenoaksmag. com/features/100_feat1.html>.

Critical Questions: Building Worker Power and a Vision of Organizing in Ontario

Deena Ladd and Sonia Singh

IN THIS CHAPTER, WE REFLECT ON OUR EXPERIENCE AS ORGANIZERS AT Toronto's Workers' Action Centre (WAC). We explore how WAC is developing a vision for organizing that addresses the nexus of migration and precarious employment, as well as its impact on immigrant and racialized communities in Ontario. We outline key tensions and questions in our organizing and how our model has developed, reflecting on the strengths and limitations, in hopes that our experience is useful for others grappling with similar issues.[1] WAC was founded in 2005, bringing together two organizations, Toronto Organizing for Fair Employment and the Workers' Information Centre. As a worker- and membership-based organization, our mandate is to improve the lives and working conditions of people in low-wage and unstable employment. Through our phone line, support services, and organizing with workers facing violations of their rights, we have been on the front lines dealing with the reorganization of labour markets and the growth of precarious work.

As other chapters outline, migration and labour market policies are inextricably linked. Labour markets are being completely restructured, resulting in increased precariousness of work, as well as immigration status.

---

1   This chapter builds on collaborative research with organizers and leaders of the Workers' Action Centre, the Caregivers' Action Centre, and Justicia for Migrant Workers, as well as an ongoing capacity-building research project with community-based organizations in Ontario. Our reflections for this chapter took place between March 2012 and December 2013. We are grateful to all the members, leaders, and organizers of these organizations who have participated in these projects, for their insights and analysis. We also acknowledge the organizers and allies who provided valuable feedback.

Racialized and low-wage workers face a labour market characterized by racialization and instability such as increased use of temporary foreign worker programs, the downloading of business costs onto individual workers through misclassification of their employment status, a move to independent contract work, and the growth of temporary agencies (Workers' Action Centre 2007; Block and Galabuzi 2011). In the last ten years, precarious work has increased in Toronto and surrounding areas by 50 percent (Lewchuk et al. 2013), while temporary worker programs have rapidly expanded (Preibisch 2010). The percentage of minimum wage workers has more than doubled since 2003, with women, new immigrants, and racialized workers more likely to earn minimum wages (Block 2013). Employment standards violations are widespread. In a recent study, one in three low-wage workers surveyed had experienced unpaid wages in the previous five years (Workers' Action Centre 2011). These shifts are a result of both employer practices to move work beyond the scope of protection and active state re-regulation (Thomas 1995; Bernhardt et al. 1998; Vosko 2000, 2006).

Pushing Open the Space for Organizing

Meanwhile the state has expanded its role in tightly managing the delivery of community and social services. Settlement programs, English as a second language programs, job search and employment support, youth training, and women's and community programming are all almost completely government funded.

As DeFilippis et al. (2010) have described, the ability of what traditionally used to be grassroots community-based organizations to determine what services and community programs are needed has vastly diminished. In our experience, these organizations now respond to the government's agenda of which programs will be delivered, how they will be managed, and whether the organization is "achieving its targets." Only then will funding be renewed. This tightly managed process combined with state-imposed expectations of board governance structures and corporate partnerships for programs, year-to-year project-based funding, little or no core funding, and strict reporting rules has resulted in great fear of displeasing government funders. Community agencies that follow the state's mantra get rewarded with expansive contracts, which sends a chilling message to the rest of the sector to stay away from advocacy and support a business-delivery style of working.

Community services require workers to adapt to and comply with economic conditions rather than challenge systemic inequities. Many community members are routinely treated as clients, customers, or users of a service. This shapes people's notions of community-based space and services where there is no sense of getting involved in a meaningful way. Many community members without full status get no access to services at all. A recent report found that one third of community agencies surveyed would report a service user to immigration authorities if they learned they were undocumented (Sidhu 2013).

Frontline workers may want to integrate community-driven programming, but find little institutional support for community organizing. We feel that basic skills and analysis of community-building; organizing; and challenging immigration policies, racism, and systemic inequities are being lost. In recent years some initiatives have emerged that seek to build resident engagement programs, community peer research programs, and some participation in broader networks, but these are very much at an initial stage. The few grassroots groups that do not receive state funding and are doing community organizing are often volunteer-based and face challenges sustaining their work and capacity. It is critical to mention this context as WAC's model challenges the normative experience of many workers who turn to community agencies with a problem. When people arrive at WAC, they are interacting in a very different space where they are encouraged to not only participate but to take leadership in workers' rights struggles.

Hemmed in by Traditional Union Models

Those of us trying to build a new model of organizing also face the flip side of a union movement that has had major difficulties addressing the insidious rise of precarious employment and the vital interconnections of race, citizenship, and low-wage work. Massive job losses in recent years and a deterioration of conditions for workers who have little protection on the job is creating a real urgency for increased enforcement and expanded protections. The majority of Ontario's workers rely on employment standards. Only 28 percent of Ontario workers are unionized,[2] leaving most workers on their own to enforce their minimum employment rights. Low-wage and precarious workers are least able to negotiate fair wages and working

2   Ontario's union density is below the Canadian average of 31 percent. Statistics Canada. 2009. *Labour Force Historical Review 2008* (Table Cd3T09an) (Cat. No.71F0004XCB).

conditions in nonunionized workplaces, which are most in need of effective and inclusive employment standards.

Where do workers go? Unions have very little connection to community programming and services that connect to workers outside of the workplace. Hundreds of thousands of workers have now lost their membership and connection with their union since the recession and grapple with a new world of work where temp agency work and basic labour violations are the norm. In this context, opening up the space to imagine a different kind of organization for workers and a way of organizing is vital.

Our organizing must address the nexus of migration and labour market regulation in order to understand how race, migration, and immigration status intersect to shape workers' experiences, the sectors they work in, and the choices faced when looking for work. This helps us to understand what economic power workers have to organize for better wages and working conditions in their workplaces and what political and social power they have in their community. This analysis assists us in thinking through how to support workers to challenge violations of employment standards and the strategies needed to address the root causes of exploitation. In order to understand organizing possibilities that can tackle the growing precariousness of work and systemic inequities in the labour market, we have to integrate demands that focus on citizenship status, race, and equity. We also need to be clear on the kinds of alliances we need to build across race and citizenship status and not allow categories of immigration status created by governments to define working-class struggles (Syed and Prior 2012).

Decline of Social Safety Net

A critical feature of the attack on workers and low-income communities has been the unraveling of a basic social safety net and denying access to full immigration status. The attacks on social assistance and employment insurance (EI), and a four-year freeze in Ontario's minimum wage resulted in a massive decline of workers being able to access basic benefits and training. When accessing these vital pieces of the safety net becomes impossible, workers are pushed from one bad job to another. Income security programs are also increasingly pushing people into precarious jobs through workfare policies, which are racialized and gendered processes (Vaillancourt 2010; Soss et al. 2011). For example, we increasingly see women of colour streamed into low-paying personal support worker jobs through the limited EI and social assistance retraining programs they can access.

Many WAC members move from temporary jobs to EI, to social assistance, to another temporary job, and then find themselves unemployed again and on social assistance. Workers struggling to deal with the exploitative conditions of the Temporary Foreign Worker Program (TFWP) have also become connected to WAC. When workers are forced to leave migrant jobs, they face an untenable situation of having to work underground while they wait for a new Labour Market Opinion (now Labour Market Impact Assessment since 2014), which can take as long as seven months. In this time, access to basic support and services is extremely limited and workers become even more vulnerable to exploitation. Opening the doors to the centre during this difficult time since the recession (2008/2009) has been critical in ensuring bridges are built between workers. Just because workers have become disconnected from accessing full-time jobs or even stable work does not mean that they are disengaged from wanting to struggle for decent work.

Movement-Building Model

A new organizing model that can build power in low-income communities, with migrant and precarious workers, and challenge the current deterioration of wages and working conditions must be rooted in a movement-building model. At WAC, this model has four important components that work to build a strong organization and a vibrant and engaged membership to fight for change.

The first component is base-building—striving to ensure that all of our services, outreach, and educational workshops work toward the broader objective of building a base of workers who are connected to organizing. Second, we want to ensure our organizing challenges structural economic power by building a working-class movement within a democratic framework. WAC is a membership-based organization. We want workers who come to us with a workplace problem to join and get involved in our organizing committees, board, campaign, outreach, and media work. So it is critical to think through how to build leadership, share skills, and ensure democratic decision-making. The third component is developing an organizing strategy that will leverage change for low-income, precarious, and migrant workers. The final component is alliance-building with a wide variety of allies and supporting the self-organization of workers in different sectors and across Ontario. As we have grappled with our evolving work and organizing, some key tensions and questions have emerged that we will explore here.

Focus and Scale of Organizing

When facing the massive attack on basic rights and social services we must ask ourselves where to focus our organizing. What strategies are most effective in rebuilding precarious workers' power? What strategies affect the most number of workers? Many worker centres in the United States have focused on broad-level policy and legislative change across sectors. Others have drilled down into a specific sector to have maximum impact. Fine (2006) writes that the strengths of the worker centre model in the United States include the ability to mobilize immigrant and low-wage workers into effective policy campaigns for improved wages and working conditions and bring issues of precarious work and immigration into public debate. In describing worker centre organizing in Los Angeles, Milkman (2010) writes that the centres' public policy wins have been impressive considering their small size and grassroots nature.

As WAC's work has developed, we have taken a multisectoral organizing strategy that seeks to win concrete gains that benefit workers, build confidence among our members, and build leadership through campaigns. We have emphasized strengthening the provincial Employment Standards Act and its enforcement as a way to rebuild a floor of rights in Ontario for all workers to address challenges of precarious work and migration. The results of this focus reflect Fine and Milkman's analyses of where worker centres can win gains that belie the relatively small organizing base.

In 2007, we launched the Ontario Needs a Fair Deal Campaign. We successfully built a coalition that won a 40 percent increase in the minimum wage to $10.25 per hour [increasing to $11.40 in October 2016]. In 2009, we won new protections for temp agency workers and, working with migrant worker groups such as the Caregivers' Action Centre, new protections for live-in caregivers under the Employment Standards Act (ESA). The government also announced an investment of $10 million to hire new employment standards officers. Our Stop Wage Theft Campaign, launched in 2011, built on these wins and called for expanded protection for low-wage workers and a crackdown on wage theft. Over this period, we have seen a shift at the Ontario Ministry of Labour from processing claims for unpaid wages to a greater emphasis on proactive enforcement and employer compliance. In December 2013, legislation was introduced by the Liberal minority government that would bring in new protections against wage theft and, critically, would make temp agencies and client companies jointly liable for ESA violations. At the time of writing this chapter, the bill had reached second reading, but a provincial election triggered by the opposition meant it could not proceed.

We have also attempted to challenge and shift the dominant narrative on precarious work. Policy makers and government often try to individualize the systemic issues workers face where being racialized, a woman, or an immigrant is reduced to being a "vulnerable worker" rather than vulnerability stemming from labour and immigration policy, racism, and systemic labour and human rights violations. We have pushed back against this paternalism and focused our campaign work to address the structural and systemic issues facing workers. Using a direct action model to expose violations has been an important element in shifting this narrative. The leadership of workers coming forward to expose conditions of precarious work has created greater visibility on the changing nature of work. As Milkman (2010) writes, these moral and discursive shifts are important outcomes along with legislative and policy wins.

While we celebrate these wins, we also reflect on the limits to building worker power through an organizing strategy that emphasizes improved regulation of the labour market and is not rooted in traditional collective bargaining models. The government often responds to our organizing for improved protections by bringing in piecemeal legislative and policy reforms. For example, while temp agency workers won expanded protections in 2009, workers are unable to enforce rights due to the nature of the employment relationship and the ongoing gaps in protection. So our organizing work has continued to push for equal pay for equal work and tools to hold employers liable for violations. In this context, the proposed expansion of liability to client companies is an important and precedent-setting win. At the level of individual workplaces, when we take on bad bosses owing wages through direct action, in most cases workers have already left the job. While we often support workers to win back their wages, violations very likely continue for workers still on the job.

These realities expose the tensions of improving standards through broad legislative change. While these gains are important wins in the present context of challenging restructuring, it is important that we are clear on the limitations. Analyzing these limitations collectively gives us an opportunity to expose the role of the state and build an analysis and understanding of how the current political and economic system does not work for workers.

Fine (2006, 2011) grapples with the extent to which worker centres with small membership bases can build true economic power for precarious workers that goes beyond policy reform, outlining new strategies and alliances that have the potential to overcome key limitations. Examples of worker centre sectoral organizing in the United States demonstrate exciting strategies to build power across a sector and within workplaces. In 2012, WAC hosted a collaborative research project with members and leaders from WAC, the Caregivers' Action Centre, and Justicia for Migrant Workers to learn from some of these new organizing models.

Using a sectoral approach, these US worker centres have been able to win concrete victories for low-wage and precarious workers. Domestic Workers United (DWU) won a precedent-setting Domestic Workers' Bill of Rights, which expanded protection for domestic workers across New York State. The New York Taxi Workers Alliance's organizing has increased taxi workers' wages by 17 percent. The Coalition of Immokalee Workers' (CIW) organizing has raised farmworkers' wages in the heart of tomato production in Florida and created a new set of protections and mechanisms for enforcement that allow workers to address violations without fear of reprisal. This expansion of protection challenges a larger neoliberal erosion and evasion of labour standards.

Each organization has overcome barriers to organizing with migrant and precarious workers to build representative structures that create an industry-wide voice for precarious workers in their sector. Many organizations spoke about how their organizing had made an invisible workforce visible.

The sectoral approach of many worker centres promotes industry analysis and a mapping of power relations in each sector. Through their campaigns, worker centres have been able to analyze where they can build leverage within each industry. This has been supported by generating worker-focused research on low-wage industries, such as the in-depth research and restaurant worker surveys the Restaurant Opportunities Centre has used to build their analysis on the restaurant industry.

Could a sectoral approach in Toronto be a tool to support workers to improve conditions across an industry and to build power within their workplaces? Many of the workers WAC works with are moving in and out of sectors, and in and out of employment. Workers who started in manufacturing and temp agency jobs are now working as personal support workers or in service sector jobs. Others have been unemployed for a long time after the manufacturing downturns, moving from EI to social assistance. Migrant workers who can get status, such as caregivers and some Low-Skilled Pilot Project workers, move out of caregiving or farm work as soon as they can. In this sense, a clear focus of sectoral organizing becomes more challenging to identify. In Ontario, union density remains relatively stable due to a high percentage of public sector unionization. However, that density over time has become less sector specific and more competitive between unions, which has made it difficult to work collaboratively to take precarious work on a sectoral basis and raise standards.

In this context, the strategy of rebuilding the provincial floor of rights to challenge employers' power in the workplace remains an important focus. Raising legislative standards and the capacity of the Ministry of Labour to effectively enforce them is key to reaching the broadest number of workers. Yet our experience with US groups raised critical questions about the degree to which these broad policy reforms can build power for workers in individual workplaces and sectors. However, the current nationwide fight for a $15 minimum wage in the United States illustrates the potential for campaigns that combine workplace actions and community mobilizing to challenge employers and government policies. As the challenges to organizing in individual workplaces intensify, it is important to think about other ways for workers to increase their economic power. What kinds of broad-based and sectoral bargaining models could help bring a collective voice to low-wage and precarious workers? In the United States, DWU and the United Workers Congress (formerly the Excluded Workers Congress) are exploring how alternative models of collective bargaining could work within the sectors they are organizing in (Domestic Workers United et al. 2010; Excluded Workers Congress 2010). Wial (1993) suggests worker associations could be tools for preunion formations or federated craft union structures across industries. Hill (2007) explores how binational unions could build representation for migrant workers on both sides of the border, while Gordon (2011) explores the concept of transnational labour citizenship.

In Ontario, sectoral bargaining was a topic of policy debate in the early 1990s before the Harris government attack on collective bargaining and employment standards (Fudge, Baigent, and Ready 1993; Eaton 1994). We need to bring these discussions back into our campaigns alongside demands for basic standards for migrant and precarious workers. It is critical to explore these strategies to shape longer-term organizing demands.

Building a Membership-Based Organization

The capacity to build membership participation and leadership among low-wage and immigrant workers is identified as a strength of the worker centre model (Tait 2005; Cranford et al. 2006; Fine 2006; Choudry and Thomas 2012). WAC's organizing model focuses on winning concrete improvements in workers' lives and building a strong membership and base. WAC's membership comprises approximately 250 members with 75 workers active in campaign development through the participation of two organizing committees in downtown Toronto and Scarborough.

We devote a lot of energy to membership and leadership development through integrating new members, training, public speaking, shadowing of workshops, and meetings and feeding that into the development of our campaign organizing. Members feel an ownership of our campaigns and our wins. Our campaign demands and overall frameworks are generated through twelve to eighteen months of discussions and campaign development. Thus campaign work can be incredibly labour intensive and slow. The pace at which we can move on new and emerging issues is sometimes limited.

Working with migrant and precarious workers, who often move back home or to other cities for work, is an ongoing challenge. Many workers who have become active leaders in WAC have had to leave because of work permits expiring, because of deportations, or simply because the challenges of surviving in Toronto become too great. However, our model of engaging members in long-term campaign and leadership development has resulted in a core of members, many who have been leaders over several years. We have wanted to fight complacency within our organizing by making sure members want to be active participants. We consciously opted for annual membership—members must choose to remain involved each year. While building a solid membership structure has been crucial, we wonder about our impact with such a small membership, and what leverages are needed for it to grow larger and stronger in terms of numbers and political development.

An ongoing issue for worker centre and other grassroots organizing models that do not have the democratic representational structure of a traditional union (however hierarchical it may be) is the degree of active involvement of workers in determining strategy and making decisions. Milkman (2010) argues that many worker centre campaigns tend to become staff-led. But a few centres have membership and leadership-building at the core of their work, from providing services to speaking out on issues to alliance-building. In some cases, these centres have found it challenging to then also have the capacity to run campaigns.

We believe that it is critical to strive toward a dual strategy of campaign/policy organizing and leadership development. Without connecting campaigns and membership development, we risk having a base of members disconnected from gaining experience of campaigns, strategy, and organizing. There will be a strong membership but one that does not get shaped by campaign organizing or by challenging power. However, the realities of implementing this on a daily basis are often difficult.

We constantly try to reflect on how we include members in making decisions on campaign development and strategy. However, this becomes difficult when situations emerge between the monthly meetings that need quick responses, or when an issue that we are organizing around breaks in the media. We have struggled with how to move quickly but with accountability back to members and leaders. We have tried a variety of approaches—steering committees, check-ins, premeetings—all of which are helpful but when members come from across the city, speak different languages, and move in and out of employment, consistency for a smaller group to meet between larger meetings is very challenging. That is why it has always been important to have a staff that reflects our membership. We put a lot of resources into internships, mentorship, training, and other supports to move members into staff and other leadership positions.

These challenges underscore why we believe that we cannot go from campaign to campaign. A movement-building strategy is critical with longer-term campaigns helping to support this. The interconnections between base-building, organization, and campaigning are needed to combat the dynamics of organizing within a system that does not value workers' experience and leadership. We have seen how workers become changed through such experience, which translates into transforming family relationships, workplace struggles, and connections with community-based institutions and other structures.

These challenges and tensions raise critical questions about how we define success around membership development—is it only about numbers, or about the depth of involvement and leadership in campaigns? It is easy to view success as having active spokespeople for campaigns and media or having members in key decision-making roles. We have been challenged and intrigued by the work of Asian Immigrant Women Advocates (AIWA, California), which prioritizes grassroots leadership training as a core strategy of building immigrant women workers' power (Chun et al. 2010).

We are expanding our understanding of membership and leadership to capture a range of abilities that can include a person's ability to take on issues in their lives, feel confident to lead a meeting, organize a workshop, or support other workers to challenge their bad boss. These are all skills that members can build through joining WAC, but we seldom stop and think about these changes and assess them as supporting organizing or building a strong movement.

Multiracial Organizing

A multiracial organizing model allows us to build alliances between workers across both race and the spectrum of work, unemployment, and migration. Labour market restructuring not only limits workers' choices, options, and power, it also restricts opportunities to build solidarity with workers across race, ethnicity, and citizenship status, whether it is migrant workers who are told not to interact with other workers outside their workplace, or racialized divisions of labour within workplaces.

Organizing across race and immigration status is a constant work in progress. We have tried different tools such as creating language-specific spaces for workers to get connected with other members of their community through WAC. Having organizers on staff that speak the languages of low-income immigrant communities in Toronto and ensuring translation at member events and organizing meetings is essential to building a multiracial organization.

Building solidarity and alliances between members means constantly challenging and deconstructing mainstream narratives of migrant workers stealing jobs and the stigmatization of welfare recipients, as well as taking on homophobia, Islamophobia, and racism. It also requires discussions of ongoing colonialism and our role in building alliances with Indigenous Peoples as immigrant workers and workers of colour. While many organizations we met with in the United States talk about doing this alliance-building through the emerging coalitions such as the United Workers Congress, it is a strength of our model that we are able to make these connections through the diverse experiences of our own members.

Chun (2009) explores how wider common narratives are a source of symbolic power and a critical basis of workers' associational power in low-wage industries. She outlines how worker organizing that borrows from past social movement repertoires can build symbolic leverage especially for workers who have little economic power through traditional union models of bargaining. We struggle with what social movement historical leverages we can pull from in our context when workers don't share a common workplace, sector, ethnic or racial background, migration experience, or even geographic neighbourhood location. Most of our members' sense of isolation is multilayered. It comes from their immigration experience and systemic discrimination in the labour market but also from being incredibly marginalized because of precarious work or employment status.

It is an ongoing challenge to build the cohesion that comes from a single community, language, or history of migration. US organizations organizing in one community can draw on common identities and narratives of struggle (see, for example, Ghandnoosh 2010). Many WAC members have been in Canada for less than ten years, were not here for the major labour market restructuring of the 1990s, and are shocked to learn about the rolling back of basic rights that occurred. Meanwhile, members bring very diverse experiences of organizing with them; how do we build a culture of organizing from these? When analyzing the sources of symbolic power in our work we have realized we need to focus on creating a new organizing culture that weaves common values and desires for decent work, connections with migration experience and building solidarity between members. We build a new commonality of experience through the injustice of not being paid, moving from job to job, fighting back on unpaid wages, and winning concrete victories.

Geographic Spaces of Organizing: Provincial Versus Neighbourhood Organizing

The community and/or neighbourhood location of organizing is a key focus of understanding worker centre and community unionism models (Cranford et al 2006). Jayaraman and Ness (2005) describe how neighbourhood organizing is combined with workplace organizing to address a wider range of issues affecting workers' lives and can involve more creative tactics when it takes place outside the workplace. Choudry and Thomas (2012) write that by being based in communities, worker centres can build on preexisting community networks in a way that is challenging for traditional union models. The geographic spaces of organizing determine both our scale of reach and potential alliance-building.

WAC faces the challenge of not being located in a specific neighbourhood while trying to build a base of members from across Toronto, and at the same time having a focus of provincial legislative campaigns. We see the strengths of neighbourhood and community organizing strategies to build power in specific communities in models such as the Workplace Project in Long Island and Make the Road in Queens, NY, as well as Montreal's Immigrant Workers Centre.

Racialized communities and immigrants comprise over 50 percent of the population and are scattered all over the Greater Toronto Area (GTA). There are definitely pockets of immigrant communities across the city, but that does not necessarily correspond to how people become WAC members. Our members span from Mississauga to Scarborough to North York to downtown. Our office is in the city centre, close to transit in order to get the widest reach for workers across the GTA. Many of our members must travel an hour to come to our office. When members come together in monthly organizing meetings, there is a lot of pressure to make these very productive and jam in a lot of discussion and decision-making. However, we also organize our actions and campaign work at a neighbourhood level in multiple locations. This greatly stretches our resources and capacity, but this is the reality of organizing in Toronto.

Our strategy around rebuilding a basic floor of rights also requires supporting other groups to form and mobilize and to build a movement across the province. Strong alliance-building means supporting, mentoring, and nurturing other grassroots groups of workers that are self-organizing. It has been important for WAC to work with the Caregivers' Action Centre, providing training and support to assist in organizational development, outreach, and involvement in decision-making in networks on broader migrant worker issues. We have also supported the development of the Migrant Workers Alliance for Change, a coalition of migrant rights, labour, and community groups in Ontario. We have provided ongoing support to other groups starting to form fledgling worker centres in Sudbury, Peterborough, St. Catharine's, and other locations, as well as training and support to community agencies wanting to start integrating workers' rights issues or community organizing in their work.

We are spearheading a minimum wage campaign in cities across Ontario, which could provide a vehicle to build relationships and strong alliances in advancing the struggle of working people.[3] We see an emerging confidence in groups in over twenty-five cities to plan actions and see themselves part of a growing network to push for the minimum wage. The campaign is laying the groundwork for developing relationships, trying out different strategies, and organizing stronger actions that can keep building for the next one. Through the experience of the minimum wage campaign, we see that this may be the first time that the local district labour council is taking on something that is not considered to be a traditional union issue. The support and strategizing to help make this happen is critical to begin bridging the divide between the union movement and community. All of these relationships can begin to support pushing worker organizing across Ontario, which will allow us to be stronger in pushing deeper legislative and sectoral demands.

Moving Forward

WAC has encountered tensions and limits related to scale, pace of change, and ability to build power in individual workplaces and specific sectors. But we have been able to explore new models of organizing that address the realities of precarious work across the labour market for migrant and racialized communities. One strength of our model has been the flexibility to experiment with different strategies and to test what it means to build a culture of organizing that can help seed new movements, and how to build alliances across experiences of migration and precarious work. We think it is important to define and value success in many different ways. Success

---

3   See <http://15andfairness.org/>.

can be raising standards and wages, but it is also building alliances and solidarity across multiracial communities and a feeling of place. Success is winning legislative change and a voice at work, but as Acsana, one of our members, states, success is also fostering hope and courage among the people who walk in our doors. Given the current context, we believe that hope and courage to join a struggle for better wages and working conditions is an essential element for building a strong movement and power in our workplaces and communities.

References

Bernhardt, Annette, Heather Boushey, Laura Dresser, and Chris Tilly (eds.). 1998. *The Gloves-Off Economy: Workplace Standards at the Bottom of America's Labor Market*. Ithaca: Cornell University Press.

Block, Sheila. 2013. *Who Is Working for Minimum Wage in Ontario?* Toronto: Wellesley Institute.

Block, Sheila, and Grace-Edward Galabuzi. 2011. *Canada's Colour Coded Labour Market: The Gap for Racialized Workers*. Toronto: Canadian Centre for Policy Alternatives.

Choudry, Aziz, and Mark Thomas. 2012. "Organizing Migrant and Immigrant Workers in Canada." In Stephanie Ross and Larry Savage (eds.), *Rethinking the Politics of Labour in Canada*. Halifax: Fernwood Publishing.

Chun, Jennifer Jihye. 2009. *Organizing at the Margins: The Symbolic Politics of Labor in South Korea and the United States*. Ithaca: ILR Press.

Chun, Jennifer Jihye, George Lipsitz, and Young Shin. 2010. "Immigrant Women Workers at the Center of Social Change: AIWA Takes Stock of Itself." *Kalfou*, Inaugural Issue. <aiwa.org/wp-content/uploads/2014/08/KalfouArticle_SocialChange.pdf>

Cranford, Cynthia J., Tanya Das Gupta, Deena Ladd, and Leah F. Vosko. 2006. "Thinking Through Community Unionism." In Leah F. Vosko (ed.), *Precarious Employment: Understanding Labour Market Insecurity in Canada*. Montreal: McGill–Queen's University Press.

DeFilippis, James, Robert Fisher, and Eric Shragge. 2010. *Contesting Community: The Limits and Potential of Local Organizing*. New Brunswick: Rutgers University Press.

Domestic Workers United, National Domestic Workers Alliance, and Urban Justice Centre. 2010. *Domestic Workers and Collective Bargaining*. New York.

Eaton, Jonathan Bruce. 1994. "Labour Law Reform for the New Workplace: Bill 40 and Beyond." LLM thesis, University of Toronto, 1994.

Excluded Workers Congress. 2010. *Unity for Dignity: Expanding the Right to Organize to Win Human Rights at Work*. New York.

Fine, Janice. 2011. "Worker Centers: Entering a New Stage of Growth and Development." *New Labor Forum* 20, no. 3 (Fall).

_____. 2006. Worker Centers: Organizing Communities at the Edge of the Dream. Ithaca: ILR Press/Cornell University Press.

Fudge, Judy, John Baigent, and Vince Ready. 1993. "Labour Needs Sectoral Bargaining Now." *Canadian Dimension* 27, no. 2 (March/April).

Ghandnoosh, Nazgol. 2010. "Organizing Workers Along Ethnic Lines: The Pilipino Workers' Centre." In Ruth Milkman, Joshua Bloom, and Victor Narro (eds.), *Working for Justice: The L.A. Model of Organizing and Advocacy*. Ithaca: Cornell University Press.

Gordon, Jennifer. 2011. "Citizens of the Global Economy: A Proposal to Universalize the Rights of Transnational Labor." *Labour Forum* 20, no. 1 (Winter).

Hussan, Syed, and Nate Prior. 2012. "Constructed Categories: Avoiding the Race to the Bottom." *Briarpatch*, November 4.

Jayaraman, Sarumathi, and Immanuel Ness. 2005. "Introduction." In Sarumathi Jayaraman and Immanuel Ness (eds.), *The New Urban Immigrant Workforce: Innovative Models for Labor Organizing*. Armonk: M.E. Sharpe Inc.

Lewchuk, Wayne, et al. 2013. *It's More Than Poverty: Employment Precarity and Household Well-Being*. Toronto: McMaster University and United Way Toronto.

Milkman, Ruth. 2010. "Introduction." In Ruth Milkman, Joshua Bloom, and Victor Narro (eds.), *Working for Justice: The L.A. Model of Organizing and Advocacy*. Ithaca: Cornell University Press.

Preibisch, Kerry L. 2010. "Pick-Your-Own Labor: Migrant Workers and Flexibility in Canadian Agriculture." *International Migration Review* 44, no. 2 (Summer).

Sidhu, Navjeet. 2013. *Accessing Community Programs and Services for Non-Status Immigrants in Toronto: Organizational Challenges and Responses*. Toronto: Social Planning Toronto.

Soss, Joe, Richard C. Fording, and Sanford F. Schram. 2011. *Disciplining the Poor: Neoliberal Paternalism and the Persistent Power of Race*. Chicago: University of Chicago Press.

Tait, Vanessa. 2005. *Poor Workers' Unions: Rebuilding Labor from Below*. Cambridge: South End Press.

Thomas, Mark. 2009. *Regulating Flexibility: The Political Economy of Employment Standards*. Montreal: McGill–Queen's University Press.

Vaillancourt, Julie. 2010. *Ontario Works—Works for Whom? An Investigation of Workfare in Ontario*. Halifax: Fernwood Publishing.

Vosko, Leah F. 2006. "Precarious Employment: Towards an Improved Understanding of Labour Market Insecurity." In Leah F. Vosko (ed.), *Precarious Employment: Understanding Labour Market Insecurity in Canada*. Montreal: McGill–Queen's University Press.

_____. 2000. *Temporary Work: The Gendered Rise of a Precarious Employment Relationship*. Toronto: University of Toronto Press.

Wial, Howard. 1993. "The Emerging Organizational Structure of Unionism in Low-Wage Services." *Rutgers Law Review* 45 (Spring).

Workers' Action Centre. 2011. *Unpaid Wages, Unprotected Workers*. Toronto.

_____. 2007. *Working on the Edge*. Toronto.

A Jeepney Ride to Tunisia— From There to Here, Organizing Temporary Foreign Workers

Joey Calugay, Loïc Malhaire, and Eric Shragge

When twenty-six-year-old Mohammed Bouazizi of Sidi Bouzid, Tunisia, walked out his door on December 27, 2010, he may have been motivated by the goal of buying a pickup truck. Mohammed was luckier than most young people in his town. While many of his peers were educated but unemployed, he could earn a living by selling vegetables and provide for his family. After years of pushing his small vegetable cart, he must have been excited at the prospect of developing his small business with the purchase of that pickup truck. Just several hours later, Mohammed was in front of the provincial headquarters pouring gasoline all over himself. Earlier that morning, his cart was confiscated, and he was given a fine and then abused and insulted by a local police officer. After officials refused to see him while trying to file a complaint, he returned to the headquarters where corrupt local officials "lorded" over the citizens of Sidi Bouzid and set himself on fire (Abouzeid 2011).

The fire Bouazizi lit sparked the flames that rushed first through Tunisia and then several other North African countries. Cities and towns burned with protests, the people's desire for change fueling the storm later to be dubbed the Arab Spring. Millions like Mohammed Bouazizi had suffered enough of the corruption, autocratic rule, and especially the poverty and high unemployment that was slowly killing their families and their dreams.

But revolution is often two steps forward and one step back. While the people of Tunisia, among other places, learned a great lesson about people-powered progress, years of maldevelopment do not go away so easily. Several years after their uprising that toppled the Western-backed dictator Ben Ali, Tunisians continue to flock overseas in search of jobs and a future for their families.

One of their destinations is Canada where they arrive through its Temporary Foreign Worker Program (TFWP), which puts them to work as temporary foreign workers (TFWs) in such sectors as health care, information technology, food and meat processing, manufacturing, agriculture, and hospitality. Each job is classified "low-" or "high-skilled"— sometimes arbitrarily—by the government. There are four main TFW programs: professional TFWs (now Stream for High-Wage Positions); the Caregiver Program (formerly known as the Live-in Caregiver Program, LCP); the Seasonal Agricultural Worker Program (SAWP); and the Low-Skilled Pilot Program (now Stream for Low-Wage Positions and Agricultural Stream). Theoretically, this program is designed to fill jobs that employers cannot fill locally. But, in practice, it serves as a means for employers to draw on Tunisians and others displaced by political upheaval and economic deterioration, a labour pool disciplined by insecurity and necessity to work and then discarded. In 2012, almost 109,000 people were working in Canada as TFWs,[1] including over 11,000 in Quebec.[2]

In 2008, for the first time, more TFWs came to Canada than new permanent residents. Recent media stories on the "abuse" of the program focus on the lack of opportunities for Canadian workers. Quite problematically, this critique assumes that Canadian workers would take these jobs if it were not so easy for employers to recruit TFWs.

This chapter reflects on the experiences of Montreal's Immigrant Workers Centre (IWC) in working to support individuals and groups of workers under the TFWP.[3] The IWC has prioritized working with TFWs in many types of employment and in different regions and cities of Quebec, learning many valuable lessons. Here we will discuss groups of workers

---

1   Statistics Canada, "Canada - Foreign Workers Present on December 1st by Yearly Sub-Status," *Facts and Figures 2012—Immigration Overview: Permanent and Temporary Residents, Temporary Residents*, <cic.gc.ca/francais/ressources/statistiques/faits2012/index.asp>.

2   Immigration et Communautés Culturelles Québec, "Caractéristiques des immigrants temporaires de la catégorie des travailleurs étrangers, effectifs au Québec, 2007 à 2012," *Portrait Statistique, L'immigration au Québec*, p. 18, <micc.gouv.qc.ca/publications/fr/recherches-statistiques/Portraits_Immigration_Temporaire_2007_2012.pdf>.

3   For history and background on the IWC, see Eric Shragge, *Activism and Social Change: Lessons for Community Organizing*, 2nd ed. (Toronto: University of Toronto Press, 2013).

in the high- and low-skilled categories, an often arbitrary distinction that produces important consequences and challenges for TFWs. The TFWP renders workers vulnerable to employer threats to terminate their jobs and status. Workers, who often support families in their home countries, are essentially bound to their employers. Most are not informed either about their employment rights or some of the complexities of status including, for high-skilled workers, the possibility of applying for permanent residence in Canada.

The defence of TFWs is complicated by such factors as whether a worker is designated high- or low-skilled, which has implications for the possibility of permanent status; the size of the group of workers (e.g., individual jobs as cooks or collective work as landscapers); and their invisibility and distance from places where there are stronger community organizations and unions. Ideally, the aim is to build associations of workers with their own leadership and capacity to represent themselves and defend their collective interests against employers and the state, supported by allies such as unions and community organizations—but we are a long way from that. While workers' vulnerability and isolation makes organizing difficult, we describe steps and processes undertaken by the IWC to work toward the broader ideal.

Why Do People Join This Program?

To defend workers in the TFWP, we must ask why people leave their countries and why the TFWP is one of the few available migration options. We must also recognize that TFWs are often recruited by agencies and do not necessarily understand the specific dimensions of the TFWP (e.g., who pays for transport, accommodation, and other costs of living, and the possibility of applying for permanent residence), and that recruiters may not adhere to program requirements.

A slow death, that's how Filipino migrant worker Louis (interview, Migrant Voices Project, April 2011) described what he and his family were going through before deciding to leave the Philippines. But it was not the slow death of poverty and lack of steady employment that finally did it for Louis. It was the threat of a quick and sudden death texted to his cell phone from what he can only surmise as military death squads in his region. The threat was no doubt the result of his labour activism as a local union president in a Southern Tagalog semiprocessing auto-parts plant.

Watching his home getting smaller as he drove away in a jeepney, Louis was sad to leave. He describes feelings of guilt when recounting his decision to leave "the fight" behind. Many of his colleagues in the union do not have this option. He remembers his young son and his wife who was pregnant with their second child. If not for them, he would have stayed and taken his chances, even with the death threats.

A year later, Louis was walking in two feet of freshly fallen snow on the frozen streets of Granby, Quebec. He and his Filipino migrant coworker, Jaime, worked the graveyard shift. Living about three kilometres from their job site, they had to walk to work in the middle of the night in the cold of Canadian winter given the deficiencies of public transport in Granby.

Their boss was happy with their work. Unlike their coworkers on the day shift, the two machinists were each able to operate two machines and produce more parts per worker within their given shift. They were an efficient team, paid up to 15 percent less than non-TFWs with the same experience and tasks. Six months into their first contract, Louis, Jaime, and two other foreign workers were sent back to the Philippines during a period of what the employer explained as a "slow-down in the economy." As soon as the employer saw orders for machine parts increase, he hired them back after they had been stewing with no income or employment insurance for several months in the Philippines. It was a profit-making dream come true. Cheap, flexible, and docile labour—at least, so management thought. We return to this story later.

Some Fundamental Critical Analyses of the Temporary Foreign Worker Program (TFWP)

The TFWP has become a central axis of employment policies, as well as a driving force of the neoliberal Canadian economy.[4] The global strategy of lowering labour and production costs inevitably and increasingly impacts the labour standards of the Canadian workforce, forcing them to accept atypical and precarious work,[5] and leading to the creation of an "underclass of foreign workers" (Montpetit 2012), Canada is experiencing a high rate of unemployment, which significantly questions the discourse around temporary labour shortages as well as the government commitments to a "Canadian workers first" employment priority (Yerochewski et al. 2013).

---

4   Martin Cook translated this section from French to English.
5   This constraint is equally a result of the restriction and conditioning of access to social protection policies, where the logic corresponds to an incentive to work for beneficiaries.

Fundamentally, we question these employment policies as they impose incentives for, if not obligations on, unemployed Canadians to work. The discourse clearly endorses precarious work through the advent of "McJobs," stigmatizing the unemployed who might dare to refuse these low-skilled and underpaid jobs through the suggestion that they are responsible for the use of TFWs. With a patriotic tone, the discourse also suggests that Canadian workers are prioritized in a sort of labour market competition with TFWs. This implicit competition affects both the unemployed and the wider Canadian workforce.

Employer needs heavily influence Canadian im/migrant selection processes, which reveals a form of "privatization of immigration" as analyzed by Boti and Guy (2012) in their film *The End of Immigration*.[6] Through these immigration policies, the Canadian government indicates that it is less concerned with the integration and participation of citizens in economic, social, political, and cultural life, than exploiting the labour of those who are forced to return home after their contracts have ended. Canada's ongoing selection of a competent, experienced, skilled,[7] young, and thus particularly "productive" workforce, deprives countries of origin of human resources essential for socioeconomic development. All that Canada offers TFWs are the prospects of returning to their country once the contract expires or is terminated.

The TFWP creates precarious employment and immigration status with marginal access to social rights. Most work permits for TFWs are restrictive—valid for a specific work contract and tied to a single employer. One quickly realizes that this situation does not benefit workers, many of whom say it is impossible to express their discontent against abuses such as forced and unpaid overtime work, unsafe conditions, lack of access to health care, arbitrary withholding of wages, harassment, and threats of deportation.[8] They fear job loss because with it comes the loss of their work permit and immigration status.

Furthermore, TFWs face many challenges in benefiting from the rights and protections theoretically associated with work. The IWC has

---

6   <multi-monde.ca/en/the-end-of-immigration/>.

7   For skilled temporary foreign workers, job vacancies require a formal education or formal training such as a university degree, a college diploma, vocational training, or an apprenticeship; CIC.

8   These examples have been documented by professionals and volunteers from the IWC called upon to defend the rights of TFWs.

documented cases of ill or injured TFWs where the administrative processing of a health and safety benefit application has been delayed for several years. The forced departure of beneficiaries to their countries at the end of their contracts puts an end to the coverage of medical treatment costs and compromises their recovery. Other difficulties workers face include language barriers and lack of knowledge of their rights. Moreover, the IWC has come across numerous TFWs who are denied employment insurance (EI) benefits because they do not have valid work permits, even though they fully contributed to the EI scheme (see Ramsaroop's chapter). Individual casework is necessary to ensure that EI rights are respected; however, it cannot go beyond the ninety days of "implied" immigration status. The problem is even more acute for workers who are fired prematurely and unexpectedly, who sometimes have incurred debts in order to finance their trip to Canada, and who must therefore find a new job as soon as possible.

Worker Centres: The New Face of Labour Organizing

Founded in 2000, the IWC has two interrelated sets of priorities—organizing an association of temporary agency workers and working with TFWs, in addition to supporting other workers confronting a range of employment and migration issues. There are several reasons for this focus. First, increasing numbers of agency workers and TFWs were coming to the centre for help with labour and immigration issues and questions. Second, these forms of work have increased dramatically over recent years, particularly in immigrant communities, part of the wider restructuring of the labour market, with growing precarious situations. We will continue with stories of TFWs, followed by a discussion of the organizing process and related challenges.

Take the example of one TFW—Muhammad Ali—as he calls himself while posing with his fists up. The group sitting around the table in the IWC is delighted with Muhammad's antics. It is a welcome respite from his more serious and poignant story about his home country of Tunisia and his experience working as a TFW in a fast food restaurant. Sitting with him are IWC organizers and Neil, an Indonesian worker who was trafficked by a Montreal restaurant while on a student visa and made to work alongside Indonesian TFWs as specialized Indonesian cooks. The group swaps stories and experiences, a method of building a collective in preparation for setting up a TFW campaign committee to push for better protection for migrant workers in Quebec.

Those same stories were written up by the workers themselves and presented to a coalition of precarious workers' groups and organizations initiated by the IWC in May 2013. The coalition's purpose was to meet with Quebec Labour Ministry officials to advance demands for better protection and access to services for TFWs and other precarious workers. Muhammad and Neil, representing the TFW committee, helped organize and spoke at a public forum, made media statements, and presented their cases to the ministry.

They were also invited to speak about the campaign at schools, union meetings, and organizational events, helping to build solidarity and allies for their cause. Building an active and committed leadership core of workers is an important stage in the IWC's organizing work. The IWC believes that a base of affected workers must be mobilized and become active in solving *our* social problems. This work means building a movement of workers supporting each other and in solidarity with other movements.

The process of organizing TFWs requires ongoing research that is concrete and can support the organizing process. One challenge facing organizations working with TFWs is locating them. Often workers are isolated both in terms of housing and workplaces. The way the IWC has been able to contact workers is described below, but a more systematic understanding of where workers are located is required. Because employers have to apply for a Labour Market Impact Assessment (LMIA) in order to receive government approval to bring in workers, monitoring and analyzing these applications is key to knowing who is using the program and in which sectors. This knowledge will help with targeted outreach and meeting workers. Sensitizing unions, community associations, and religious groups about the program and the availability of help for TFWs is another means to reach workers.

The goal of the second area of research is to document the conditions of work, housing, and issues related to migration such as the role of agencies and transportation costs. Specific knowledge helps prepare organizers in identifying issues. The best source for this information is the workers themselves, but a system of documentation would help build a systematic critique of the program and prepare for engagement with new arrivals. A related area of research concerns policy: better understanding of the complex intersection of labour and migration, and the shifting policies and regulations that comprise the TFWP. These include the multiple policies that shape the program, including worker eligibility for benefits such as EI. The IWC has prepared a manual but it is limited because of policy differences between provinces and shifts over time. Tools are required that should be made accessible and easily available. At the same time, ongoing research is required to make sure information is up-to-date. This research has the potential to provide information for test cases such as whether or not someone in the TFW is eligible for EI or benefits if there is a workplace accident and the worker cannot return to work.

The Organizing Process

Below is a breakdown of the steps in organizing based on the IWC's experience. This is not to be understood as sequential. The challenge is for the organizing process to build a group/organization of workers who can represent themselves in the fight for improved conditions, and challenge the temporary and vulnerable status associated with the program.

1. FINDING CONTACTS AND BUILDING A BASE

The starting point of any organizing is to build relationships between the organizer and those s/he is attempting to organize. TFWs provide a major challenge. The workers are hidden insofar as their presence is not announced and other outreach such as meeting workers near their workplace or in the community will not necessarily lead to contact with TFWs. The IWC has been able to reach workers through community contacts. However, this can only happen if there is an awareness in the community and unions that the TFWP exists and that the IWC is working with TFWs to defend their rights. For this to work, a program of community outreach and education, either formally or through individual contacts, is a precondition. For example, there was a group of TFW landscapers in suburban Montreal living in the same apartment complex as a former live-in caregiver worker. She knew about the IWC through her affiliation with its sister organization PINAY and connected them. For several summers, the IWC was able to meet these workers and discuss issues related to work, housing, and immigration. The IWC had also worked with a group of Tunisians in Chicoutimi. The brother of one worker, a TFW in another town, was laid off and was introduced to the IWC by his brother. Other groups of workers have found the IWC through friends or the Internet, as did the workers at a computer games company, discussed below. Systematic education of allied community organizations, religious groups, and unions is vital for organizing. Most community groups and unions do not have the knowledge of the TFWP to help people in it and many in the union movement see the use of the program solely as an attack on their members. It is through these organizations that finding TFWs is possible, and it will help build alliances for campaigns through education.

2. How to Engage—First Steps

TFWs arrive as dependent or tied to employers. This relation makes them more vulnerable than most workers and not willing to risk confrontation with their bosses. Further, many are neither clear about the nature of the TFWP and the complex policies that shape it nor the labour standards that theoretically govern their working conditions. Further, why should these workers trust an outside organization such as the IWC that is agitating on labour rights? Part of the answer rests with the previous discussion and on how TFWs are introduced and by whom. The second part is to begin the process of relation-building with less threatening tactics. For example, for those TFWs who arrive classified as skilled workers, workshops on the immigration process meet their interests and provide valuable information. This can lead to further discussions about the nature of their jobs and create relations of trust so that abuses can be confronted. Labour standards workshops can help workers judge whether or not their jobs are abusive. The IWC has produced a basic manual that covers the TFWP and related concerns to help prepare workers. Contesting working conditions for workers in this program implies high risk, but understanding their situations is the starting point.

3. The Role of Individual Work in Pushing the Boundaries and Setting Precedents

The TFWP works better in theory than in practice. Workers face severe problems when they lose their jobs or are injured and can no longer work. Two cases illustrate the complex interrelationship of benefits and precarious migration status. Regardless of their status, all workers in the TFWP contribute to EI and pensions, and pay taxes.

This was certainly the case for Val, from Bangladesh, a cook in an Indian restaurant in Montreal's South Shore. He was actively recruited by an Ottawa-based recruitment agency, which in turn was contracted by the restaurant to hire a temporary foreign worker cook. Val was charged thousands of dollars for the recruitment process, for which he was referred to moneylenders in his hometown for a loan. This is supposedly illegal under the TFWP but is common practice, which the worker can rarely challenge if they want to work.

Val's employer confiscated his passport and made him live in his basement and do gardening and household chores for months, working over sixty hours per week without overtime pay or a pay stub explaining deductions and calculations of hours. After all this, Val had finally secured repayment funds when, close to the end of his first contract, his employer asked for hundreds of dollars to renew his contract and work permit. When he refused, he was fired a few days before the end of his work permit and told to pack his bags.

Referred to the IWC by a member of Montreal's Bangladeshi community involved in the IWC's textile campaign, Val fought back. The centre helped him to apply for EI while he awaited the results of his complaint and looked for other work during the ninety-day grace period given to TFWs at the end of a work permit.

At first, Service Canada, which administers EI, refused Val because his employer only reported a certain amount of hours lower than what was needed to apply for EI for the first time. After Val and the IWC appealed this based on the fact that the Commission des Normes de Travail (Quebec's Labour Standards Commission, CNT) agreed with Val that he was owed money for several hundred unpaid hours worked, Service Canada refused him again because he did not have a valid work permit. Val and the IWC also appealed this decision—this time to the EI Board of Referees—and won, arguing that it was absurd to ask TFWs to have valid work permits before receiving EI because it would mean that they had already found employment in order to be issued a permit and thus no longer needed EI; and that it was also absurd for foreign workers to fulfill obligations that we all have but deny them access to the rights and benefits that all workers should have in Canada.

Service Canada, which seemed adamant about denying foreign workers access to EI, appealed this win, but it is not the final word on the matter for the IWC. Val's case was fought on principle. And Val, who at many points just wanted to let it go, was encouraged to go forward, not because he wanted the financial support from EI that should have been afforded to him but because the IWC's position was that his case was precedent setting.

Val continued to fight on the front lines of labour violations against TFWs and fought to get his temporary status reinstated based on the fact that he should have the right to stay while he had a judicial proceeding underway (and was backed by a letter signed by the CNT president supporting Val's request to stay in Canada). Val also used his case to highlight the problems inherent in the TFWP and found the courage to speak to the media. This helped to raise awareness among the general public and acted as encouragement for other workers to come forward. Indeed, several of Val's contacts brought their complaints to the IWC when they saw a newspaper article about his experience.

Collective Action

Building a mass movement among immigrant and migrant communities also means building their organizational capacity. This organization is expressed through their ability to make collective decisions democratically, by taking collective leadership in clarifying their common issues and uniting around their common demands. It also means their ability to mobilize for collective action. Often, collective action starts with a question to an individual: Are there others in your workplace experiencing the same situations?

This question has continuously produced situations where IWC organizers are in a room filled with some thirty, forty, or eighty workers, their spouses, their children, and other relatives and acquaintances. Their individual workplace problems are actually a common collective problem with far-reaching implications beyond their workplace and into their communities, homes, and neighbourhoods. For example, the IWC has worked with linguistic-testers, hired to check language in computer games to be marketed internationally. Over thirty of these foreign workers met at the CNT's lobby to demand that it approve their complaint for remuneration for collective dismissal without the proper notice period. These workers—some of whom had arrived less than two months earlier and were just settling into their new environment—were dismissed by their employer, giving them one or two weeks to leave the country by providing them with plane tickets home (which the company was legally bound to do). Thinking that would be the end of it, the company hoped that this time frame would discourage workers from looking into their rights. That would have been the case had it not been for one worker who came forward.

At the CNT lobby, negotiations between building security and CNT administration began with the CNT's usual instructions to file individual complaints online. The problem with this suggestion was that some of the newer workers had done just that prior to occupying the lobby. They were refused because they had not secured the required number of months of employment with the same employer. However, under Quebec's collective dismissal laws, all workers dismissed within a given period are owed several weeks of compensation in lieu of notice periods, amounting to eight to ten weeks of pay. The company hoped to avoid this situation by not registering the closure of their Montreal lab to the Quebec government and justifying it as a move of locations.

The workers' determination prevailed and the CNT allowed up to six workers representing several of the nationalities involved to file a collective dismissal on behalf of the laid-off TFWs. Along with a sympathetic CNT investigator, they devised a plan to use their social networking savvy and created a Facebook group to keep connected even after they had to leave Canada.

Almost two years later, they won their fight, with most of them receiving between four thousand and six thousand dollars in compensation—an amount justifiably owed to the workers that would have continued to line the pockets of the owners had the workers not undertaken collective action.

Concluding Comments

Our chapter addresses two questions—who speaks for TFWs and how do we position ourselves in defending their rights? We have discussed the IWC's organizing approach in building relationships and supporting workers who can take public action to defend and extend the rights of TFWs. The goal of this process is, first, to organize workplace committees where there are TFWs so that workers can develop knowledge and analysis and then become contacts for other workers. Education is a key aspect of local work. Workers are not equipped with details of the TFWP and the services and benefits to which they are entitled. Further, for those workers in the skilled category, and who want to stay permanently, the process of immigration is complex, and sharing information is the basis of forming local committees. From these local committees, the goal is to build a larger body that brings together workers in both low- and high-skilled categories to represent themselves and advance political demands with IWC support. This is not a quick process, and there are organizations that while lacking a TFW base, remain willing to speak on behalf of these workers. In contrast, the IWC stands committed to organizing TFWs. This is a slow, time-consuming process with modest results. But as the TFWP expands, and as the IWC becomes better known among TFWs, we believe in the prospects of organizing these workers. One aspect of this is that there has been initial contact and workshops with groups and then little contact until a problem arises—lay-offs, immigration problems, etc.—at which point contact is renewed. We do not believe that advocacy groups and community organizations can by themselves demand and win a program of reform. TFWs need to build power through organization and struggle in their own interests. A national movement is required but the challenges in building this are immense, given the variety of workers, their isolation, and their different nationalities. Alliances between workers themselves and allies are necessary to build a broader movement to win the slogan "good enough to work, good enough to stay."

Finally, we will comment on an important tension that emerged in Spring 2013 when the public learned that RBC was using the TFWP to train workers with the idea of sending them back to India and performing their functions there, thus taking jobs with them. The consequence of this revelation was pressure on the government, which resulted in a tightening of the Labour Market Opinion (now LMIA) process for employers. However, the public debate leaned toward an anti-immigrant stance—that they were taking "Canadian" jobs and the government should allow these foreign workers as a last resort. Even some unions that defend the rights of TFWs adopted a similar position.

An example of this is found in the United Steelworkers' Give Everyone a Chance for Canada's Future campaign, which sought much-needed changes to the TFWP and to the Harper government's low-wage model of economic development by:

> ensuring that Canadians and permanent residents are given genuine
> opportunities to fill job vacancies before employers can bring in
> temporary workers;
>
> insisting that employers provide training for Canadians and per-
> manent residents for available jobs before being allowed to hire
> temporary workers;
>
> eliminating the creation of a two-tier workforce where many tem-
> porary foreign workers are subject to abuse and exploitation by
> ensuring that all temporary workers have a clear path to Canadian
> citizenship and have the same rights as permanent residents; and
>
> increasing oversight and enforcement of the TFWP. (United
> Steelworkers, n.d.)

This position, despite the acknowledgement of the two-tier labour market, focuses on "Canadian" workers' needs for training and jobs. However, a deeper analysis reveals three additional factors that need to be taken into account. First, we should understand the role of migration in Canadian history, as other contributors to this volume suggest. One of the major ways immigrants to Canada have been perceived is as an easily exploit-able and expendable source of labour—from the Irish who built canals and the Chinese who built railways, to domestic workers imported from the Caribbean and the Philippines. This is the legacy—superexploitation of immigrants to build Canadian infrastructure and the service economy with little in the way of adequate compensation or rights. Second, the empha-sis on the TFW obscures the ongoing conditions of immigrant labour in Canada; that is, a highly educated labour force filling the lowest-paying jobs with little hope of upward mobility. Finally, the broader context creates the conditions for migration. People are pushed out of their home countries because of changing economic and social conditions. The TFWP exploits this global displacement as contemporary migration policies supply capital with an easy pool of labour to draw from. The critique of the TFWP we share is far more complex than simply protecting Canadian workers first and promoting training. Understanding the TFWP as the internationalization of what Marx called the "reserve army of labour" makes the stakes greater for all and the defence of TFWs a priority for the conditions of *all* workers.

Louis Pagaling, one of the machinists in Granby, introduced earlier in this chapter, explains he and his coworkers joined together and pressed management to concede to several demands, including housing that was cheaper, had more appropriate private spaces, and was within reasonable walking distance to and from work. More importantly, they achieved a raise to their hourly rate that was the same as the rates of non-TFWs with the same seniority. Louis calls this a victory for all of the workers in the plant. It means that the employer must treat all workers the same, regardless of race, nationality, or immigration status, and the removal of a two-tier system in their workplace that management can use to lower standards across its workforce. Louis knows this from his experience as a labour organizer in a unionized plant in the Philippines, where he had encountered labour flexibilization through the hiring of contract labourers as a form of union busting. As a union organizer, he and his comrades knew they had to reach out to the casual workers and fight together for better work conditions, including the ability of temporary casual workers to gain a permanent position. Their militant union activism put Louis in danger and contributed to his decision to leave his country. Muhammad also understands the sacrifice. He too came from a country full of strife. Both feel that they have come full circle. Their journeys eventually led them to the same conclusion: workers from the Philippines to Tunisia to all workers within the borders of Canada must organize.

References

Abouzeid, Rania. 2011. "Bouazizi: The Man Who Set Himself and Tunisia on Fire." *Time*, January 21. <content.time.com/time/magazine/article/0,9171,2044723,00. html>.

Citizenship and Immigration Canada. 2011. "Summary Report: Temporary Foreign Worker (TFW) Program—Consultations with Stakeholders." <cic.gc.ca/english/department/consultations/tfw-consultations-stakeholders/index.asp>.

Employment and Social Development Canada. 2013. "Harper Government Announces Reforms to the Temporary Foreign Worker Program—Ensuring Canadians Have First Chance at Available Jobs." News release, April 29. <news.gc.ca/web/article-en.do?nid=736729>.

Give Everyone a Chance for Canada's Future website. United Steelworkers (USW). <everyoneschance.ca>.

Marx, Karl. 1976. *Capital,* vol. 1. Translated by Ben Fowkes. New York: Penguin.

Montpetit, Caroline. 2012. «Le Canada a créé une sous-classe de travailleurs étrangers» ("Canada Created an Underclass of Foreign Workers"). *Le Devoir,* October 6. <http://www.ledevoir.com/societe/actualites-en-societe/360873/le-canada-a-cree-une-sous-classe-de-travailleurs-etrangers>.

"RBC Replaces Canadian Staff with Foreign Workers." 2013. *CBC*, April 6. <cbc.ca/news/canada/british-columbia/rbc-replaces-canadian-staff-with-foreign-workers-1.1315008>.

Yerochewski, Carole, et al., 2013. "Réformes de l'assurance-emploi et de l'aide sociale—Des machines à produire pauvreté et sous-citoyenneté" (Interview of Diane Finley at CPAC TV about the reform of employment insurance) *Le Devoir,* April 18. <ledevoir.com/politique/canada/375937/des-machines-a-produire-pauvrete-et-sous-citoyennete>.

Organizers in Dialogue

**Joey Calugay, Jill Hanley, Mostafa Henaway, Deena Ladd,
Marco Luciano, Adriana Paz Ramirez, Chris Ramsaroop,
Eric Shragge, Sonia Singh, and Christopher Sorio**

IN MAY 2013, ORGANIZERS FROM ACROSS CANADA HELD A DIALOGUE AT THE
Immigrant Workers Centre (IWC) in Montreal to discuss strategies,
models, and dilemmas of migrant and immigrant worker organizing.
Here we reproduce an excerpt of the dialogue traversing such themes as
building leadership, community versus workplace organizing, organizational sustainability, possibilities and limitations of organizing models,
and alliance-building. We have attempted to maintain the conversational
flow of this discussion, given the interconnections between these topics.
Participants included: Adriana Paz Ramirez and Chris Ramsaroop (Justicia
for Migrant Workers, BC and Ontario (Justicia)); Sonia Singh and Deena
Ladd (Workers' Action Centre, Toronto (WAC)); Christopher Sorio and
Marco Luciano (MIGRANTE-Canada); Joey Calugay, Mostafa Henaway,
Jill Hanley, and Eric Shragge (IWC).

The IWC (see also chapter 8) was formed in 2000 as a community-
based workers' organization in Montreal's diverse, working-class neighbourhood of Côte-des-Neiges by Filipino-Canadian union and former
union organizers, and other activist and academic allies. Two of the found-
ers (including Marco Luciano) had been union organizers who found that
much of their recruitment and education to support a union drive had to
happen outside the workplace, which proved difficult. The organizers also
critiqued the unions; for them, once the unions got a majority of workers
to sign cards and join up, the processes of education and solidarity built
into the organizing process were often lost as union "bureaucrats" came to
manage the collective agreement. Providing a safe space where workers

could discuss their situation, the IWC was intended to operate as a community-based workers' organization in which workers themselves would drive the agenda.

Founded in 2002, Justicia for Migrant Workers is a volunteer-run political collective comprising labour activists, educators, researchers, and students based in Ontario and BC. Justicia strives to promote the rights of migrant farmworkers including those without status. For Justicia, "promoting workers' rights entails fighting for spaces where workers themselves can articulate their concerns without losing their work or being repatriated. We start with workers' knowledge and concerns and collectively devise strategies to make necessary changes. We see ourselves as allies and strive for a movement that is led and directed by workers themselves."[1]

Formed by sixteen Filipino migrant organizations in 2010, MIGRANTE-Canada is an alliance of Filipino migrant and immigrant organizations in Canada. It has member organizations in BC, Alberta, Winnipeg, Toronto, Barrie, Ottawa, Montreal, and New Brunswick. MIGRANTE-Canada is a member of MIGRANTE International, an international alliance of progressive organizations comprising overseas Filipinos and their families, established in 1996.

Founded in 2005, the Workers' Action Centre is a worker-based organization in Toronto that is committed to improving the lives and working conditions of workers in low-wage precarious employment (see also chapter 7).

Chris Ramsaroop, Justicia: I want to bring up three points: 1) Each one of us has a different way of thinking about multiracial organizing—both the obstacles to it and also how we continue to strive for it; 2) White supremacy is always a difficult issue; some people see it as an academic discussion and it can be difficult with white allies and non-allies to put forth how it relates to our work and how we can counter it; 3) Solidarity work and the idea of community support is so critical within all of our communities but class divisions and paternalism can influence and hinder our work. What type of strategies could we use in relationship to multiracial coalition-building but also countering paternalism?

Deena Ladd, WAC: People have been so focused on trying to find work, then just getting paid. And the kinds of daily crap that everybody

---

1   <justicia4migrantworkers.org/>.

faces: racism, lack of respect, indignity on the job, the humiliation of having to beg for your wages—that stuff can't be taken lightly in terms of what it does to people's sense of being able to resist and fight back. It comes back to building that culture of organizing. It's not just learning how to put forward your demands when you're in a meeting with the government or being able to speak to the media. It's also about creating a culture that says, "We're in this together, this is our fight." It's a shared commonality of experience, a place where we can catch our breath and challenge people on politics, develop political awareness but also connect to each other through cooking, eating, dancing. So that people can rebuild against their sense of isolation and marginalization.

Adriana Paz, Justicia: With migrant farmworkers, the level of isolation is more intense. This is the nature of the program and they are geographically isolated. For us, the place to start organizing workers is through building trust, a relationship, a community. [Migrant worker programs were] never meant to [build] a community. They don't have relatives here; they rotate every year. How do we create a community? When we talk about a culture of organizing we must have community first and then, within that, continued organizing. The challenges are huge. Workers come and go; work tensions and dynamics don't stop at the farm—they continue in the house. There is competition, betrayal; they police each other. That's how colonialism works, by internalizing oppression and racism, and the program itself works to promote the colonized mind, the colonized body.

As organizers we face the same things. But when we go to the farms, workers see that we have power—we are citizens or permanent residents, we won't be deported, we speak the language well, we are locals living there. But as racialized organizers with no resources we also face marginalization. How do we reconcile those intersections, recognizing that the situation the workers are in is very different than ours, but that sometimes we find ourselves struggling with the same types of marginalization?

When we create moments with a lot of personal sacrifice—going to the farms, trying to create a community that doesn't exist because the system is [designed] to abolish it—when workers expose a condition or speak up, then we reach out to our white or nonwhite allies—organizations with money, the [funders], or lawyers that would be able to carry forward a case—all of our work is completely erased. Those workers were able to [go] public because of months creating a relationship, in restaurants, parking lots, talking by phone. People don't just speak up when they feel a huge sense of injustice; they need to feel supported. They need even a small sense of community behind [them].

Marco Luciano, MIGRANTE-Canada: It's important for us to understand as organizers what the real problem is before we establish long-term strategies and short-term tactics for organizing. Otherwise burnout happens all the time. If we're not focused on where we're going and what we're doing, the next step is, "I['ve] got to step back and just take care of my family." But my family is organically entrenched in the society where I live, in my community. True, it is a fragmented community but the same class exploits—not community groups, or ethnic groups, or Filipinos—here this class exploits Filipinos but it exploits migrants in the Philippines, pushing people to come to countries like Canada. It's important to understand the dynamics of migration and that lingering question in Filipino migrants' heads: "What the hell am I doing here in the first place? Why did I have to migrate, to come to Canada?" It boils down to one answer: "I have to put food on my table back in the Philippines."

Socioeconomic conditions in countries such as the Philippines push people out while countries such as Canada pull people in, drawing them to a "better life" and a "better future." This is the dream of all migrants—to become a Canadian citizen, to become a permanent resident. It's important to understand those dynamics because otherwise our organizing will be a revolving door—service and they leave, service and they leave. They'll settle for that whole concept of being a Canadian.

Filipinos in Canada send approximately $2 billion of remittances per year to the Philippines, about 10 percent of the total of what Filipino migrants [globally] send back home, which is approximately US$20 billion. There's an economy that's benefiting from this labour migration, so there's no way that the Philippine government will stop sending people outside, wherever they go.

For countries such as Canada, it's like a fishpond. There's a whole pool [of workers] that the Philippine government is putting out there.

With MIGRANTE we principally address day-to-day issues, that people get deported or fired from work. We do referral servicing like others, we refer them to WAC or to other providers. We also do a lot of organizing work, principally education. In terms of organizing let's not lose touch with the bigger picture because there are institutions and structures putting this all together behind our backs, while we're servicing Filipina caregivers or Mexican and Caribbean farmworkers—and it's important to address those as well.

Sonia Singh, WAC/Justicia: It's really interesting to hear Adriana and Marco's points about building community, whether farm by farm, seeing community with a transnational lens that stretches across borders or recognizing that some worker centre models are very different than the model needed to work in the countryside or transnationally. This highlights the importance of redefining our base geographically when we're talking about how we organize. This raises bigger questions of how we define organizing and how we connect individual sites and acts of resistance, whether it is caregivers taking action in a home or the farm as a site of resistance. When we ask ourselves how we connect all these different points, how are we envisioning the steps that take those individual acts to collective resistance?

Deena: Building a sense of community and building a culture of organizing is the same thing. I don't separate them. When somebody dealing with unpaid wages comes in who's never been involved in our organization before, we ask them to talk about their experience and get support from members to do a delegation visit and a direct action. They haven't built a relationship yet but there is a culture of organizing that can help build that sense of solidarity. So members will do a direct action for someone even if they have no idea who they are. They just met them but they'll be out the next day visiting them at their workplace. Through that form of direct action, for the worker who is owed their unpaid wages, they're dealing with a community that's come out to support them and if they're incredibly marginalized and isolated and have never been involved in something like that, that's an incredibly positive experience [that] builds hope because our community can be there for them.

One of our members was dealing with a job scam—within a couple of weeks, members had formed a committee to help deal with it, building a culture of organizing and a sense of community at the same time. [For many workers] it's this complete feeling of divide and rule and [they are] not meant to form any sense of solidarity or commonality as workers. You can understand the structures of labour market restructuring in a global sense, but also in a domestic sense—how it is fracturing communities, sometimes on ethnic/racial lines, but also in the status as workers, employment status, and then citizenship (and the nexus of those issues). There's the challenge of building a community where there's no language, no commonality of immigration experience. People are not coming from the same country; there's no shared language, no culture, no work experience, no sector.

Mostafa Henaway, IWC: We're trying to build a real, long-term struggle and see that these people are critical to wage any broader struggle to challenge capitalism in North America or in Canada and challenge Canadian imperialism, that means immigrant and migrant workers—and this is the thing about the racialization and marginalization of both organizers and organizations—we become self-marginalized. One of our major tasks is to show the rest of the left, whether the labour movement or the trade union movement more specifically, that class has fundamentally changed. That you can't sit there and look to the same institutions and organizations, and at people's orientations and strategies and not realize that *class has fundamentally changed.*[2]

Capital is very dynamic, very ingenious. Like when Adriana was talking about the farmworkers. So you gain a victory for more rights for people under the SAWP program, but then they just change who they bring. You see that all the time. Then they just bring people under the Low-Skilled Pilot Project. Less rights, less scrutiny; they'll never come back, they can't put up a fight. Capital is always changing and dividing. This agency work, precarious work in general, low-wage work, all the migrant worker programs, undocumented workers and recent arrivals who might be on social assistance—but that's only a third of the way to the poverty line—so also working under the table. You're not talking about a marginal population anymore, [but] a major chunk of the working class, particularly in urban settings.

In terms of our job, people are generally quite isolated and we have false notions of communities where it's like, "Oh yeah, that mosque or church or temple." But a lot of people, especially working poor in precarious work because of the way that wages are structured, don't identify with those institutions a lot of the time. They might show up for an hour or two. But there's actually opportunity to build a different sense of community,

---

2 Henaway contests notions that predominantly white, predominantly unionized workers comprise the working class, represented by unions. He is arguing that the transformation of work, and the racialization of workers in Canada means that the working class now is much more diverse; spans a range of immigration status; and includes contexts considered marginal, precarious, and unorganized—which are growing.

along class lines [rather than ethnic/racial/religious or cultural notions of community].

Christopher Sorio, MIGRANTE-Canada: I always say that our members, including me, allow ourselves to be exploited for eight to ten hours in order to resist capital and exploitation. Principally we came to this country to find work, to build a better life. When it was established in 1996, MIGRANTE International's slogan was: "We dream of a society where families are not separated." Now when I look at our slogans it's linking the struggle of our people to the homeland. I think it's right because we're not dreaming anymore. Our everyday life of organizing, mobilizing, and fighting exploitation makes us part of that struggle. The presence of Filipinos in countries like Canada is not by accident, but goes back to a deep reason— there are no decent jobs or industry in the Philippines. There is massive unemployment and an absence of genuine land reform that addresses the need of the landless people. That becomes the foundation of the reason why we're pushed to leave our country. Some of us have to come here and leave behind our families and then are reunited eventually in maybe five, six, seven, eight, nine years.

I was lucky because I came here as an immigrant. But that distinction of immigrant and migrant is blurred and we can't say one is different from the other because of the concept of unfree labour. Your status doesn't prevent you from being exploited. We see that in our everyday lives. We have nineteen member organizations of MIGRANTE-Canada across this country. The challenge of organizing this is not easy because all of us also work. And the core group of organizers are challenged to carry on that fight, that resistance, and also by how to help the people who need our help. By the time MIGRANTE-Canada finds out about exploitation or the need for support, it's already an extreme case.

We have a 1-800 hotline that could be the lifeline between us and people who need our support. But we are challenged. How do we help free the unfree, when we ourselves are part of that unfree practice? Organizing is becoming a full-time job; it's not like years ago when we'd say we'd do it on the weekend or, "I'll see you tonight." That doesn't happen. Our work is interrupted by phone calls and people saying, "We need your help and we need it now." How do you do that?

Plus we've got to look at the Philippines. Our struggles here are not separate from the struggles of our people in the homeland—which one comes first is like a balancing act. Do we attack the Canadian government's immigration policy? Or do we address the labour export policy of the Philippine government? How do we connect the two, and let people realize that the very reason that labour export policy exist[s] is because of globalization? That the feminization of migrants is not [accidental]. The reason why women are the preferred workforce of migration is because of their discipline in remittance. Men can choose to send money or not but women cannot make that decision. They have to do it; they have no choice.

If you want to address and help migrants the first thing you['ve] got to know is the framework of labour export policy, the omnibus migrant act,[3] because the state that you are dealing with is operating within these parameters. It's not about "justice" or "human rights"; it's about addressing that act to see how it exploits people.

Joey Calugay, IWC: We talk about struggles and contradictions, so what are we talking about? Are we talking about race? Is it a race war, a race struggle? A class struggle, a class war? I'd like to address the issue of contradictions. Are we talking about antagonistic contradictions? Or contradictions that we can find ways to resolve? It's a framework to look at building alliances, organizing among workers and the contradictions among them. It's a framework to look at the community and its contradictions, including class contradictions within communities. As an organizer I can define what my strategy and tactics are through that sort of analysis. When we tried to conceive of IWC as a community group—as community activists and community organizers—Marco, my brothers, other friends were there. Many of us there were implicated in union organizing. The union SVTI-UNITE had heard about our student organization, approached us, asked us to help them organize Filipino workers in the textile industry.[4] In that process, we realized the limitations of that organizing and realized something else too—there were contradictions among workers by ethnicity or cultural background.

Because we started organizing outside the union's model with workers in community organizations that included their whole families, some workers who were not Filipinos approached us, asking, "How come the

3 Philippines: Amendment to Omnibus Rules & Regulations Implementing the Migrant Workers and Overseas Filipinos Act of 1995.
4 SVTI-UNITE (Union of Needletrades, Industrial and Textile Employees) merged with HERE (Hotel Employees and Restaurant Employees International Union) in July 2004 to form what is now known as UNITE HERE.

Filipinos are so solid in their position inside the union struggle or unionization struggle?" Some would ask to come to the meetings, so we said, "Maybe we should set up an immigrant worker centre and approach other community groups and organizers who had the same idea." We set up IWC because we needed to build a community to resolve the antagonistic contradictions among workers and build a militant community to focus that antagonistic contradiction on struggles between classes. I think that continues in our work at the centre. We're trying to build that militant community to fight back. We have no illusions that the state will look out for workers [or] that everybody in our community is for social change or stands with the workers in the community. There's a tendency for us organizers to forget—our enemy seems so big but they're really not and our friends seem so small but they're really not. We're actually the majority, a small minority of society is in control and imposing the barriers and challenges to what we feel is just.

Marco: We often get asked, "Why do you organize Filipinos only in MIGRANTE? You should be organizing other migrant groups or be part of migrant groups." Our response is firstly, "Yes we are," although the membership of MIGRANTE are Filipinos. And we address the daily issues we face in Canada, always linked to supporting people in the Philippines addressing their socioeconomic conditions. Our issues might not be the same as other groups. Secondly if you're organizing on an ethnic level there's a natural magnet. Filipinos congregate automatically. When they come here, they look for a church; they don't necessarily believe in that church but they look for a place where fellow Filipinos are. So it's important for us to acknowledge that and be part of that community and those being built.

This isn't the end of the organizing. We ensure that we're part of a bigger community too, whether more long-term alliances or short-term campaign-based coalitions. On the other hand, we ensure that these small struggles are made part of a bigger picture. When MIGRANTE comes in we try to explain the global aspect of migration. My position in MIGRANTE is the global representative in Canada. I sit in the international committee and then we share experiences. In terms of strategies and tactics, we recognize the importance of the people's needs. It's really hard for us to talk above their heads. It's important to be part of the community to understand both anecdotal and one-on-one communications with people.

Christopher S: For MIGRANTE we say what an alliance is—our member organizations—and we differentiate that from those organizations' memberships. We believe that there is independence and initiative within these alliances, and while we have a general call for nation-wide campaigns, we always look at the capacity of our member organizations to be able to respond. Because that's what's going to make the campaign work. Some could respond with a statement, some with mobilizations or mass demonstrations. Others could do conferences, a dance number, [or] fundraising. We can't discount it when people say their resistance is based on cultural presentation; that's their resistance—some do it in poetry, others in mobilizations. We always say, "How does this contribute to the exposition of the problem; how does it contribute to mobilization and raising awareness?"

We say we've failed when we don't recruit people because our purpose in launching campaigns is to expand our membership and raise awareness. But you're always fighting against time, especially for the live-in caregivers. We saw a period of growth in our mass organizations, mostly with caregivers. But then, as they complete their programs and transition to permanent residence, we lose them. We ask ourselves, why are our organizers lost in this process? Is it a part of their transition to get organized and then later assimilate and integrate and say, "I'm a Canadian now and I need my weekend"? A few core organizers say, "OK, just like gardening, let's go back, look for new seeds; let's plant new seeds again."

Mostafa: One critical thing for the centre is the space that we're sitting in. When we talk about power or being sustainable I think [having] a space that's large enough and usable has been really important. So [at] IWC it's not just us who organize out of here; it's the South Asian Women's Community Centre youth, Dignidad Migrante, the Mexicans United for Regularization, PINAY (Filipino Women's Organization in Quebec); it's other activists' meetings, whether on Palestine, anti-Harper, etc. The fact that the centre gets used in that way is also critical in terms of alliance-building because of the actual interaction between organizers and activists from different organizations, but also a sense of ownership. If you want this to last and think this is critical you have to also participate. It might be easier for Montreal to do that in terms of rent control and geography but I think it's been really critical.

Marco: How do we sustain the organization? We still live in a capitalist society where we pay rent so I think it is an important discussion that sometimes we place under the table because of our engagement with campaigns and stuff. How do we survive as organizers and how do our centres remain open for people to come? After a few years built with trust we gather communities together and then suddenly we shut the doors on them, so it is a disservice to the people.

Sonia: Rethinking how we build power is part of a vision of transformation. But what are those campaigns, those demands, the different models where it's a step-by-step fight; so you're building that confidence and the power to win; you're building small changes, small reforms, and updating standards, and is that enough? How do we connect that to a vision of transformative organizing? Especially when we connect this back to demands around the TFWP and see the weight, huge coercion, and barriers that it presents to building power in the first place, and the conditions it puts workers in? It would be great to come back to that question of demands and how our strategies then shift depending on that vision.

Deena: On social reproduction, a new study interviewed over four thousand workers, looking at the impact of precarious work on families.[5] It found that the impact of precarious work, combined with workers not finding work or having income security, has meant that now there's quite a big delay in having families—partners, children. So that's another dimension of how it's playing out in communities of workers. [We're] always trying to make connections that link to what's happening on the ground. For example, people understanding connections between themselves as workers and other workers migrating to help take care of their kids when they work, that they're disconnected from their families. There's many points of connection as well as contradictions.

Marco: We live in a capitalist society. The framework is not to develop your family, but to survive today in order to work the next day. It ensures that we are fragmented as a community and not united. We need to keep this challenge in mind. We're organizing in the context of a capitalist society; we are workers, migrant workers, immigrant workers, and are pretty much commodified labour. Migrant workers experience the extreme end of this just-in-time model of production and there's a whole bunch of migrant workers that come and after you dispose of them. There won't be a family and there should be a conscious effort to develop and organize that unit too.

---

5   PEPSO (Poverty and Employment Precarity in Southern Ontario). 2013. "It's More than Poverty: Employment Precarity and Household Well-being." <https://pepso.ca/>.

Mostafa: On the global level, the World Bank wrote—and this reflects the Canadian migrant worker/just-in-time migration model— that they don't want social reproduction in the host countries because migrant workers won't send money back (to Manila, Mexico, Cairo) in foreign currency, which can get cycled back into the banks in London and Washington.[6] They were very explicit that it's a national debt reduction strategy for Third World countries. The World Bank is [interested in] developing cheaper ways for people to send money back. Never making migrants feel completely comfortable where they're migrating to, just enough that they feel more attachment back home than they would in the country that they're working in. [Otherwise] that capital never actually gets sent back. So it's explicit on a global level; we don't want migrant workers to actually be able to even have that opportunity to reproduce on a much larger scale.

Marco: It's reflected in how [Citizenship and Immigration Canada] recruits migrant workers. They shut down the family class category[7] where you could sponsor your parents and grandparents so it's not a model where you build your family, but you come here to work pretty much, right?

Joey: The concept of social reproduction, family, and private property in a capitalist system is so skewed. We touched on that when we were talking about domestic workers—why women's work is so undervalued and they're so exploited. How this is used in a way that [talks] about being part of families can be helpful; but it's part of the chains as well because it's the same thing that bosses use in the workplace, "You're all part of our family in this company. You should protect this company," but it's part of that exploitation. The concept of family, private property, and social reproduction has to be looked at that way from an organizer's perspective. When you're organizing live-in domestic workers and they have this concept, there's also contradictions—you're trying to say there is an exploitative relationship but at the same time many families themselves [employing]

---

6   "Migration and Remittance Flows: Recent Trends and Outlook, 2013–2016." October 2, 2013. World Bank. <siteresources.worldbank.org/INTPROSPECTS/ Resources/334934-1288990760745/MigrationandDevelopmentBrief21.pdf>. See also <imf. org/external/pubs/ft/fandd/2009/06/ketkar.htm>.

7   Citizenship and Immigration Canada. November 4, 2011. "Fourth Set of Ministerial Instructions: Temporary Pause on Family Class Sponsorship Applications for Parents and Grandparents." *Operational Bulletin* 350. <cic.gc.ca/english/resources/manuals/bulle- tins/2011/ob350.asp>.

live-in caregiver[s] are working families who are exploited. How do you build alliances with these contradictions as organizers?

Christopher S: When you speak about reproductive rights, and building societies and families, I return to MIGRANTE's original slogan: "We dream of a family that could be united and not separated." That's not happening; the emphasis has become struggle. We link our struggles because the present state of capital means you're a worker, your workplace is Canada. You know what an employer would say when you're at work—you're not supposed to have fun; it's all about work, about sending money. Labour export policy is about remittance. If we bring them together there's no remittance. The global trade of migration won't have its full benefits if remittance is taken out of that equation. To make it happen we have to separate families.

I was surprised when the immigration ministry introduced a proposal to reduce the age [of a dependant] from twenty-one to eighteen. They're changing the concept of family, reducing us to individuals and workers. That's why all these changes are taking place. The process of family-building doesn't end with that.[8] You develop alliances, and migrant workers because they're human beings break old relationships and build new ones. There's a high rate of divorce, separation. That's why, even in the Catholic Philippines, questions of divorce and reproductive rights are being put to legislation.

Chris R: I want to focus on two issues: employment insurance, and recruiters and recruitment fees [in the context of] this idea about transnational and cross-national organizing. There's been some important work in Justicia in putting demands on the Canadian state and exposing conditions here, in the Caribbean and Mexico. The alliances that we're developing in Mexico, the Caribbean, and Canada are an incredible strength not only because it's a different way of organizing, but also it's not your mainstream or traditional actors. It's people who are concerned and see the relevance of both migration and the portability of rights between countries. Justicia has been working with injured workers who've been banned from the programs. As terrible and frustrating as it is, it can also be a strength for injured

---

8   In May 2013, CIC proposed regulatory amendments to narrow the definition of "dependent child" from twenty-two years of age to eighteen and to eliminate the exception for full-time students. CIC. 2013. "Regulations Amending the Immigration and Refugee Protection Regulations." <gazette.gc.ca/rp-pr/p1/2013/2013-05-18/html/reg1-eng.html>.

workers or those willing to try to develop new demands—on the state and about injuries in the workplaces. There's potential with two categories of workers that we haven't really discussed.

As to recruiters, we're tracing and making the connections with Guatemala and Honduras, for instance, about the companies involved in Canada and the United States. The same recruiters work in the Philippines. Mapping that at the international level and building the workers' stories is another important aspect. This helps ground the work that we are developing in our local campaigns, showing the larger context, what other places are doing, what we can do within our communities.

Marco: Some concrete examples about agencies show there's a movement and victories by organizers, like regulation of agencies in certain Canadian provinces, but it's shifted and payments by migrants to these agencies are made offshore. There are agencies in Hong Kong that caregivers pay into and these offshore agencies remit money. How do you trace that on legal grounds? So it's important to trace the money.

Chris R: I was thinking about extralegal pressure points. We know the state's going to reorganize; recruiters are going to reorganize. We use extralegal tactics and keep building wherever the workers go.

Mostafa: The agencies are not mom-and-pop operations anymore—they're global. As labour becomes more globalized, companies don't want to hire directly. They go through these agencies, and they're becoming more globalized. So Manpower finds people in Hong Kong to bring here even though they came from the Philippines or wherever. They just aren't placement agency workers but they're also dealing with temporary foreign workers. By the 1990s, Manpower was one of the largest corporations in the United States, in the world even.

Sonia: I think that's a crucial piece as we're mapping where workers are. So is mapping what a corporate strategy, building on these kinds of connections and alliances, looks like. With farm work, what are the crops and the supply chains? We could look at US examples where worker centres have mapped power across the industry supply chain and then mapped the strategies and alliances they need to improve conditions across the sector. It's really interesting to hear from the Quebec experience that temp agencies are embedded in all of these parts of the labour market—like Dollarama and the role of massive distribution companies, warehouses, and distribution points.

At WAC, we know our work can't be in just one sector because we work with workers in so many areas. So how does our alliance-building come into play as we look for where we can come together? One of the things is looking at the path that migrant workers who do get status follow. We know caregivers often come to Canada with a nursing background; when they get status they go into personal support work. So what alliances could be formed with caregiver groups, with nursing unions, with racialized nurses with citizenship who face racism and discrimination at work? What alliances are supporting and learning from each other's struggles, making links across precarious work, race, and citizenship?

How does this mapping improve our alliance-building strategy and also identify corporate targets? Mapping what sectors [Labour Market Opinions] are being issued in and building the alliances needed for joint organizing campaigns, for example. Mapping that could generate interesting points of leverage, and cross-campaigns would be a good place to start.

Chris R: The objective when we started to build the centres across Ontario was to try to build community relations with different mediums, community alliances in different parts. The idea was to go back thirty years, when communities came together to say that there were problems, that one community alone was too small to challenge things. So they got different unions with different expertise to come to the table. When we started the farm work organizing that's what we wanted to do. There's a huge pie. How can we have a progressive dialogue with all these different stakeholders and say, "This isn't something that one organization can do; check your egos outside, think about what part of the pie you can undertake, and then we'll develop something together." Maybe when we're thinking about community- and alliance-building it helps to conceptualize this as this large map, with different aspects. We come around the table, [pool] our resources, and map out how to work together. That was our dream twelve years ago and maybe it's something that we can have.

Sonia: After workers contact us at WAC and we talk about their rights, we support them to calculate how much they're owed by that employer and to file a case. Workers then try to find other restaurant jobs but the conditions are the same in any place hiring migrant workers. There's a mainstreaming of ESA [Employment Standards Act] violations across the industry. The message is: "These are the conditions. There are no alternatives except to fight for your wages after you work another year." That's a huge challenge.

On casework, we've learned over time, through lots of trial and error, that we need certain structures in place in order to not get totally overwhelmed with responding to the huge need out there. We know that it's very difficult to navigate through the Ministry of Labour. We have weekly information sessions. We can provide information over the phone, but when people want support from the centre, we ask them to come to an information session. We talk about the different options—that you can file a complaint at the Ministry of Labour; this is what the process is like and we can do some basic support on that, and/or we can contact the employer directly and do a delegation visit. We find that this is an effective way to get wages in many cases.

If someone is interested in doing direct action, then we move on that right away. We had to think of a lot of ways to limit our role in doing casework because it could take all of our time. We have a secondary structural level of regular support clinics where people come to get help to file their claims, but we really encourage the direct action model where we can tie individual cases back to organizing and involving other WAC members.

Christopher S: With MIGRANTE, we're developing a movement and the organizers are just components of that movement. In case I'm gone, somebody's gone, there are people who will move forward. I think in the process of movement-building, it's important that we're fighting for a cause—for migrant workers or the Philippine people—but we're all collectively working and it's important that while we recognize the differences and the values that each one brings to the table, it's the collective strength of that movement that will move forward.

People will make mistakes, we shouldn't be afraid, that's why we have criticism and self-criticism in our structure. It strengthens us collectively to move forward. We learn from our lessons and start again.

Deena: Our organizing has evolved because of this huge context in which we're organizing. I think about where things were at in the early 2000s and where things are now; it's very different. We had masses of temporary agency workers coming forward from 2001 that built our campaign, but our membership looks very different now as workers reflect new jobs in the labour market.

Organizational structure, issues of leadership, and building a multiracial membership are inextricably linked. We've learnt some hard lessons over the years. Around five years ago we had a power struggle about how WAC should function between immigrant communities that were members. Through that experience, we learnt that a large part of our membership had an affiliation to one particular organizer, based on loyalty, common cultural and immigrant experiences, and support around individual casework. You've got organizers from particular communities, so they go out and work with those communities. Because you're dealing with time pressures, it's easier. But then it creates divisions and power struggles. Part of our reflection is the need to develop an accountable organizational structure. Because if it's only based on loyalty—connections to a person, not the mission and a vision of organizing, what you're trying to change— it can easily fall apart. That is important, putting in place an accountable membership structure and making people seriously think it's an important decision to belong to an organization.

It is important to create a buffer between organizers and members also to shield that from funding control. That's a constant challenge and something we've tried to do in Toronto. If we're serious about developing sustainable leadership and organizers, it's important that we figure out: If our organizations go down, what are we leaving behind? What kinds of organizational skill base have we left behind for the common cause of working people's struggles? How are people strengthened by their experience of being connected to your organization and understanding how to fight back—whether it's against their employer or a woman handling the patriarchal shit she has to deal with on a daily basis, or someone dealing with welfare or employment insurance?

We take seriously a strategy of implementing a program of political leadership development—political and economic literacy—having people move through levels of leadership training step by step, which is difficult and labour intensive. We have to incorporate the fluxes and flows of the membership. That means building in different strategies intentionally year by year to look at where we're going. It's important to pull out, think through and learn from what other organizations are doing.

Marco: Prior to the founding of IWC, the discussion was do we build a centre or create membership first? There was a Friday group then, union organizers were doing house-to-house meetings to gather people and we had a meeting. When we started getting other folks involved—Jill and Eric—the discussion was about how we were gonna survive. We might survive for a year or two based on our funding, but where would we get funding? Do we compete for crumbs from the city, province, federal government? There was a conscious decision that we're gonna try to work our way and not be tied to other things just for funding.

It's important to build that constant strong volunteer base, what we call leadership—people that are committed to stay and contribute their skills. Those are skills that have value that can't be replaced. How do you ensure that IWC does not get attached to funding? There are settlement agencies and NGOs that are "good" initially, with good visions and organizers, but get swallowed by the system.

Mostafa: On leadership development and organizing models, one of the qualitative shifts for IWC in our direct action model was how to collectivize a case. If one person's having a problem, it's got to be more than one person. It worked for a moment—maybe seventy people of different ethnicities talking about globalization, NAFTA, the textile industry, and organizing demos. But it dissipated so quickly because it was a focused campaign and a focused moment. When we moved away from that we thought: "How can we build campaigns that undermine precarity in the longer term, bring people in and develop leadership?" When we moved to agency work and to temporary foreign farmworkers, it also took a lot of patience. We're only now seeing the beginnings of the fruits of this and that was three, four years ago.

Jill Hanley, IWC: Even the textile campaign—the amount of time, years of outreach in these neighbourhoods where we had one case here, one case there, and then suddenly when there was a sectoral crisis people came back in numbers, but that was years of outreach—it's amazing to think how long it takes.

Eric Shragge, IWC: Most weeks we have to decide whether we're gonna pay the rent or pay a staff member. We use Emploi-Québec to hire people short term—worker-organizers. One of the things that's worked really well are interns, social work and non–social work students. Some of them are incredible. We're working with three or four MA/PhD students who are interested in issues of precarious labour and they've been committed—they don't just research but work, sometimes two or three days a week, doing everything in the organization. But we don't have any money for core staff after years of working, trying to get unions to understand what we're doing.

Mostafa: A lot of leaders that we've been able to really develop are injured workers, workers who've been laid off or are in a transition. They're the ones who actually fought so they have a deeper understanding, but they're also slightly removed and so there's less fear. The ability to hire worker-organizers has been central to leadership development. It's not just leadership development, it's the process of learning from workers them-selves; not just mapping the economy but what organizing should mean because they're gonna have tools that you don't have.

Leadership development is a two-way street—it's giving them the space to express the knowledge and tools they already have in terms of organizing. That's been key and it's always been people from different communities. We've been able to build a multiracial organization. More agency work focused on the sectors has brought in people from different communities.

The other thing around leadership development is that many activists here run coursework, programming, etc. but that consistent programming, as small-scale as it may be—workshops, language courses, computer courses, theatre—gave them the space to develop collective leadership with a multiracial dimension. It's a culture that people are beginning to enjoy at the centre and one of the things that brings other people in.

Chris R: I think this idea about the managed migration programs—to hold up the Live-in Caregiver Program as the exemplary model on which to base everything—each one of us has consistently opposed that. We need to do further education and be even stronger in our affirmation that that's not the way to go. That's a challenge for all of us. I think we believe in alliances, we do alliance work. But we also do our own work. With Justicia—even though we talked about the critiques of the UFCW and our relationship—a lot of committees where we do work there's nobody. So there's no centre, there's nothing. Something else we bring to the table is going to places where nobody else is organizing.[9]

As Jill was saying, the only key work is the long haul. Building up those relationships takes a very long time and is transformative. Sometimes when we're doing this work, we think that we're continuing that [work]

---

9   See Ramsaroop chapter.

of people who fought slavery and indentureship; the first thing we do is provide information. We may start off the night in Simcoe. We'll say, "Did you hear what happened in Niagara? This group of Mexican women said they'd had enough of their bad employer harassing them." The guys would say, "No really, what do you mean by that?" Then we share that information [which] is then shared with other people. Then you find out that everybody's sharing the information amongst each other. That's happened through a level of trust, developed over many years.

The second thing is sustainability. We're all precarious; we do other jobs or are unemployed. The way we do our work is not ideal—there's some freedom but there's a lot of obstacles. We all want paid work, but on our own terms. It's an obstacle and part of the frustration about our organizing work.

Adriana: I want to talk about sustainability and transformative organizing. In Justicia, unlike IWC and WAC, we have no space, limited funding, everybody's a volunteer. The organization in Ontario is ten years old, in BC, eight. That's something to be proud of but also something to be worried about because it's very precarious organizing. With that freedom comes restrictions and frustrations. Even when organizations have funding and a space, you still don't know if you'll be around in six months. Although we're talking about transformative organizing, when funders want to see campaigns or stories in the media, the priorities become "what is our model" or "what are we going to do when there are these restrictions?"

At least in BC, we have made a conscious choice to focus on the places where nobody goes—to peoples' houses. We start building and opening up spaces where workers can come and relate to each other in a different environment than one of competition. Through that and relationship-building we are working on this transformative aspect of organizing. Although I don't have a polished definition, I think it has to do with how you regain confidence, regain humanity, regain dignity, regain joy, regain and share this with other people. At least to believe that you are building a sense of community or harmony in the house or farm where you are working and living. That is how you acknowledge humanity and your emotions. That is part of what makes us visible and invisible as workers and organizers; how we see a victory or success for the workers and ourselves.

What were we able to accomplish? Did we have a campaign? We do have measures that tell us we are going the right way, building up a relationship, working through cracks of resistance that aren't even acknowledged. That's transformative organizing, not only for the community and workers but for ourselves as well. As organizers, how can we transform in this process if we do not engage in it? What politics are we talking about if we're not transforming along with the people we're working with? Sometimes there are many frustrations in this work. It's not glamorous; it's invisible. What kind of emotional outlet do we develop among ourselves and with the workers to share our victories or frustrations? How can those emotions fuel us as the energy that'll keep us and the workers going for the coming seasons? Sharing information, the crucial act of connecting what workers are doing, is very important.

Chris R: Another thing is emotional trauma. All of us have lost people through injuries and deaths. That's been difficult for us to deal with and that's also part of this legacy. Just thinking about how we've made that part of our narrative, the impact this has on us, it's really critical.

Marco: While looking at the joy of organizing and internalizing this, we also need to keep the fire burning and not pour cold water on it. We're talking about emotions among organizers and the people that we're organizing to keep that anger and fire going. Why do these people die in the first place? It's important to acknowledge the victories but also keep that anger toward the system that perpetuates unbearable conditions for these workers.

Chris R: That's what is also part of telling the stories—whether this person died because of chemicals, or we find out five weeks after that someone who got banned went home with an injury that should have been taken care of. When a worker died in Norfolk County [Ontario], he had a pickup truck with tobacco on the attachment. The pickup was way too light so it was going fast; probably the guy was really tired at work—he'd had an eighteen-hour day and was trying to get his last load in. The truck turned over and he died immediately. Part of that information sharing is to say that we've talked to the family, having discussions in parking lots and bars. Then the workers have conversations with each other. People started thinking about how their workplaces [are] dangerous. Trauma is not only sadness but we can think about how to use it as an organizing tool to let people know what's happening. These things don't need to happen; what steps do we take for change?

Mostafa: In terms of organized labour we need to build alliances that go back to the flying squad model, from local to local [i.e., groups of workers mobilized at short notice for direct action]. But there's a real opportunity where people are looking for the worker centre model or new models within unions. Union activists themselves are looking for different models and alliances. There's an opportunity for us doing migrant worker, immigrant worker and precarious worker organizing [to] join up with organized labour. It won't translate into a whole lot of money; it might translate into tensions and fights, but in the long-term politically I think those are natural alliances that we need to build.

Deena: The union movement is in crisis trying to figure out how to deal with their organizing and what's happening in their sectors. At WAC we have supported building alliances with a number of unions. We supported the postal workers when they were interested in developing a courier workers centre. They started in our place and then moved into their own. Through that process, we developed links with the courier organizers. The Justice for Janitors campaign, around the subcontracting of cleaners and violations of employment standards led by SEIU,[10] was an initiative we supported. Then two years ago when OPSEU was challenging tiered wage rates within the LCBO bargaining, we were doing support work.[11]

Many unions are trying to figure out how to do better education and connect it to action where you try to build concrete alliances and develop a culture of how to organize in a different way that builds a relationship. Alliance-building can also help you raise resources for your centre and provide a base for sustainability. I think that some of our progressive allies who are trying to reform their own unions in this crisis, fighting for workers of colour/immigrant communities, are people that we have to develop alliances with. You cannot then work with them when they feel threatened by your work; they feel [it] is their territory. I think transformative organizing means having a shared vision, a mission that everyone knows—not just the organizers. How do we make that a living, breathing thing?

---

10 Service Employees International Union.
11 Ontario Public Service Employees Union; Liquor Control Board of Canada.

Unfree Labour, Social Reproduction, and Political Community in Contemporary Capitalism

Sedef Arat-Koç

THERE ARE INTEGRAL RELATIONSHIPS BETWEEN THE RESTRUCTURING OF THE labour market; the restructuring of the state under neoliberalism; and the changes in immigration policies, regulations, and practices we have seen in Canada and other immigrant-receiving countries for the last few decades. As labour market restructuring and the dismantling of the welfare state create, reproduce, and expand conditions of precariousness affecting increasingly larger numbers of people, and ease the chances of their accept-ance of degrees of unfree labour, international migration can be used as a "regulatory labour market tool" (Bauder 2006, 21), and immigration policies help to directly and actively construct "precarious legal status" (Goldring and Landolt 2012), instituting forms of unfree labour for migrant workers through denial of citizenship rights and protections. Systemic discrimina-tion, especially racism, plays a central role in the creation, reproduction, and regulation of unfree labour (Bakan, this volume).

While certain forms of unfree labour and degrees of unfreedom have never disappeared in capitalist societies, the current period represents a resurgence of unfree labour and its increasing pervasiveness of slowly replacing what have been deemed "standard" labour practices in the Fordist era. In discussing unfree labour, it is useful, as the editors and Mark Thomas (this volume) argue, to see it more on a continuum rather than in a simplis-tic binary relationship with "free labour." While this conceptualization of unfree labour helps us to see how it may be a condition shared by citizens and migrants alike, it is also important analytically to identify those who may be more likely targeted as sources of unfree labour.

Citizenship status (or denial thereof) plays an important part in the creation of conditions of vulnerability to unfree labour. While citizenship does not guarantee freedom, noncitizenship makes it very likely that it can be denied. As Goldring and Landolt (2012, 3) point out:

> Citizenship status does not necessarily correspond to citizenship practice, nor does citizenship resolve inequality—many citizens live with discrimination and poverty. However, noncitizenship, by definition, is associated with limits in terms of voice, membership, and rights in a political community, and with social exclusion and vulnerability.

Miles (1987) and Satzewich (1989, 1991) have discussed how unfree labour is not an anomaly, but rather a contemporary feature of capitalism. They have also shown how migration and racialization continue to function as central mechanisms for the creation and reproduction of unfree labour. A growing resurgence of migrant—as opposed to permanent immigrant—labour in Canada in recent decades works to complement the increasing flexibilization and precariousness in Canadian labour markets. The very rapid expansion in levels of precariousness among workers (Ladd and Singh, this volume), combined with the shift in immigration toward migrant workers means that analysis of unfree labour needs to be carried from the margins to the centre of understanding modern-day capitalism. A focus on unfree labour promises not only a better analysis of contemporary capitalism, but also contributes critically and radically to labour, antiracist, and feminist debates and activism. It can offer a focal point to address some of the biggest contemporary challenges facing labour organizing, to create solidarity beyond divisions of race, gender, and citizenship. In addition to understanding production, a focus on migrant labour also helps with a better understanding of social reproduction.

Salimah Valiani (2012) has argued that Canadian immigration policy has responded to the restructuring of the labour market through two interrelated shifts. One significant shift in recent decades has been the move from permanent to temporary migration. The other has been from a publicly determined immigration system to an employer-driven one (ibid.). It can be argued that both moves have negatively undermined rights for migrants, as the shifts have also contributed to a general decline in universally applicable labour standards in Canadian society.

Even though the official justification for the Temporary Foreign Worker Program (TFWP), since its origin in the early 1970s, has been based on the claim that it responds to temporary labour needs, in reality, the oldest running programs—i.e., those bringing in seasonal agricultural workers and domestic workers/caregivers—have represented responses to permanent shortages of labour in specific sectors. In recent years, as the TFWP has expanded to a wide variety of sectors and jobs, the falseness of their justification for the program has become even more transparent. As Nakache (2012, 91) observes, Canadian employers seem to be "using both skilled and unskilled TMWs [temporary migrant workers] to fill long-term and even permanent vacancies." The category of *temporary* migrant workers responds to employer preference for a more flexible and disposable labour force. The category helps to normalize differential treatment of migrants: "'Temporary foreign workers' are a creation of the Canadian state. That is 'temporary foreign workers' in Canada exist within a state bureaucratic classification scheme designed to hold people in a *particular* relationship of exploitation and social/political subordination" (Sharma 2012, 35).

In liberal-democratic and multicultural societies where overt racism and sexism have lost legitimacy in public policy and discourse, temporary migrant programs deny basic rights and freedoms through what may appear to be "neutral" legal means. They perform forms of labour discipline accomplished through more explicit forms of racism and coercion than in previous periods. As Paz Ramirez and Chun (this volume) point out, migrant labour programs enact "racialized forms of governing and disciplining of migrant labour through seemingly 'raceless' mechanisms such as the denial of political and economic rights, the denial of citizenship, spatial segregation, restrictions on territorial movement and movement within the labour market, family separation, and prohibition of intimate sexual relations."

Migrant Labour and Social Reproduction

Migrant workers may represent ideal workers for capitalism not just in the role they play in production, but also in social reproduction. Denied basic rights and freedoms, migrant workers do not just provide cheaper and more flexible labour for their employers. Since the 1970s, political economists have discussed how migrant labour also helps subsidize the welfare state. Whereas for citizens, social reproduction necessarily involves generational reproduction as well as needs over a life span, the "temporari-ness" of migrant workers means that they do not need to be compensated for these dimensions of social reproduction. The denial of social citizenship to migrant workers and their (forced) separation from their families create the possibility of compensating them only for the daily reproduction of workers as long as they actively worked, while transferring the responsibil-ity and costs of their families' upkeep, as well as their own, during times of unemployment, sickness, disability, and old age on to the home country (Gorz 1970; Castles and Kosack 1973; Burawoy 1977).

Treated as "good enough to work" but not "good enough to stay," migrants represent "labour only" rather than full human beings to migrant-receiving countries. The disposability of migrant workers for the "host" society implies that the costs and responsibilities for significant dimensions of social reproduction can be downloaded and outsourced to their families, communities, and countries of origin and are invisibilized to the country that has utilized their labour.

Neoliberalism involves increased invisibilization of social reproduc-tion. As the welfare state is weakened and dismantled, there is often priva-tization of some of the costs and responsibilities of social reproduction such as health care and pensions. As market orientation dominates the logic of society, politics, and public discourse under neoliberalism, there is also an ideological invisibilization of social reproduction, as its relevance to the central logic of society becomes further blurred and its social value is further diminished.

Migrant domestic workers and caregivers present an especially ironic case for the invisibilization of social reproduction. The Live-in Caregiver Program (LCP), through the general restrictions imposed on migrant workers against migrating with their families, and through the require-ment that caregivers live with their employers, has ensured that caregiv-ers keep their own families and social reproductive responsibilities in the "home country" out of sight and mind, in the society they are working in (see Koo and Hanley, this volume). Not only are migrant caregivers expected to hide their reproductive responsibilities and needs but their labour focuses precisely on meeting the reproductive needs of others. In the last few decades, as middle-class women have participated in ever-increas-ing numbers in paid employment, organization of paid work and expecta-tions of workplaces in Canada and the United States have not changed in ways to accommodate family responsibilities. Worse, they have become more demanding. As the hours of work that most workplaces have come to expect of their full-time employees have increased in recent decades (Ehrenreich and Hochschild 2003, 3), domestic workers/caregivers are often employed and preferred over public sources of care to provide the longer hours and flexibility to cover employers' needs. In this context, migrant caregivers seem to be the dream workers of a neoliberal society/economy as they not only invisibilize their own social reproduction, but also that of their employers (Arat-Koç 2006).

Cindi Katz (2001, 709–10) discusses the specific challenges that the current period of neoliberal globalism, a "vagabond capitalism," poses for social reproduction, suggesting that an emphasis on social reproduction may provide a critical lens to see and address problems with globalized capitalism:

> The phrase vagabond capitalism puts the vagrancy and dereliction where it belongs—on capitalism, that unsettled, dissolute, irresponsible stalker of the world. It also suggests a threat at the heart of capitalism's vagrancy: that an increasingly global capitalist production can shuck many of its particular commitments to place, most centrally those associated with social reproduction, which is almost always less mobile than production. At worst, this disengagement hurls certain people into forms of vagabondage; at best, it leaves people in all parts of the world struggling to secure the material goods and social practices associated with social reproduction. Insisting on the necessity of social reproduction provides a critical arena, as yet undertheorized, within which many of the problems associated with the globalization of capitalist production can be confronted.

There are a number of different ways in which unfree labour may help address issues of social reproduction. Writing about the reemergence of gang labour in British agriculture recently, Kendra Strauss (2013) sees this as a response to tensions between capital accumulation and social reproduction. She shows how unfree workers may not just be cheap for their own employers, but that through the lower prices of food they make possible, they may help lower general costs of social reproduction and lower wages in the larger economy. The widespread use of seasonal migrant workers in Canadian agriculture suggests a similar relationship between unfree migrant labour and social reproduction. While the cheaper costs of unfree labour to employers and the state help lower food prices and social reproduction costs for others, by refusing to extend social benefits such as employment insurance to migrant agricultural workers, the Canadian state effectively eliminates the possibility of sharing costs of social reproduction transnationally (Ramsaroop, this volume).

Contesting Unfree Labour: Challenges and Strategies

In bringing together academics and activists, this volume contributes not only to research and analysis of unfree and migrant labour, but also to the discussion and creative solutions to challenges of organizing and struggling to end conditions of unfreedom. Even as conditions of precariousness have started to affect significant numbers of workers and migrant labour programs have rapidly expanded, contesting unfree labour has been challenging in a number of important ways.

One of the serious obstacles has had to do with the fact that certain sectors of work, such as agriculture and domestic, have specifically been excluded from protective labour legislation. Even when they become formally covered by labour legislation, this is only partial as they are often excluded from certain provisions such as freedom of association and collective bargaining rights (Thomas, this volume). Further, immigration law and citizenship status often undermine labour protections where/when they may be legally available for migrant workers (Smith 2015a). This is due to the fact that any actual enjoyment of the labour protections is impossible as long as migrant workers are tied to specific employers and deportation remains a real threat (Smith 2013).

Another challenge concerns the fact that even when social movements have pushed for progressive policies and legislation, many of the conceptions of, and policies on, equity have generally ignored unfree labour. Even as the liberal democratic states have occasionally responded positively to demands to end gender and racial discrimination and to address equity, they have done so in contradictory ways, often denying equality precisely to those who are most vulnerable to systemic discrimination. Abigail Bakan (this volume) analyzes a curious policy pattern in Canada in which employment equity programs have not only failed to extend to racialized migrant workers, but have also coexisted with other policies and programs that actively enable and promote systemic discrimination. Focusing on the LCP that was introduced roughly around the period that the Employment Equity Act (EEA) came into effect, Bakan highlights the contradiction between the two, and observes that the "precarious and temporary conditions associated with the LCP are becoming more generalized, while the approach to systemic discrimination that calls for redress, inscribed in the EEA, is diminishing."

The traditional industrial union model has been especially weak in organizing around and addressing issues of precariousness, race, and citizenship status (Ladd and Singh, this volume). Sometimes, even when unions address some issues concerning migrant workers, wrong tactics have been used. When the United Food and Commercial Workers union (UFCW) recently intervened on behalf of seasonal workers, they challenged the stipulations of the Employment Insurance Act requiring migrant workers to pay employment insurance (EI) premiums, as their temporary work permits did not allow them to claim EI benefits. Chris Ramsaroop (this volume) argues that the strategy of the union has been problematic: rather than questioning and struggling to change the legal structures that prevent racialized migrant workers from accessing basic labour benefits, "the UFCW's legal challenge reaffirms the subordination and exploitation that workers face." Instead of the shortsighted strategy of the union seemingly legitimizing the status quo, Ramsaroop argues for a transnational approach to EI that may benefit agricultural workers even after they return to their country of origin.

Given the legal and practical obstacles to unionization, migrant worker justice initiatives have emerged addressing rights of migrant farmworkers. Besides providing education for migrant workers and the larger community on labour rights, these initiatives engage in advocacy and campaigns to improve labour rights and to address injustices of differential status (Thomas, this volume).

Grassroots community-based organizations, especially those based on social justice principles, have in the 1970s and 1980s provided viable alternatives to organizing at the workplace or sectoral level, supporting and advocating for racialized migrant workers. However, in the last two decades, some of these organizations have moved from a grassroots orientation to being driven by state priorities and agenda. As government funding has shifted from core funding to short-term project-based funding and as governments have punished organizations doing advocacy work by denying them funding while providing generous funds to those organizations that follow government agendas, these have sent "a chilling message to the rest of the sector to stay away from advocacy and support to a business delivery style of working" (Ladd and Singh, this volume). In this context, grassroots organizations that refuse to tow the government line or work within the new framework continue their work on a volunteer basis. They, however, face the real possibility that their service and advocacy may not be sustainable.

As Calugay, Malhaire, and Shragge (Immigrant Workers Centre (IWC), Montreal) and Ladd and Singh (Workers' Action Centre (WAC), Toronto) discuss (this volume), besides providing support and services to precarious workers and migrants, worker centres aim to establish a sense of collectivity and community among them. Different from models based in a workplace, a sector, or in a single community, this model organizes workers across differences of workplace/sector, employed/unemployed status, race, language, and citizenship status. Instead of collective bargaining models, worker centres use a movement-building model, building a base of workers and a movement working for change. As noted, both the IWC and the WAC have been involved in campaigns to improve provincial labour legislation and its enforcement.

In addition to the numerous difficulties of organizing workers who do not have an apparent sense of community and campaigning for the government to make improvements in legislation, the real challenge in contesting unfree labour lies with creating a sense of solidarity in the larger Canadian society. However, the objective reality that precariousness is rapidly expanding and becoming a more generalized condition does not automatically lead to a sense of political solidarity with precarious and/or migrant workers. On the contrary, periods of the wildest forms of capitalism and crisis may sometimes be exactly the same periods when divide and rule, and deepening material deprivation on the part of workers can work to prevent people from being in solidarity with one another. Divisions actively cultivated or reinforced by employers and by the state on the basis of legal status and race often have a real divisive impact on the political identities of people who otherwise share similar social/economic conditions.

Ultimately, the success of any campaign for migrant workers is dependent on building political consciousness and support in the wider public, a social/political movement that pressures change in state policies and practices. As long as nationalist discourse on citizenship creates and reinforces "ideological borders" (Sharma 2012), there is a tendency to normalize differential treatment of migrants and racialized groups. Even as overt racist thinking has become illegitimate in liberal multicultural discourses, "ideological borders" between citizens and noncitizens have helped legitimize the racialized treatment of migrants on the basis of their legal status. Thus, what we often find simultaneously in many Western states recently is coexistence of a significant expansion in the numbers of migrant workers entering the countries and powerful anti-immigrant discourses. Even though these two are seemingly contradictory, there is a relationship between them. "Anti-immigration discourse, by continually constructing the immigrants as unwanted, works precisely at maintaining [their] economic viability to . . . employers. They are best wanted as 'unwanted'" (Hage 2000, 135).

Bonnie Honig (1998, 2003) addresses some of the ideological challenges in the way of solidarity with immigrants. Analyzing popular discourses on immigrants in the US context, she identifies a central ambiguity toward immigrants in a nation defining itself as a country of immigrants. She refers to the fact that discourses on immigrants are often simultaneously based in xenophilia and xenophobia. She argues that the figure of the "good" immigrant is often used in the United States to celebrate the virtues and values attributed to the nation; to show the disenchanted that the regime is worthy; and to discipline the poor, the domestic minorities, and the unsuccessful immigrants by showing them that the system is fair. According to Honig, the myth of immigrant America, in its various versions—capitalist, communal/familial, and liberal—represents a xenophilic embrace of immigrants by either depicting them as hardworking and upwardly mobile; as embodying conservative "family values"; and/or as those having "chosen" and being enchanted by America for its liberal democratic values. Ironically, Honig (1998, 3) points out, *"nationalist xenophilia tends to feed and nurture nationalist xenophobia as its partner"* (emphasis in original):

> the dream of a national home, helped along by the symbolic foreigner, in turn animates a suspicion of immigrant foreignness at the same time. "Their" admirable hard work and boundless acquisition

put "us" out of our jobs. "Their" good communities, admired by some, look like ethnic enclaves to others. "Their" voluntarist embrace of America reaffirms but also endangers "our" way of life.

To return to a discussion of labour organizing in Canada, there are many examples, historical and contemporary, that show that the very same qualities of migrants and immigrants that make them desirable to employers and the state—hardworking, reliable, flexible, and (forced to be) accepting of more dangerous and less favourable conditions of work—have been seen as threats to other workers and constituted excuses for racism among workers and unions. Honig's (1998) sobering analysis is a further reminder of the enormity of challenges in establishing solidarity in contexts of nationalism and racism.

In a climate of neoliberalism and nationalism that fragment people in various (and sometimes contradictory) ways, contesting unfree labour needs new and creative strategies for solidarity and development of a new sense of "self." As discussed, the dispersion of "unfree" workers across sectors and categories of citizenship/noncitizenship means that the worker centre model may provide a new sense of community (Calugay, Malhaire, and Shragge; Ladd and Singh, this volume). Even as the union model may not have proved to be the most effective one to organize migrants and precarious workers, it is important that unions engage more actively in campaigns to support their rights, rather than seeing them as competitors. In a neoliberal climate of downward spiral, a race to the bottom in social rights, this may be the only strategy for unions to protect their own members.

The project of constituting new identities also involves the creation of new public memories against the dominant nationalist ones. As Paz Ramirez and Chun (this volume) point out, employers of agricultural workers in BC have been successful in dividing racialized workers by simultaneously using differences of ethnicity, language, and citizenship status, and by repressing the public memory of organizing among South Asian workers in the 1970s and 1980s. This suggests that one strategy toward solidarity needs to involve workers, activists, and academics working together to reveal "subjugated histories" and linking these across time and space to "create sites of collective memory." Canada has had a long history of using unfree labour from various sources, including Europe. Even though many of these histories have already been documented, they lose any radical potential when incorporated into romantic national narratives of immigrant upward mobility and immigrant "whitening." Reinterpreting, reframing, and linking these histories could help to build multiracial solidarity, and subvert national narratives that normalize these experiences and present them as a necessary part of immigration and nation-building.

A final strategy needs to include organizing at a transnational and international level. As Ramsaroop (this volume) argues in relation to EI, the strategy can include unions or migrant justice organizations working across national boundaries to pressure governments to develop specific policies and protections. In addition to campaigns for changes in policy and legislation, transnational organizing can help develop different notions of community and solidarity across borders.

The diversity, complexity, and changes in the nature of labour markets in the present moment call for creative approaches to organizing. As the expansion of precarious and unfree labour (notwithstanding recent changes to the TFWP) pushes the significance of im/migrant workers' struggles from the margins to the centre of labour politics, there have emerged a number of models working from the local to the transnational level that promise to overcome differences on the basis of race, gender, and citizenship. While new models emerge, labour unions also need to rethink their strategies. In addition to creativity, the rethinking would benefit from historical perspectives on labour organizing and reflection on strategies that produced substantive change and those that did not. As Butovsky and Smith (2007) argue, not only has business unionism failed to produce effective strategies for change, so has social unionism. Although social unionism has developed alliances with groups targeted by neoliberals and neoconservatives, such as the poor, women, and minorities, it has invested in a liberal rights-based and legalistic strategy, and overruled more effective strategies such as direct action (ibid.).

Butovsky and Smith (2007) offer an important critique of the "rights-based" approach adopted by contemporary unions, especially as such an approach reinforces the bureaucratic and hierarchical nature of trade unionism. However, their inability to take seriously the existing resistance of migrant workers arguably replicates longstanding racialized stereotypes of worker docility (Smith 2015a). The challenge remains: how do we consolidate, broaden, and fortify the forms of migrant worker struggle currently undertaken? As many contributors in this book suggest, in the context of the need for renewal of an explicitly oppositional politics, one way forward is for organized labour to situate im/migrant worker struggles at the centre and not at the margins. In so doing, there is much to be learned from the experiences of alternative forms of organizing and action of groups such as the Workers' Action Centre, the Immigrant Workers Centre, Justicia for Migrant Workers, and MIGRANTE.

References

Arat-Koç, Sedef. 2006. "Whose Social Reproduction? Transnational Motherhood and Challenges to Feminist Political Economy." In Meg Luxton and Kate Bezanson (eds.), *Social Reproduction: Feminist Political Economy Challenges Neo-Liberalism*. McGill–Queen's University Press.

Bauder, Harald. 2006. *Labour Movement: How Migration Regulates Labour Markets*. Oxford: Oxford University Press.

Burawoy, Michael. 1977. "The Functions and Reproduction of Migrant labour: Comparative Material From South Africa and the United States." *American Journal of Sociology* 81, no. 5.

Butovsky, Jonah, and Murray E.G. Smith. 2007. "Beyond Social Unionism: Farm Workers in Ontario and Some Lessons from Labour History." *Labour / Le Travail*, no. 59 (Spring).

Castles, Stephen, and Godula Kosack. 1973. *Immigrant Workers and Class Structure in Western Europe*. London: Oxford University Press.

Ehrenreich, Barbara, and Arlie Russell Hochschild. 2003. Introduction to *Global Woman: Nannies, Maids, and Sex Workers in the New Economy*. New York: Metropolitan Books.

Goldring, Luin, and Patricia Landolt. 2012. "The Conditionality of Status and Rights: Conceptualizing Precarious Non-Citizenship in Canada." In Luin Goldring and Patricia Landolt (eds.), *Producing and Negotiating Non-Citizenship: Precarious Legal Status in Canada*. Toronto: University of Toronto Press.

Gorz, Andre. 1970. "Immigrant Labour." *New Left Review* 61.

Hage, Ghassan. 2000. *White Nation: Fantasies of White Supremacy in a Multicultural Society*. Annandale, NSW: Pluto.

Honig, Bonnie. 2003. *Democracy and the Foreigner*. Princeton, New Jersey: Princeton University Press.

_____. 1998. "Immigrant America? How 'Foreignness' Solves Democracy's Problems." *Social Text* 16, no. 3.

Katz, Cindi. 2001. "Vagabond Capitalism and the Necessity of Social Reproduction." *Antipode* 33, no. 4.

Miles, Robert. 1987. *Capitalism and Unfree Labour: Anomaly or Necessity?* London and New York: Tavistock.

Nakache, Delphine. 2012. "The Canadian Temporary Foreign Worker Program: Regulations, Practices and Regulation Gaps." In Luin Goldring and Patricia Landolt (eds.), *Producing and Negotiating Non-Citizenship: Precarious Legal Status in Canada*. Toronto: University of Toronto Press.

Satzewich, Vic. 1991. *Racism and the Incorporation of Foreign Labour: Farm Labour Migration to Canada Since 1945.* London: Routledge.

_____. 1989. "Unfree Labour and Canadian Capitalism: The Incorporation of Polish War Veterans." *Studies in Political Economy* 28.

Sharma, Nandita. 2012. "The 'Difference' That Borders Make: 'Temporary Foreign Workers' and the Social Organization of Unfreedom in Canada." In Patti Tamara Lenard and Christine Straehle (eds.), *Legislated Inequality: Temporary Labour Migration in Canada.* Montreal and Kingston: McGill–Queen's University Press.

Smith, Adrian A. 2015a. "Racialized in Justice: The Legal and Extra-Legal Struggles of Migrant Agricultural Workers In Canada" *Windsor Yearbook of Access to Justice* 31, no. 2.

_____. 2015b. "Troubling 'Project Canada': The Caribbean and the Making of 'Unfree Migrant Labour.'" *Canadian Journal of Latin American & Caribbean Studies* 40, no. 2.

_____. 2013. "Pacifying the Armies of Offshore Labour in Canada" *Socialist Studies* 9, no. 2.

Strauss, Kendra. 2013. "Unfree Again: Social Reproduction, Flexible Labour Markets and the Resurgence of Gang Labour in the UK." *Antipode* 45, no. 1.

Valiani, Salimah. 2012. "The Shifting Landscape of Contemporary Canadian Immigration Policy." In Luin Goldring and Patricia Landolt (eds.), *Producing and Negotiating Non-Citizenship: Precarious Legal Status in Canada.* Toronto: University of Toronto Press.

About the Contributors

Editors

Aziz Choudry is an associate professor in the Department of Integrated Studies in Education at McGill University and visiting professor at the Centre for Education Rights and Transformation at the University of Johannesburg. He is author of *Learning Activism: The Intellectual Life of Contemporary Social Movements* (University of Toronto Press, 2015), coauthor of *Fight Back: Workplace Justice for Immigrants* (Fernwood, 2009), and coeditor of *Learning from the Ground Up: Global Perspectives on Social Movements and Knowledge Production* (Palgrave Macmillan, 2010), *Organize! Building from the Local for Global Justice* (PM Press/Between the Lines, 2012), *NGOization: Complicity, Contradictions and Prospects* (Zed Books, 2013), and *Just Work? Migrant Workers' Struggles Today* (Pluto, 2015). He serves on the board of the Immigrant Workers Centre, Montreal.

Adrian A. Smith is an activist-scholar with interests in the legal regulation of labour migration in historical and contemporary forms. He has published in the *Canadian Journal of Law and Society* and *Socialist Studies* and is currently completing a manuscript tentatively entitled *Migration, Law and Development* situating Canada's temporary labour migration programs in global history and socioeconomic development. He is a member of Justicia for Migrant Workers (J4MW). In July 2011, Adrian joined Carleton University's Department of Law and Legal Studies.

Contributors

Sedef Arat-Koç is an associate professor in the Department of Politics and Public Administration and a member of the School of Graduate Studies at Ryerson University, contributing to graduate programs in Immigration and Settlement Studies, Policy Studies, and Communication and Culture. Her research interests include imperialism in the Middle East; Turkish society and politics in a period of neoliberalism and post–Cold War geopolitics; immigration policy and citizenship, especially as they affect immigrant women; transnational feminism; and the politics of multiculturalism and antiracism.

Abigail B. Bakan is a professor and chair of the Department of Humanities, Social Sciences, and Social Justice Education at the Ontario Institute for Studies in Education, University of Toronto. Her books include *Negotiating Citizenship: Migrant Women in Canada and the Global System* (with Daiva K. Stasiulis), winner of the 2007 Canadian Women's Studies Association Book Award; and *Critical Political Studies: Debates and Dialogues from the Left* (coeditor with Eleanor MacDonald). Her articles have appeared in *Race and Class*, *Social Identities*, *Rethinking Marxism*, *Socialist Studies*, *Atlantis*, and *Studies in Political Economy*.

Joey Calugay was born in the Philippines during the tumultuous years leading up to the declaration of martial law by the dictator Ferdinand Marcos. His activism has included union organizing in Montreal's textile and garment industry. He is currently a community organizer for the Immigrant Workers Centre and is a part-time filmmaker.

Jennifer Jihye Chun is an associate professor in the Department of Sociology at the University of Toronto, Scarborough. Her current research focuses on immigrant women workers and community organizing; contentious labour politics in South Korea; and the nexus between work, travel, and language among mobile Korean youth. She is the author of *Organizing at the Margins: The Symbolic Politics of Labor in South Korea and the United States* (Cornell University Press, 2009).

Jill Hanley is an associate professor at the McGill School of Social Work. Her research focuses on access to social rights for migrants with precarious status and she is an active member and a cofounder of the Immigrant Workers Centre.

Mostafa Henaway is a writer and community organizer and has worked at the Immigrant Worker Centre, Montreal, since 2007. He is active in campaigns on temporary agency workers, temporary foreign workers, and laid-off textile workers. In Toronto he organized with the Ontario Coalition Against Poverty and the Toronto Coalition of Concerned Taxi Drivers. He has a book chapter in *Organize! Building from the Local for Global Justice* (PM Press/Between the Lines, 2012) on immigrant and migrant worker organizing, and has coauthored articles in *Canadian Dimension*, *Global Labour Journal*, and *Labour, Capital and Society*. He holds a master's degree from the Global Labour University.

Jah-Hon Koo is a PhD candidate in social work at McGill. His dissertation explores labour process and power relations in the workplaces of live-in caregivers. Prior to his doctoral studies, he worked in a migrant workers centre in South Korea.

Deena Ladd has been working to improve wages and working conditions for primarily racialized, low-wage women and immigrant workers for over twenty years in Canada. She was an organizer with the International Ladies Garment Workers Union (now known as UNITE HERE) for seven years, working with garment workers; home-based workers; and social service, retail, and manufacturing workers. Deena is a cofounder and coordinator of the Toronto Workers' Action Centre. She teaches a community engagement practice course at Ryerson University and is active in supporting the development of the Migrant Workers Alliance for Change, the Caregivers' Action Centre, worker organizing efforts in various cities across Ontario, and the leadership of workers in low-wage and precarious jobs.

Marco Luciano, now based in Alberta, was a union representative for the Canadian Union of Public Employees (CUPE) Local 1281 in Toronto for several years. He is also an organizer and activist. An advocate on migrants' rights for over fifteen years, Marco is currently the Canada Global Council representative for MIGRANTE International, an international alliance of one hundred organizations in over twenty-two countries. He cofounded MIGRANTE-Canada, a chapter of MIGRANTE International (with seventeen member organizations from British Columbia, Alberta, Manitoba, Ontario, Quebec, and the Maritimes), and is a cofounder of the Immigrant Workers Centre, Montreal.

Loïc Malhaire is a PhD student in the Applied Human Sciences program at the Université de Montréal. His current research focuses on the working poor in Canada and particularly the role of policies regarding the situation of immigrant workers working through temporary agencies and temporary foreign workers. He is a member of GIREPS (Groupe interuniversitaire et interdisciplinaire de recherche sur l'emploi, la pauvreté et la protection sociale) and the Immigrant Workers Centre, Montreal.

Adriana Paz Ramirez is a Bolivian community organizer and popular educator with over ten years of experience working in social justice issues. She is a cofounder of, and an organizer with, Justicia for Migrant Workers in British Columbia, a national grassroots organization advocating for migrant farmworkers' social, economic, and labour rights. She recently finished an MA in the sociology department at the University of British Columbia.

Geraldina Polanco is an assistant professor in sociology at California State University at Northridge. Prior to this she was a Social Sciences and Humanities Research Council of Canada postdoctoral fellow at York University's Centre for Research on Latin America and the Caribbean. For her doctoral study she conducted a transnational, multisited project on the recruitment and employment of Filipino migrant workers in western Canadian Tim Hortons restaurants. Her current research further analyzes the changing landscape of work and migration, taking Mexico and the Philippines as comparative cases to explore how low-waged, service sector worksites and labour markets are transnationally organized under migrant worker programs.

Chris Ramsaroop is a founding member of Justicia for Migrant Workers, a grassroots collective of community, labour, and migrant activists who organize with migrant workers for change. Alongside his organizing work, Chris participates in the executive of the Asian Canadian Labour Alliance.

Eric Shragge taught for almost forty years in universities, the last twelve in the School of Community and Public Affairs at Concordia, and is now a volunteer staff member at the Immigrant Workers Centre. He has authored, coauthored, and edited books on various aspects of community organizing and development, including *Activism and Social Change: Lessons for Community and Local Organizing* (Broadview Press, 2003), *Fight Back: Workplace Justice for*

Immigrants (2009), and *Contesting Community: The Limits and Potential of Local Organizing* (2010).

Sonia Singh currently works for Labor Notes but was until recently an organizer with the Workers' Action Centre (WAC), Toronto. Sonia is also a member of Justicia for Migrant Workers, a collective that supports outreach and organizing with migrant agricultural workers, and has been supporting the development of the Migrant Workers Alliance for Change, a coalition of grassroots migrant worker organizations, community groups, unions, workers, and community members.

Christopher C. Sorio, the secretary general of MIGRANTE-Canada, is a founding member of MIGRANTE-Ontario. A former political prisoner and torture victim during the martial law years of Marcos in the Philippines, he received US$1000 compensation in May 2011 for being a victim of human rights abuses. As a migrant advocate he has worked with migrant stakeholders and groups of caregivers to lobby Canadian parliament for changes to the temporary foreign worker program.

Mark Thomas is an associate professor in the Department of Sociology and a codirector of the Global Labour Research Centre at York University. He is the author of *Regulating Flexibility: The Political Economy of Employment Standards* (McGill–Queens, 2009), coeditor (with Norene Pupo) of *Interrogating the New Economy: Restructuring Work in the 21st Century* (University of Toronto Press, 2010), and coeditor (with Deborah Brock and Rebecca Raby) of *Power and Everyday Practices* (Nelson, 2012). His current projects examine the connections between labour standards enforcement and precarious employment, and labour organizing in the context of economic crisis and austerity.

Index

"Passim" (literally "scattered") indicates intermittent discussion of a topic over a cluster of pages.

PM Press was founded at the end of 2007 by a small collection of folks with decades of publishing, media, and organizing experience. PM Press co-conspirators have published and distributed hundreds of books, pamphlets, CDs, and DVDs. Members of PM have founded enduring book fairs, spearheaded victorious tenant organizing campaigns, and worked closely with bookstores, academic conferences, and even rock bands to deliver political and challenging ideas to all walks of life. We're old enough to know what we're doing and young enough to know what's at stake.

We seek to create radical and stimulating fiction and non-fiction books, pamphlets, T-shirts, visual and audio materials to entertain, educate, and inspire you. We aim to distribute these through every available channel with every available technology—whether that means you are seeing anarchist classics at our bookfair stalls; reading our latest vegan cookbook at the café; downloading geeky fiction e-books; or digging new music and timely videos from our website.

PM Press is always on the lookout for talented and skilled volunteers, artists, activists, and writers to work with. If you have a great idea for a project or can contribute in some way, please get in touch.

PM Press
PO Box 23912
Oakland CA 94623
510-658-3906
www.pmpress.org

FRIENDS OF PM

These are indisputably momentous times—the financial system is melting down globally and the Empire is stumbling. Now more than ever there is a vital need for radical ideas.

In the eight years since its founding—and on a mere shoestring—PM Press has risen to the formidable challenge of publishing and distributing knowledge and entertainment for the struggles ahead. With hundreds of releases to date, we have published an impressive and stimulating array of literature, art, music, politics, and culture. Using every available medium, we've succeeded in connecting those hungry for ideas and information to those putting them into practice.

Friends of PM allows you to directly help impact, amplify, and revitalize the discourse and actions of radical writers, filmmakers, and artists. It provides us with a stable foundation from which we can build upon our early successes and provides a much-needed subsidy for the materials that can't necessarily pay their own way. You can help make that happen—and receive every new title automatically delivered to your door once a month—by joining as a Friend of PM Press. And, we'll throw in a free T-shirt when you sign up.

Here are your options:
- $30 a month: Get all books and pamphlets plus 50% discount on all webstore purchases
- $40 a month: Get all PM Press releases (including CDs and DVDs) plus 50% discount on all webstore purchases
- $100 a month: Superstar—Everything plus PM merchandise, free downloads, and 50% discount on all webstore purchases

For those who can't afford $30 or more a month, we have Sustainer Rates at $15, $10, and $5. Sustainers get a free PM Press T-shirt and a 50% discount on all purchases from our website.

Your Visa or Mastercard will be billed once a month, until you tell us to stop. Or until our efforts succeed in bringing the revolution around. Or the financial meltdown of Capital makes plastic redundant. Whichever comes first.

Organize! Building from the Local for Global Justice

Editors: Aziz Choudry, Jill Hanley & Eric Shragge

$24.95
ISBN: 978-1-60486-433-5
9 by 6 ∙ 336 Pages

What are the ways forward for organizing for progressive social change in an era of unprecedented economic, social, and ecological crises? How do political activists build power and critical analysis in their daily work for change?

Grounded in struggles in Canada, the United States, Aotearoa/New Zealand, as well as transnational activist networks, *Organize!: Building from the Local for Global Justice* links local organizing with global struggles to make a better world. In over twenty chapters written by a diverse range of organizers, activists, academics, lawyers, artists, and researchers, this book weaves a rich and varied tapestry of dynamic strategies for struggle. From community-based labor organizing strategies among immigrant workers to mobilizing psychiatric survivors, from arts and activism for Palestine to organizing in support of Indigenous Peoples, the authors reflect critically on the tensions, problems, limits, and gains inherent in a diverse range of organizing contexts and practices. The book also places these processes in historical perspective, encouraging us to use history to shed light on contemporary injustices and how they can be overcome. Written in accessible language, *Organize!* will appeal to college and university students, activists, organizers and the wider public.

"To understand the world, you have to try to change it. That's what the authors of this fine set of essays and meditations have taken to heart. The result? Some of the best insights on power, organizing, and revolution to be found."
—Raj Patel, author of *The Value of Nothing*

Continental Crucible: Big Business, Workers and Unions in the Transformation of North America, Second Edition

Richard Roman and Edur Velasco Arregui
Foreword by Steve Early
Preface by Mel Watkins

$19.95
ISBN: 978-1-62963-095-3
9 by 6 • 192 pages

The crucible of North American neoliberal transformation is heating up, but its outcome is far from clear. *Continental Crucible* examines the clash between the corporate offensive and the forces of resistance from both a pan-continental and a class struggle perspective. This book also illustrates the ways in which the capitalist classes in Canada, Mexico, and the United States used free trade agreements to consolidate their agendas and organize themselves continentally.

The failure of traditional labor responses to stop the continental offensive being waged by big business has led workers and unions to explore new strategies of struggle and organization, pointing to the beginnings of a continental labor movement across North America. The battle for the future of North America has begun.

"This insightful, revealing, and passionate book is a must read for workers and union activists all over the world in their efforts to develop strategies to overcome neoliberalism. The creation of a single North American and global labor market by NAFTA and neoliberal globalization has created both the bases and the necessity for workers and unions to move beyond nationalism and chauvinism."
—Alejandro Álvarez, socioeconomist and professor at the Faculty of Economics–Universidad Nacional Autónoma de México (UNAM, National Autonomous University of Mexico), member of the Trinational Coalition in Defense of Public Education and of the '68 Pro-Democratic Liberties Committee

New Forms of Worker Organization: The Syndicalist and Autonomist Restoration of Class Struggle Unionism

Editor: Immanuel Ness
Foreword by Staughton Lynd

$24.95
ISBN: 978-1-60486-956-9
9 by 6 • 336 pages

"...a real contribution to labor's rebirth."
—FRANCES FOX PIVEN

Bureaucratic labor unions are under assault. Most unions have surrendered the achievements of the mid-twentieth century, when the working class was a militant force for change throughout the world. Now trade unions seem incapable of defending, let alone advancing, workers' interests.

As unions implode and weaken, workers are independently forming their own unions, drawing on the tradition of syndicalism and autonomism—a resurgence of self-directed action that augurs a new period of class struggle throughout the world. In Africa, Asia, the Americas, and Europe, workers are rejecting leaders and forming authentic class-struggle unions rooted in sabotage, direct action, and striking to achieve concrete gains.

This is the first book to compile workers' struggles on a global basis, examining the formation and expansion of radical unions in the Global South and Global North. The tangible evidence marshaled in this book serves as a handbook for understanding the formidable obstacles and concrete opportunities for workers challenging neoliberal capitalism, even as the unions of the old decline and disappear.

"As the U.S. labor movement conducts its latest, frantic search for 'new ideas,' there is no better source of radical thinking on improved modes of union functioning than the diverse contributors to this timely collection. New Forms of Worker Organization *vividly describes what workers in Africa, Asia, South America, and Europe have done to make their unions more effective. Let's hope that these compelling case studies of rank-and-file struggle and bottom up change lead to more of the same where it's needed the most, among those of us 'born in the USA!'"*
—Steve Early, former organizer for the Communications Workers of America and author of *Save Our Unions: Dispatches from a Movement in Distress*

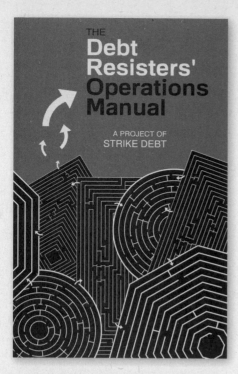

The Debt Resisters' Operations Manual

Editor: Strike Debt

$16.95
ISBN: 978-1-60486-679-7
8 by 5 • 256 Pages

Over the last thirty years, as wages have stagnated across the country, average household debt has more than doubled. Increasingly, we are forced to take on debt to meet our needs—from housing, to education, to medical care. The results—wrecked lives, devastated communities, and an increasing reliance on credit to maintain our basic living standards—reveal an economic system that enriches the few at the expense of the many.

The Debt Resisters' Operations Manual is a handbook for debtors everywhere to understand how this system really works, while providing practical tools for fighting debt in its most exploitative forms. Inside, you'll find detailed strategies, resources, and insider tips for dealing with some of the most common kinds of debt, including credit card debt, medical debt, student debt, and housing debt. The book also contains tactics for navigating the pitfalls of personal bankruptcy, and information to help protect yourself from credit reporting agencies, debt collectors, payday lenders, check cashing outlets, rent-to-own stores, and more.

Written and edited by a network of activists, writers, and academics from Occupy Wall Street, additional chapters cover tax debt, sovereign debt, the relationship between debt and climate, and an expanded vision for a movement of mass debt resistance.

That debt is neither inevitable nor ethical is one of the powerful assertions of Strike Debt, whose brilliant manual is both a practical handbook and a manifesto for a true debt jubilee: an economic rebirth in which the indebted are freed and financial institutions are reinvented."
—Rebecca Solnit, author of *A Paradise Built in Hell: The Extraordinary Communities That Arise in Disaster*